Race and Politics in New York City

Race and Politics in New York City

Five Studies in Policy-Making

EDITED BY

Jewel Bellush
and
Stephen M. David

PRAEGER PUBLISHERS
New York • Washington • London

PRAEGER PUBLISHERS
111 Fourth Avenue, New York, N.Y. 10003, U.S.A.
5, Cromwell Place, London S.W.7, England

Published in the United States of America in 1971
by Praeger Publishers, Inc.

© 1971 by Praeger Publishers, Inc.

Library of Congress Catalog Card Number: 70-101653

Printed in the United States of America

For
Bern and Janet

Preface

This book is designed to give the reader an opportunity to re-examine some fundamental and long-accepted conclusions concerning power, influence, and decision-making in America's cities. Its main intent is to question the findings of a group of political scientists, the pluralists, who, writing about cities during the 1950's, had considerable impact not only on the profession but also on academic thought and activity in general.[1] From their research, these political scientists concluded that a pluralistic pattern of decision-making characterized the governing of American cities and that this pattern would enable these urban centers to accommodate and respond to the new demands they would encounter in the future.

Yet, only a few years after the publication of the pluralists' studies, American cities were plunged into serious conflicts involving their black citizenry. The emergence of these conflicts and, more importantly, the manner in which urban political systems dealt with them have caused doubts concerning the pluralists' notion that our cities are governed in a democratic and responsive manner. The purpose of this volume is to explore these fundamental questions and to examine the validity of some of the most significant conclusions reached by the pluralists.

It would seem the height of folly for political scientists to continue subscribing to a political theory that has left us so unprepared for the events of the 1960's and, perhaps, the 1970's. Instead, our task should be to analyze critically the works of the pluralists in order to determine where they went astray. Hopefully, this volume will aid in that endeavor.

In the introductory chapter, the editors have analyzed the

major shortcomings of the pluralist model. In the five chapters that follow, cases are presented in the substantive policy areas of health, education, welfare, housing, and police. Although the controversies discussed are limited in locale to New York and are centered upon the ability of one urban political system to deal with the demands of a particular population group, the editors believe that the implications of these conflicts are far broader. These cases are intended to capture the way the government in one city—whose problems are similar to those faced by all large urban centers and whose political system was characterized as pluralistic by political scientists writing in the 1950's—dealt with the demands of groups that were essentially newcomers to the political process.[2]

In their writings, the pluralists expressed confidence that urban government would be as responsive to the demands of black citizens as it had been to the claims of the immigrant groups that had preceded them.[3] The case studies included here, however, document that the pluralists' confidence was unfounded: New York City's political system has proved resistant and inflexible in the face of the demands emerging from the newly politicized black community. The difficulties this community has encountered in what is considered the most "liberal" city in the United States force us to question whether the political system of New York, or any other large city, can be said to have been correctly described by the pluralist school.

Since the case studies in this volume are intended to portray the response of New York City's political system to the demands made upon it by the black community, it would seem logical that the controversies selected should be those that the black community felt were most important. We agree with those pluralists who have argued that it is not the function of researchers to let their own value preferences determine what is important for a group of city residents.[4] Pluralists have also correctly pointed out that some issues are more important to a given group than others and that this affects the extent to which they will seek to influence a particular decision.[5] For example, one can suspect that welfare is more important to the black community than air pollution, and, accordingly, that blacks will commit more of their resources to influencing welfare policies.

Although the editors had no survey data to indicate which local controversies in the 1960's were most salient to black New Yorkers, we did have the Kerner Commission findings, which point out policy areas that black communities across the nation felt to be most important. We therefore sought to select one case from each of these issue areas. All of our case studies are in policy areas of concern to the black community and all but one are in the issue areas most mentioned in the Kerner Commission survey.[6] Although we sought to follow the pluralists criterion for "important" decisions when selecting each case, we were constrained by the availability of data and of knowledgeable authors.[7] We believe, however, that this volume captures many of the issues that were of major importance to New York's black community during the 1960's.[8]

The cases are written in accord with a certain pattern. First, each piece identifies the active participants in the decision-making area on some substantive issue; second, as full an accounting as possible is made of the behavior of the key actors during the unfolding of the policy conflict, with particular emphasis placed on the strategies and tactics employed to influence the decision; and, finally, the specific outcomes of the conflict are determined and analyzed. The authors of these studies have been keen observers of the urban scene in their particular field of interest for a good number of years, at times actively participating in the politics of the issue. Consequently, not only are they the most informed people we could find, but each writer brings a distinctive point of view. As a result, each is responsible for his or her own work. In addition, the writers do not necessarily share each other's views.

Because of the unique combination of expertise and differing perspectives, this volume can be used to stimulate discussion and debate on a variety of issues. As illustration of these uses, we offer a few examples:

(1) To examine conflicting solutions to the race problem. In recent years, the goal of "community control," which involves a redistribution of governmental authority through lodging important segments of power in the community, has been advocated on behalf of our black citizenry. Almost all of the cases provide data relevant to an analysis of the consequences of this proposal. Moreover, the differing perspectives of the contributors on this solution put the alternatives into sharp focus and enable constructive analysis of the viability and drawbacks of this solution.

(2) To examine differing views on leadership. At any point in

time, there are always many citizens who believe that our problems are due to a lack of leadership. Yet, almost invariably, the meaning of the term "leadership" and the consequences of different styles of leadership fail to be discussed. The differing perspectives on leadership offered by the cases included here can help to sharpen our perspectives in this area and provide an opportunity for comparative analysis of leadership styles.

(3) To evaluate the role of professionals in decision-making. Increasingly, we live in what many authors are calling a "technocratic age"—a time when more and more of the important decisions are being made by experts and technicians. At the turn of the century, the progressives viewed the process of professionalization as an important device for improving the quality of government in the city. The displacement of the "dirty" and "corrupt" political "bosses" by the efficient, neutral, competent experts has continued to be warmly hailed and encouraged. The consequences of this displacement are heatedly debated in this volume.

It is hoped that this volume will prove of interest to both teachers and students of urban political systems. While the primary intent of *Race and Politics in New York City* is to raise questions concerning the prevailing theory in the field, there is another and perhaps more important aim: It is hoped that these case studies will promote further interest in the policy outputs of our city governments. To this end, each study, in its conclusions, discusses the policy consequences of the resolution of the conflict. It is time for students of urban affairs to make the study of public policy a central concern. The study of the consequences of policies implemented by urban governments (as well as of policies rejected) should be high on the agenda of urban political scientists in the decade to come.

We cannot begin to list the many colleagues and friends who have helped us, often unknowingly, on this volume. Their suggestions and reactions to our ideas are reflected in the content of the book. We would like specifically to thank our contributors for their efforts, their patience, and their understanding in working with us to produce this case book. We would also like to thank two students—Louise Bisogno and Ivory Robinson—for their important services on behalf of the book. Our editor, Marian S. Wood, played many roles, all with considerable skill. Our greatest debts are to the two individuals to whom the book is dedicated. Without their unflagging support and encouragement, this volume would have been impossible.

Notes

1. For a more detailed description of the conclusions of these political scientists, see the opening pages of the Introduction. Throughout this volume, these political scientists will be referred to as pluralists. In so doing, we are aware that their methodological approaches, empirical conclusions, and normative statements were not always in agreement. However, there are major similarities in their writings, and we therefore feel justified in considering their works as constituting a school.
2. See Wallace S. Sayre and Herbert Kaufman, *Governing New York City* (New York: Russell Sage Foundation, 1960).
3. Robert A. Dahl, *Who Governs?* (New Haven, Conn.: Yale University Press, 1961), pp. 34–36, 293–95.
4. The best-known and most persuasive argument to this effect is found in Nelson Polsby, *Community Power and Political Theory* (New Haven, Conn.: Yale University Press, 1963). Polsby, at many points, attacks the writings of sociologists (who had concluded that a small elite dominated decision-making in the cities) for imputing a "false class consciousness" to groups in the community. Instead, Polsby, along with other pluralists, argued that the overt activity of groups in the community is the only reliable indicator of the feelings and demands of the different interests in the cities. See Polsby, p. 116 *et passim*.
5. Edward C. Banfield, *Political Influence* (Glencoe, Ill.: The Free Press, 1961), pp. 331–32.
6. The Kerner Commission interviewed approximately 1,200 people in twenty cities that had undergone race riots in 1967. (The twenty cities were "a representative group of cities that experienced some sort of disorder in 1967.") U.S., National Advisory Commission on Civil Disorders, *Report* (New York: Bantam, 1968), p. 576. The 1,200 people came from three groups: public officials; the private sector (businessmen, labor, and so forth); and "the disorder area (residents, leaders of community groups)." *Ibid.*, p. 577. The representatives of the black community were asked to indicate their major grievances. The commission published a ranking of those grievances that appeared to have the greatest significance for the black community. They concluded that six areas of grievance were of greatest concern to the black community; namely, police practices, unemployment and underemployment, inadequate housing, inadequate education, poor recreation facilities, and an unresponsive political structure. Four of the five controversies in this volume cover four of these areas. A fifth case study in the area of employment had been planned and written for the volume. However, last minute unforeseen developments prevented the publication of this study. The only case study that is not in one of the

six issue areas is the controversy over the delivery of health services—an
area of grievance further down the list compiled by the Kerner Commission. For a description of the methodology and results of this survey,
see *ibid.*, pp. 143–50.

7. For a description of the criteria used by the pluralists in selecting "important decisions," see Polsby, *op. cit.*, pp. 95–96.

8. The editors feel that the inadequacies in the selection process and the
small number of cases prevent us from drawing any reliable conclusions
about the character of the city's political system. However, the importance
of these controversies to the black community and their coverage of many
issue areas constitute impressive evidence and permit us at least to begin
to question the validity of a number of the pluralist findings.

Contents

Race and Politics in New York City

1. Introduction: Pluralism, Race, and the Urban Political System

STEPHEN M. DAVID

AND JEWEL BELLUSH

It was not until the late 1950's that political scientists began to give serious attention to the study of community power and influence. Up to that time, sociologists had held a monopoly of the field, while political scientists had been preoccupied with promoting "good government" prescriptions for city management and with writing dry texts. By and large, those early sociological studies had concluded that a power elite, representing an upper class (whose definition varied from study to study), governed American communities. Party officials and civic and labor leaders were said to hold places subordinate to this upper-class elite.[1] These conclusions were arrived at by a variety of approaches. The best known placed primary reliance either on analysis of the resource bases (sources of power) of the elite or on identifying reputed influentials in the community.[2]

Political scientists, almost en bloc, attacked such findings, complaining that sociologists had failed to verify these conclusions

3

about the role and character of a "power elite." The major thrust of this attack was that the studies had not proved elites used their power to rule local communities; instead, sociologists had relied on potential sources of power or reputed influence, rather than on actual acts of power.[3] To avoid this error, political scientists set to work to study actual decisions made by local government officials. In this way, they hoped to determine the most influential actors and to reveal what constituted the patterns of power in American cities. Concentrating on the "case study approach" (as their method of reconstructing government decisions came to be known), they hoped to uncover the loci of power in various urban centers.[4]

Most of these studies arrived at a conclusion sharply different from that reached by the sociologists: A pluralistic, rather than hierarchical, pattern of decision-making was the real shape of urban power. Political scientists, perceiving urban political systems to be made up of a myriad of small special-interest groups having widely differing power bases and undertaking a multitude of strategies on decisions salient to them, were able to conclude that no single power elite dominated the full spectrum of decision-making; instead, there existed a relatively wide sharing of power among leaders and groups tending to specialize in one or a few issue areas. Believing these multiple centers of power to be the norm, they argued that no single group constituted an all-encompassing power elite. The various centers, or clusters, of power provided the political system with discrete, functional arenas, each public activity operating separately with a different constellation of interests. While accepting the sociological claim that the active, interested, affected groups (always a minority of citizens) dominated the policy process, the advocates of pluralism contended that what eventually evolved into public policies was the result of bargaining and compromise; participants were constrained, checked, and balanced either by other leaders or by those they led.[5]

Thus, as the 1960's began, political scientists had designed a new pattern of urban decision-making that challenged the prevailing power elite model. The pluralists, as this group of political scientists came to be called, were initially widely praised for their studies. Their reliance on the case method to test the validity of their conclusions was considered a major improvement upon the methodology used by the sociologists. Moreover, their findings fitted the optimistic mood of the country during those years, when the process of accommodation and compromise in an open system seemed to be confirmed by daily events.

The events of the 1960's, however, forced many academics to take a closer look at the works of these political scientists. The black revolution, student rebellions, the peace movement, mounting concern for the plight of such groups as the Indians, migrant laborers, and the poor whites of Appalachia—these events raised fundamental questions about the ability of our political systems to function in an open, democratic, and responsive manner. Problems such as these could not be denied or ignored, and the prevailing political theory that could not explain them came into question.

The earliest major critique came from a group of scholars disturbed by the pluralists' sole reliance upon the case study technique, which they believed to be inadequate in the determination of the distribution of power in a given locality. These critics, holding that there were limitations inherent in the very methodology of the pluralists, described three types of situations in which a would-be participant could fail to act (though affected by the policy) and hence would not be represented in a case study reconstruction of the governmental decision.

In each of these situations, groups fail either to initiate a controversy or to promote certain positions that are in their self-interest. The first occurs when a group feels it lacks sufficient influence to affect governmental policy and thus takes no action to promote its interests. In the second, a group fails to initiate or participate in political controversies because it fears the use of sanctions were it to choose to get involved; the history of America is replete with examples of actions—such as lynchings of Southern blacks or police raids on "extremist" groups—taken to discourage political involvement. The last occurs when community norms, which are supportive of the interests of particular groups, lead either to the failure of a group to initiate a controversy or to the exclusion of a whole range of alternatives during the course of a conflict. In this last type of situation, the norms are accepted by government officials and nongovernmental groups alike. In all three cases, those groups that are advantaged by the non-occurrence of the controversy or by the failure to consider certain alternatives have exercised influence on government officials without any action on their part. Yet, such use of power never comes within the purview of the case study approach.[6]

Criticisms of the pluralist school have not been limited to

attacks on their methodology. In this volume, the case study approach of the pluralists is employed to raise questions about the validity of some of their most significant conclusions concerning the nature of urban political systems. While the limitations of these case studies have been noted in the preface, they do provide data that are contrary to a number of the findings of the pluralist school.[7] These pluralist findings can be broadly categorized thus: (1) Urban political systems are open and responsive; (2) there exists a workable model for decision-making; and (3) functional islands of decisions can be perceived. It is to these categories that the remainder of this chapter is devoted.

Openness and Responsiveness of the Political System

Although the pluralists have conceded that differential influence exists within the American political system, they have also maintained that no significant groups are left out of the system. This view has been expressed in a variety of ways: Robert Dahl has written that any active and legitimate group can usually "make itself heard at some crucial stage in the process of decision";[8] Nelson Polsby expresses the same view, when he states that, in our pluralistic systems, "the claims of small, intense minorities are usually attended to";[9] in summing up New York City's political system, Wallace Sayre and Herbert Kaufman found it to be open and responsive, available "to all the inhabitants of the city and particularly to the active participants in the contest for the stakes of politics."[10]

The pluralists, generally drawing these conclusions from their analyses of the processes and the policy outcomes of decision-making, have maintained that most citizens most of the time are politically apathetic, getting involved and organizing themselves effectively only when their "primary goals" would be affected by political activity. The classic exposition of this pluralist view appears in Dahl's description of the metal-houses controversy in *Who Governs?*.[11] In that case, a working-class, poorly educated, politically apathetic Italian community in New Haven organized itself and succeeded in preventing the construction of metal houses, which were intended as residences for blacks, in the neighborhood. These otherwise apolitical people quickly formed a civic association and were able to muster large numbers to appear at meetings of the Board of Aldermen and the Board of Zoning Appeals. At the conclusion of his description of the controversy, Dahl wrote that it illustrated several durable characteristics of the political system—most especially, that involvement in political activities occurs when there is a threat to the primary goals of an individual or group; at such times, the affected citizens will quickly and effectively organize themselves. Sayre and Kaufman wrote in a similar vein about New York:

> Some inhabitants of the city have been slower than others to make use of the weapons the political system places within their grasp, but most—even immigrants from lands with altogether different traditions—have learned quickly, and there are not many who accept passively whatever the system deals out. They have learned that governmental decisions of every kind in the city are responsive to the demands upon the decision centers.[12]

Pluralists have also maintained that each participant in a political controversy almost invariably receives some satisfaction from its outcome. Thus, Sayre and Kaufman wrote that "if there is any single feature of the system of government and politics ... that may be called ubiquitous and invariant, it would seem to be the prevalence of mutual accommodation. Every program and policy represents a compromise among the interested participants."[13]

The validity of the pluralists' views can be challenged at a number of points. To begin with, in their analysis and conclusions concerning political activation the pluralists argued that political involvement is conditioned upon a threat (be it government action or inaction) to primary goals. When such a threat does not exist, citizens are apathetic, the assumption being that their greatest desires (for example, security, sex, love, food, self-esteem) are best attained by channeling their efforts into nonpolitical activities.[14] This view of the cause of political activation led the pluralists to describe the apathetic state of the general populace in our cities as indicating satisfaction with the prevailing political system. According to pluralist reasoning, since the system was open for those groups of citizens who felt threatened, their failure to become politically involved signified their general approval of the actions of public officials.[15] Such reasoning is, however, simplistic. The pluralists failed to consider a crucial question: How does the citizen become informed of governmental action (or inaction) that would threaten his primary goals? Nor did they consider the processes involved in informing the citizen that public action could actually help in dealing with his daily problems. Put another way, the pluralists used an individual, rather than a societal, perspective to analyze the hindrances to activation; they failed to realize that changes in the *political system* could affect the chances of the citizen's being informed of potential or actual governmental action. In short, the pluralists failed to see the complexity of the political processes involved in activation.

These processes—which involve informing the citizen about political issues, interpreting these issues to him, relating the problems in his daily life (of which he is very aware) to the potential or actual activities of government—must be understood before one can begin to generalize about political activation. When one reflects upon these processes, one is struck by the role that society's institutional structure plays in communicating political issues to the citizen and in shaping his frame of reference for interpreting these issues as well as the events in his everyday life. He depends upon a number of institutional factors for these functions: the existence (or absence) of groups that share interests and concerns similar to his and are able to reach him; the activities of those participants in the political system that may threaten or use sanctions against the activities of said groups; the role of television and the newspapers in informing the citizen and shaping his perceptions; and the role of various institutions—such as the school system, the police, the political party, or charitable organizations—that seek to impose their definitions of the situation upon the citizen. In short, when one begins to speculate on the processes involved in activating the citizen, one becomes aware that these processes do not resemble the simplistic model of the pluralists; instead, they are highly complex and have biases built into them. Without an analysis of these processes and built-in biases, one cannot assume, as the pluralists did, a one-to-one relationship between citizen involvement and government threats, by action or inaction, to primary goals.

One of the case studies in this volume illustrates this phenomenon of a group, very directly affected by an issue, which does not get involved in the ensuing controversy. As the housing case study shows, during the protracted conflict over placing public housing in white areas, low-income blacks played no significant role in the decision-making process. Those who supposedly were to be the prime beneficiaries of the Lindsay public housing program played an essentially passive part. Their antagonists, on the other hand, were activated. They organized effectively and were able quite literally to dictate the outcome of the conflict.

According to the pluralist model, the lack of political activity by low-income blacks would signify that the conflict did not involve the primary goals of this group. Pluralists would deny that the case illustrates that the political system is not open to all groups and would argue instead that one cannot assume that these potential public housing recipients wanted to live in white middle-income areas. Such an argument assumes that the apathy of the blacks was due to a choice on their part regarding the issue at hand. Given the long waiting list to get into public housing and the previous apathetic behavior of this group's members, it appears far more likely that their lack of involvement was directly related to their lack of awareness both of the issue and of their stakes in its outcome. In the community, there were no organized groups supporting the program that could "reach" this group; neither black middle-class organizations nor the white liberals who promoted the program had a constituency among the black poor. In all likelihood, those groups that did have a constituency among the poor—such as the churches, the antipoverty agencies, and the regular Democratic organizations—had other organizational stakes that led them to oppose any program that might lead to a dispersion of their constituents.[16] This case indicates that the pluralist conclusion concerning the inevitability of group involvement when primary stakes are involved is open to serious question.

More, however, is at stake than activation. Even if a group of citizens is politically activated, can we accept the pluralist assumptions about the spontaneous and inevitable emergence of group action and leadership skilled in the selection of strategies necessary for success?[17] The pluralists were aware that political resources and skills were differentially distributed throughout the system; yet they never seemed to have analyzed whether particular groups were *systematically* disadvantaged in their ability to organize because they lacked the requisite resources and skills. Pluralists seemed to feel that, if such communities as New Haven's Italians could rouse themselves from their usual lethargic state and organize effectively in a short period of time, any group of urban residents were similarly capable of so performing.

It appears, nonetheless, that groups initially entering the political process are at a distinct disadvantage in this regard. Such groups are usually short on funds, and material resources have been known to be among the best inducements for getting people to work for an organization, particularly if they are low income with little leisure time.[18] The best-known example of a successful organization among the low-income urban poor is the political machine, and it depended upon such material resources. But, in addition, the leaders of these organizations are often political neophytes, and the acquisition of political skills stems, in large part, from experience in the political process. If these groups come from the poorer and less well-educated sectors of the population, as is often the case, their leaders will often lack the technical and professional expertise needed to engage successfully in combat in today's urban political system.

Some of the cases in this volume point out the difficulties blacks have encountered in their efforts to organize on their own behalf. The mental health chapter describes the difficulties black residents experienced in becoming an organized force capable of challenging the relatively cohesive power alliance of Columbia University and the traditional voluntary health organizations in control of the Community Mental Health Board. The case study of the community-action program illustrates how a government program helped promote the organization and development of leadership skills among certain segments of the black community. These two cases suggest that resources such as money, technical and professional expertise, and group cohesion and the skillful use of these resources are scarce commodities among New York blacks. The reality these case studies describe is a long way from the assumption that activated citizens can easily organize and become influential in politics at any time. Once again, findings of the pluralists, upon which they based their conclusion that our urban political systems are open, come into question.

The cases in this volume raise doubts not only about the validity of pluralist conclusions concerning the activation and organization of the citizenry, but also about their conclusion that public decisions almost invariably reflect an accommodation or compromise among the contending parties. Pluralists have claimed that the interests of all the contending parties will somehow be represented in the final outcome, even if only partially. Such a conclusion is open to attack on several grounds. Surprisingly, the pluralists have generally failed to analyze the outcomes of their case studies systematically in order to determine who gained from the final decision. They have limited their efforts instead to analyzing the extent to which the participants obtained what they asked for.[19] Pluralists have argued that an index that documents the extent to which a participant gains what he demanded during the course of a controversy is preferable to one that focuses on the outcome and ascertains who gained from that decision.[20] As a result of this choice, the outcomes the pluralists analyze represent an accommodation and compromise only for those groups that participated in the controversy; only their demands, made in the course of the conflict, are included. Yet, Nelson Polsby, who has made the best-known defense of this methodological approach, has readily admitted that these factors reflect the power realities of the community.[21] In other words, when the pluralists argue that accommodation is the rule, they are, in effect, saying compromise occurs if we limit our analysis to those who had been activated and organized and to the demands they made, which were shaped by their perceptions of what was politically attainable. By so narrowing the definition of the political system we are seeking to characterize, the pluralists have provided us with a conclusion about the distribution of rewards that is of limited value. One wonders whether any political system, as defined by the pluralists, could not be said to accommodate the demands of its various participants.

Before any conclusion concerning the responsiveness of a political system can be drawn, it would seem necessary to study those conflicts that have been suppressed (whether such suppression be due to a decision of the potential initiator that his demands stand no chance of recognition or to threatened or actual use of sanctions against the initiator) and those conflicts that involve "significant" challenges to the values held by the politically dominant groups in the community.[22] There is no gainsaying the methodological problems involved in studying such events (or nonevents); yet without this kind of data, it seems premature to draw any conclusions as to the responsiveness of a political system.

Even if the pluralist approach to ascertaining responsiveness were to be used for the cases in this volume, the limited extent to which the city's political system has accommodated the demands of the black community would become apparent. Before discussing this question, it is necessary to raise a logically prior problem; namely, the value bias inherent in making any judgment about the responsiveness of a political system. The determination of whether a decision has accommodated the demands of a particular participant is a judgment based upon empirical fact *and* upon one's value preferences. It is not enough to validate empirically that a participant received something he had sought from the decision. To conclude that the participant has been accom-

modated by the outcome, one must make a judgment that the
benefits received were, in some sense, satisfactory. This judgment
should be made by the participants, not by the researcher; yet
the pluralists, after verifying that the actors in their controversies
achieved some measure of success, drew the conclusion that urban
political systems accommodated the varying demands and pressures put upon them.[23] That conclusion reflected the beliefs of
the pluralists as to what the participants in a controversy should
reasonably expect. These beliefs, of course, can be very different
from the expectations of the actors. Although it is always hazardous to generalize about the biases of a group of scholars, it does
appear that the pluralists as a group placed a high value upon
stability and upon change that comes about incrementally.[24] As a
result, a political system that rewarded all participants, both
those who supported the *status quo* and those who sought change,
was considered responsive. It was the pluralists, not necessarily
the participants (or the potential claimants) in political controversies, who were satisfied with the outcomes of urban political
systems.

Whether the groups that represented elements of the black
community were satisfied with the outcomes in the controversies
reconstructed in this volume is impossible to ascertain.[25] What
can be done is to compare the demands of these groups with the
outcomes and then, based on our biases, draw conclusions as to
the responsiveness of New York's political system.

One of the cases offered in this volume has its genesis in the
administration of Mayor Robert F. Wagner, Jr. The Wagner
Administration had responsibility for implementing the first year
and a half of the community-action phase of the poverty program.
The law required the "maximum feasible participation" of the
groups who were to be aided in the development and administration of the program. Yet, as Stephen David observes, the
Wagner Administration resisted attempts to implement the provision and made only the most minimal concessions in the direction of involving the poor.

Two of the controversies took place during 1966, the first year
of the administration of John V. Lindsay. Jewel Bellush writes
about the attempt of the Lindsay Administration to locate public
housing projects in white middle-class areas. Among her conclusions: the bulk of the new Mayor's program was never implemented. Edward Rogowsky, Louis Gold, and David Abbott
analyze the attempt to establish a Civilian Review Board as a

means of dealing with the charge of police brutality. The defeat of this attempt—its impact on the new Mayor and on the political tone of the city—is known throughout the nation.

The remaining cases describe controversies and events that took place in the latter years of Lindsay's first term. All involve the issue of community control, reflecting the change that has occurred in the demands of many in the black community. Marilyn Gittell recounts the turbulent three-year history of the attempt to impose community control upon the public school system. She concludes that the decentralization law enacted by the State Legislature does not begin to meet the demands of the proponents of community control and that the professional bureaucracy is now powerful enough to block future attempts at local control. In the struggle over community mental health services for the Washington Heights–West Harlem–Inwood area, Barbara Ehrenreich and Maxine Kenny write that the groups seeking community participation were able to prevent Columbia University from administering the distribution of these services but were unable to secure funding for community organizations providing these services. Finally, Stephen David, in his analysis of the community-action program as it was implemented under Mayor Lindsay, concludes that, while the Mayor encouraged the involvement of the poor and the use of the program to promote demands for community control of various public services, he also took a number of steps to ensure that control of the program would remain with him rather than with the poor.

These cases, each describing a controversy in a different functional area, do not present a picture of a political system responsive to the demands of black groups. If one compares, in each of these cases, the demands made by black groups with the final outcome, one finds they received very little for their efforts. This is not to say that no change occurred during the decade of the 1960's; clearly, the city's political system was not as unresponsive to the black community in the late 1960's as it had been earlier in the decade. These cases do, however, provide impressive evidence that New York City's political system was not as responsive as the pluralists had predicted.[26]

The Model of Decision-Making

Throughout the pluralist writings, a certain model of political decision-making emerges. The actors are usually individuals who represent organizations, agencies, and organized groups, but not

broad social classes. Almost invariably, there are coalitions representing the various contending parties. Participation is confined
almost exclusively to those activists who represent organized
interests. These actors communicate among themselves in a covert
manner, avoiding public notice. The conflict is resolved through
bargaining, and the resolution is usually an accommodation
among the interests of all contending parties.[27]

The case studies raise questions concerning a number of these
characteristics of the pluralistic model of decision-making. The
pluralists expected participation to be limited to the leaders of
organized groups; little consideration was given participation by
the membership. This was in accord with the pluralist belief that
most citizens most of the time were not involved in political
activities.[28] The activation and organization of the Italian community in Dahl's metal-houses case was considered a deviation
from the normal processes of decision-making. Sayre and Kaufman, listing political participants, refer to the leaders of groups
—for example, public officials, both elected and appointed; the
leaders of the political parties; the organized public bureaucracies; nongovernmental groups; and officials and bureaucrats of
other governments—with only a passing reference to the mass of
the citizenry.[29]

In this volume, however, we find larger communities of people
becoming involved in the racial conflicts of the 1960's. In the
conflict over the location of public-housing projects in white
areas, the Italian community in Corona mobilized small-home-
owners, blue-collar workers, *ad hoc* neighborhood groups, and
middle-class Jewish apartment-dwellers. The more massive style
of the 1960's is best exemplified in the well-known conflicts over
the establishment of a Civilian Review Board and over the
attempt to initiate community control of the schools in Ocean
Hill–Brownsville.

This larger number of participants also cast doubt on the
pluralist finding that conflicts almost invariably take place between small, well-organized groups. Instead, the character of race
politics appears to be more and more a social-class or social-
group phenomenon. In the controversy over community control
of education, the Ocean Hill–Brownsville conflict was not merely
a clash between an experimental school district and the United
Federation of Teachers (UFT); it became a clash between large
segments of the black community and large segments of the white
community, particularly its Jewish grouping. The controversy

over the establishment of a Civilian Review Board exhibited similar tendencies, with the Catholic, rather than the Jewish, community in the forefront of the white population group opposed to the black community.

The pluralist model also stressed a covert process of communication. This means of communication among the participants allowed for and promoted compromise among them. One effect of such a strategy of secrecy is to limit the number of participants. Groups (often promoting different ends from the ones being pressed by those already participating) that might have become involved are never informed of the decision process in time. This type of communication process also enables leaders to avoid public commitments to their constituents, thereby allowing greater latitude for maneuver and compromise in the negotiations.[30]

In the 1960's, however, racial controversies had a high, rather than a low, visibility, and it was therefore much more difficult for the city's bargaining process to proceed in the traditional manner described by the pluralists. Thus, in the decentralization case, the conflict was resolved, not through quiet bargaining between representatives of the union and the community but only through a highly publicized citywide strike. In effect, this conflict was fought out in the communications media. In the case involving the location of public housing projects, the Mayor did not follow his predecessor's tactic of gaining the approval of the neighborhood leaders and the public officials whose votes were needed before announcing the placement of public housing sites. Instead, the announcement was made and the controversy fought in a very public arena, with a final outcome that cannot be called an accommodation by any stretch of the imagination.

Another aspect of the pluralist decision-making model is the existence of coalitions representing the various sets of participants. Again, the pluralists assumed that alliances were an invariant characteristic of the process and that no significant groups would encounter any particular difficulties in obtaining allies. The importance of coalitions to the pluralists is stated by Polsby: One of his five conditions for success in influencing public officials is the "capacity to form coalitions with other participants in order to achieve one's goals."[31] Yet the cases described in this volume suggest that black and Puerto Rican groups encounter considerable difficulty in gaining white allies. In these controversies, allies were limited to the New York Civil Liberties

Union, the Metropolitan Housing Council, the Citizens Housing and Planning Council, various religious groups, a small number of civic organizations, and some reformers residing largely in Manhattan. More to the point, a number of these organizations, while announcing support for black demands, often did not come through on a continuing basis; many were also confronted with membership resistance. For example, the New York Civil Liberties Union leadership, which opposed the UFT on the issue of community control of the schools, found its membership taking positions on both sides of the issue.

In short, the pluralists appear to have believed that, in describing a covert process of decision-making with limited participation, they were dealing with universal tendencies that were not likely to change: Almost all urban controversies would be marked by participation limited to the leaders of organized groups, by the absence of involvement of the mass of the citizenry, and by the use of covert processes of communication.[32] Ironically, the pluralists, who criticized the sociologists for assuming that power distributions were permanently related to the social structure, appear to have made similar assumptions about the permanence of the processes involved in decision-making. The controversies reconstructed in this volume certainly cast considerable doubt on these findings of the pluralists.[33]

To understand this belief of the pluralists in the universal tendencies of the model, one needs to know their perception of American society and its political systems at all levels of government. Nelson Polsby nicely summarized much of what they believe when he wrote:

Pluralists, who see American society as fractured into a congeries of hundreds of small special interest groups, with incompletely overlapping memberships, widely differing power bases, and a multitude of techniques for exercising influence on decisions salient to them, are not surprised at the low priority Americans give to their class memberships as bases of social action. In the decision-making of fragmented governments—and American national, state, and local governments are nothing if not fragmented—the claims of small, intense minorities are usually attended to. Hence it is not only inefficient but usually unnecessary for entire classes to mobilize when the preferences of class members are pressed and often satisfied in piecemeal fashion. The empirical evidence supporting this pluralist doctrine is overwhelming, however stratification theorists may have missed its significance for them; the fragmentation of

American governmental decision-making and of American society makes class consciousness inefficient and, in most cases, makes the political interests of members of the same class different.[34]

The pluralists assumed that the fragmented nature of American society and its political system would continue indefinitely. The basis of this assumption was their belief that the claims of all of these significant small competing groups would continue to be accommodated. The responsiveness of the political system would make it unnecessary, in the words of Polsby, "for entire classes to mobilize when the preferences of class members are pressed and often satisfied in piecemeal fashion."[35]

Yet, within a decade of the pluralist writings, broad social classes did appear on the political scene. While this is not the place to work out the complex causal chain that accounts for the changes described in this section, the inability of urban political systems—as well as of political systems at other levels of government—to respond to the demands of black groups is probably of major importance. The failure to respond to the claims of the civil rights organizations in the early 1960's, claims that had a long history prior to that time—such as the demand by the NAACP for the location of public-housing sites in white areas (as described in the scattered-site case), and the demand by the NAACP and CORE for a public committee to review police actions (as described in the Civilian Review Board case)—presumably led to increased dissatisfaction within the black community. This dissatisfaction, in turn, led to the organization of new black groups promoting different goals (for example, community control), to attempts by the older, more established groups to broaden their support, and, most importantly, to a growing sense within the black community that they shared a common fate in the political arena. The movement toward a unified black community has, in turn, led to a mobilization of its opponents and to the kind of political controversy unforeseen by the pluralists.[36]

Functional Islands of Decisions

The pluralists argued that there were different political arenas whose boundaries were determined by functional policy areas. Each of these arenas involved different public officials who were influenced by different nongovernmental interest groups. What little overlap existed among these functional areas was provided by city-wide officials and a few interest groups whose concerns spread over a number of functional areas, but the dominant characteristic of the political system was the relative autonomy of each functional area. Herbert Kaufman neatly presents the core of the argument:

> Each consists of a complex of decision-making "islands." From each such island emanates a flow of decisions and actions embodying the stakes and prizes of politics. The flow from any given island is only loosely related to the flow from all the others; all are, by the same token, relatively autonomous. Every island is composed of a cluster of participants especially concerned with the types of decision that issue from it.[37]

Based upon these findings concerning the degree of autonomy of the functional areas and the minimal overlap of the areas by city-wide officials and nongovernmental actors, these political scientists concluded that the system was pluralistic because there was no single power elite dominating decision-making. Instead, political influence was spread among the actors in the various functional areas. The pluralists, however, never made any attempt to determine the distribution of influence *within* these policy areas. By reconstructing only "important" decisions in each functional area surveyed rather than "representative" controversies, they ruled out such a possible determination.[38] Their choice made sense in light of their goal of determining whether a power elite existed in a particular community. Presumably, if such elite existed, it would more likely appear in "important" rather than in "trivial" issues. By limiting their focus to the "big," rather than the "representative," decisions, the pluralists could not obtain the data necessary to draw any conclusions concerning the patterns of influence within the functional areas.

Several consequences flow from this failure. The most important, as presented by the case studies in this volume, is that we cannot assume that the system is responsive to all groups merely because a power elite fails to exist. The pluralists, by spreading their net over the entire framework of urban decisions, felt satisfied that enough groups, enough pressures, enough interests, enough actors were absorbed by the subsystems to guarantee responsiveness. But how can the responsiveness of the system be judged without considering the possible controlling influence of particular groups over each functional area? What guarantee does one have that there is, for all participants, adequate access to those making official decisions in each functional island?

The cases in this volume do more than raise these questions. They suggest that, in various functional areas, there are elites who are capable of placing severe constraints on—or preventing public officials from accommodating—the demands of groups promoting antagonistic goals. The school bureaucracy and teachers were highly effective against the proponents of community control, as was the police officialdom in its conflict with groups concerned about police brutality. Although no generalized conclusions can be drawn about the patterns of influence in the various functional islands covered by the case studies, the controversies do uncover the existence of a number of potential elite groupings that are able to determine the responsiveness of the system in their area.

Finally, the existence of functional islands of decision has a built-in bias against those who desire to change the *status quo*. In the current urban political system, there is an obvious fragmentation of authority and power. This fragmentation, as many pluralists have pointed out, provides participants, both those favoring and those opposing change, with a variety of points of access. Because, however, any demand for change almost invariably requires the approval of a number of public officials, it is necessary for those who wish to alter the *status quo* to achieve access to all these officials. On the other hand, the supporters of the *status quo* can prevent or limit the scope of change by achieving access to one or, at most, a few of the officials involved in the controversy. In short, our fragmented urban political systems make reform more difficult to obtain. As Sayre and Kaufman concluded in their description of New York's political system: "One consequence of this ordering of the city's political relationships is that every proposal for change must run a gauntlet that is often fatal. The system is more favorable to defenders of the *status quo* than to innovators. It is inherently conservative."[39]

In summary, while the pluralists made a significant contribution when they discovered the existence of these functional islands of decisions, their assumption that such areas promoted the responsiveness of urban political systems is open to question. The pluralists made little or no attempt to ascertain the patterns of influence within the areas they surveyed. As the cases in this volume suggest, elite groupings in these areas, capable of closing the system to antagonistic groups, appear to exist. Finally, it is hard to ignore the possibility that the very existence of this dispersion of authority and power serves those who support the *status quo,* thereby making the system less responsive to those promoting change.

Conclusion

The response of the New York City political system to the demands of the black community during the 1960's raises a number of significant questions concerning some of the conclusions reached by the pluralist school. The optimism of the pluralists in regard to the system's openness and responsiveness; their belief in the primacy, if not universality, of a particular decision-making process that promoted the accommodation of conflicting interests; their conclusions about the pluralistic nature of the system based on their findings that a power elite fails to exist— all such aspects of pluralistic thought are challenged by the findings of these case studies. As the editors have indicated, the cases are not intended as a rigorous test of the findings of the pluralists; nonetheless, their coverage of a number of functional areas as well as the importance of the controversies described make these studies a source of impressive data refuting the pluralist school. At the very least, these cases should elicit questioning and, eventually, the testing of these conclusions that emanated from the dominant school of thought among urban political scientists. In other words, the concern of our volume is not merely to question pluralist conclusions in regard to black city dwellers; it is to call into question the pluralist beliefs per se and to test their applicability to all of the various groups existent in our urban areas—be they students, ethnic groups, or any other as yet uncounted minority.

Our interest in the case studies, however, has not merely been limited to raising questions of concern within the academic community. As citizens as well as academicians, we are interested and troubled by the public-policy implications of our cases. The underlying theme of the cases—as well as of this essay—has been the inability of the city's political system to accommodate the demands of its black citizens—an inability we suspect is not unique to New York. As a result, the black community, in growing numbers, is turning inward and rejecting the legitimacy of institutions and norms associated with the white world. Increasingly, we are becoming aware that we are confronted with a crisis of authority. Increasingly, institutions associated with the white world are finding it difficult to obtain the allegiance of black Americans through consent and are, more and more often, being forced to resort to coercion in order to rule.

This is not the place—nor has it been the intent of the book—to deal with underlying issues involving the legitimacy of existing institutions. We are, however, concerned with the prospect that violence will be resorted to as an alternative strategy unless urban institutions somehow become more responsive to black demands. The resort to violence appears unavoidable unless fundamental changes occur. The increase in mass disruptions, arson, and vandalism in public places, particularly schools; the rise of paramilitary groups; and the increasing number of blacks who answer "yes" to questions regarding their willingness to resort to violence make the possibility of "urban guerrilla warfare" more likely. At least tactically, guerrilla attacks against white persons and property anywhere in a city can be successfully undertaken by relatively few members of the black community. The response of the white community to these actions is fairly predictable: It will be massive, punitive, and repressive.

Whether our political system will be able to avoid these consequences is difficult to answer. The heart of the problem is that we need to know more about the black and white communities. We need to know what actions of our political system would satisfy black citizens and forestall their resorting to violence. Because the decisions that most public officials can make in this area are constrained by what their white constituents will permit, we also need to know more about what governmental programs the white community will support. Because the orientations and opinions of the two communities are not static, we need to know the conditions under which they are subject to change.

Unfortunately, it is this kind of knowledge that is lacking among political scientists. We lack this knowledge because the pluralists chose to concentrate their attention on the behavior of elites rather than on that of the masses. Yet, it is an understanding of the latter that is essential if we are to make wise choices in these times.

This chapter has stressed the inadequacies of the pluralist school; its members can expect better treatment from those who will look at their contributions from the perspective of intellectual history. The role pluralists played in redirecting the orientation of urban political scientists, away from the sterile efforts of the "good government" prescriptionists who preceded them and toward the direction of describing and explaining urban political systems, will be applauded. They will also be praised for their concern for methodology and empirical theory and for their writings on elite activity during a particular period in the history of our cities. At the same time, they can expect to be criticized for universalizing their conclusions and limiting their concern to the activities of political elites. We can only hope that future political scientists will both appreciate the contributions of the pluralists and transcend their limitations.

Notes

1. This conclusion was reached in an excellent analysis of their literature by Nelson W. Polsby, *Community Power and Political Theory* (New Haven, Conn.: Yale University Press, 1963), pp. 8–10.
2. *Ibid., passim.*
3. *Ibid.*, particularly ch. 6.
4. Among the best known of these studies were Robert A. Dahl, *Who Governs?* (New Haven, Conn.: Yale University Press, 1961); Wallace Sayre and Herbert Kaufman, *Governing New York City* (New York: Russell Sage Foundation, 1960); Edward Banfield, *Political Influence* (Glencoe, Ill.: The Free Press, 1961)—although Banfield didn't primarily use the case study method for this purpose so much as for showing the workings of influence; and Frank J. Munger, *Decisions in Syracuse* (Bloomington: Indiana University Press, 1961).
5. Lewis Froman, Jr., *People and Politics* (Englewood Cliffs, N.J.: Prentice-Hall, 1962), pp. 49 ff. The pluralist approach has also attracted the attention of European scholars, and, in fact, several have applied it to community studies abroad. See for example, *The New Atlantis*, No. 2 (Winter, 1970), which is devoted to current work on community power in several European countries.
6. Peter Bachrach and Morton S. Baratz, "Two Faces of Power," *American Political Science Review*, LVI, 4, pp. 947–52; Shin'ya Ono, "The Limits of Bourgeois Pluralism," in Charles A. McCoy and John Playford, eds., *Apolitical Politics* (New York: Thomas Y. Crowell, 1967), pp. 99–123; Todd Gitlin, "Local Pluralism as Theory and Ideology," *ibid.*, pp. 124–45. For a critique of this school of thought, see Richard M. Merelman, "On the Neo-Elitist Critique of Community Power," *American Political Science Review*, LXII (June, 1968), pp. 451–60.
7. See final note of the preface to this volume.

8. Robert A. Dahl, *A Preface to Democratic Theory* (Chicago: University of Chicago Press, 1956), p. 145. See also Dahl, *op. cit.* (note 4), p. 228.
9. Polsby, *op cit.* (note 1), p. 118.
10. Sayre and Kaufman, *op. cit.* (note 4), p. 720.
11. Dahl, *op. cit.* (note 4), pp. 192–98.
12. Sayre and Kaufman, *op. cit.* (note 4), p. 721.
13. *Ibid.,* p. 714.
14. Dahl, *op. cit.* (note 4), ch. 19.
15. *Ibid.,* pp. 309–10.
16. See the discussion in Martin Meyerson and Edward C. Banfield, *Politics, Planning & the Public Interest* (Glencoe, Ill.: Free Press, 1955), pp. 100–102, concerning the opposition of similar groups in Chicago to the location of public housing in white areas.
17. Dahl, *op. cit.* (note 4), pp. 197–98.
18. This argument is persuasively made by Peter B. Clark and James Q. Wilson, "Incentive Systems: A Theory of Organization," *Administrative Science Quarterly,* (September, 1961), pp. 129–66. This same analysis is made by Bellush and Hausknecht in their analysis of urban renewal politics. See Jewel Bellush & Murray Hausknecht, eds., *Urban Renewal: People, Politics and Planning* (Garden City, N.Y.: Doubleday, 1967), pp. 278–86.
19. This methodology was followed by Dahl in *Who Governs?* See his description on pages 332–36 of the appendix of that volume. The rationale for this approach is found in Polsby, *op. cit.* (note 1), pp. 132–36.
20. Polsby, *op. cit.* (note 1), pp. 132–36.
21. *Ibid.,* pp. 134–35.
22. This argument is covered more extensively by Peter Bachrach and Morton S. Baratz, *Power and Poverty* (New York: Oxford University Press, 1970), part one.
23. Sayre and Kaufman, *op. cit.* (note 4), pp. 712–14.
24. Polsby, *op. cit.* (note 1), p. 134; Dahl, *op. cit.* (note 4), ch. 28; Sayre and Kaufman, *op. cit.* (note 4), pp. 736–38.
25. This statement is made with the knowledge that few, if any, groups in a political controversy will ever admit—because of the possible consequences upon their future political activities—that they were satisfied with the results.
26. The editors again refer the reader to their earlier reference on the limitations in using these case studies for purposes of generalization. See final note of this volume's preface.
27. For a description of some of the aspects of this model, see Sayre and Kaufman, *op. cit.* (note 4), pp. 712–14.
28. See the discussion in this chapter on the pluralist views toward citizen apathy.
29. Sayre and Kaufman, *op. cit.* (note 4), ch. 3.

30. For an illustration of this point, see the description of how secrecy aided the promoters of urban renewal, by Jewel Bellush and Murray Hausknecht, "Entrepreneurs, and Urban Renewal: The New Men of Power," in Bellush and Hausknecht, *op. cit.*, p. 221.

31. Polsby, *op. cit.* (note 1), p. 137.

32. After describing this controversy, Dahl wrote that "conflict of this intensity is a rarity. Ordinarily, political decisions move along in an atmosphere of apathy, indifference, and general agreement." *Op. cit.* (note 4), p. 198.

33. Other political scientists have made similar observations. The best known are those of Lowi, when he wrote that the process varies according to the types of public policies at stake. See Theodore J. Lowi, "American Business, Public Policy, Case Studies and Political Theory," *World Politics* XVI (July, 1964), pp. 677–715.

34. Polsby, *op. cit.* (note 1), p. 118.

35. *Ibid.*

36. Much of the difficulty of the pluralists on this point is perhaps explained by Jacobs and Lipsky, when they criticized the pluralists for their almost exclusive focus on elite activity rather than on other strata in local politics. Attention to this latter realm might have forewarned the pluralists of possible changes in the political system. See Herbert Jacobs and Michael Lipsky, "Outputs, Structure, and Power: An Assessment of Changes in the Study of State and Local Politics," in M. D. Irish, ed., *Political Science: Advance of the Discipline* (Englewood Cliffs, N.J.: Prentice-Hall, 1968), pp. 236–38.

37. Herbert Kaufman, *Politics and Policies in State and Local Governments* (Englewood Cliffs, N.J.: Prentice-Hall, 1963), p. 110.

38. For a discussion of the reasons the pluralists chose to reconstruct "important" decisions, see Polsby, *op. cit.* (note 1), pp. 95–96.

39. Sayre and Kaufman, *op. cit.* (note 4), p. 716.

2. Welfare:
The Community-Action
Program Controversy

STEPHEN M. DAVID

The Economic Opportunity Act, popularly known as the "war on poverty," became law in August, 1964. While the act contained six titles, its best known and most innovative feature was contained in Title II: "Urban and Rural Community-Action Programs." Title II provided that local communities throughout the country could develop and administer programs that would offer, in the language of the act, "services, assistance, and other activities of sufficient scope and size to give promise of progress toward elimination of poverty or a cause or causes of poverty." Under the terms of the act, 90 per cent of the costs of these local community-action programs would be paid by the federal government.

Title II further specified that such programs were to be "developed, conducted, and administered with the maximum feasible participation of residents of the areas and members of the groups served"—the famous "maximum feasible participation" clause. On the basis of this clause, the Office of Economic Opportunity (OEO) was subsequently to stress, in administering the law, the participation of the poor in community-action programs. For many observers, this clause was both the most novel and the most controversial feature of the Economic Opportunity Act, and its implementation has generated widespread conflict among administrators, politicians, and the poor themselves.

Even before the passage of the act, however, the concepts underlying this clause were provoking considerable controversy. Indeed, most of those who were associated with promoting the inclusion of the clause had been, since the early 1960's, involved in projects that struck at the very core of the professional welfare bureaucracy's perceptions of the problems of poverty.[1] Focusing on the problem of juvenile delinquency, the Ford Foundation (in its Gray Areas project) and the President's Committee on Juvenile Delinquency had, between 1960 and 1964, funded a total of seventeen demonstration projects in large cities throughout the country. These demonstration projects were based on a conception of the problem of delinquency in which environmental changes, rather than individual treatment, were seen as the most productive method of approach. Hence, the projects were designed to change the policies and practices of institutions involved in the lives of ghetto youths.[2]

The staffs of these various projects maintained close liaison with each other, so that, by 1964, they were able to exert a strong influence on the formulation of the poverty program—an influence that was to lead to the community-action program and the "maximum feasible participation" clause. In so operating, they contradicted the accepted notions held by the social-welfare profession, which generally interpreted poverty as the result of individual, rather than environmental, deficiencies. For the social-welfare professionals, poverty was the product of emotional problems that prevented the individual from availing himself of the opportunities offered by American society. To cure these emotional (mental) problems, social workers standardly advocated the increased use of casework on an individual basis so that, case by case, individuals would be made better able to function in the society.

To proponents of community action, poverty was less the result of individual pathology than of structural barriers, of institutions that were involved in the lives, yet unresponsive to the needs, of the poor. The psychological problems associated with poverty were the result, then, of the failure of these institutions. Thus, while the poor were told that anyone who worked hard could succeed, they nonetheless came out of a school system that failed to educate them to hold skilled and professional jobs, and they faced an employment market that used racial discrimination to prevent them from achieving jobs and promotions. Deviant and delinquent behavior could then be explained as resulting from the inability of the poor to achieve culturally accepted goals by the use of legitimate means and existing institutions.[3] For those ghetto residents who chose not to rebel, the psychological consequences of their failure to achieve these goals—a failure interpreted by them as a reflection of their own inferiority—were different but equally severe.[4] Given this perspective, community-action proponents could argue that concentrating on the psychological problems of the poor meant focusing on symptoms rather than causes. The real target of reform should be the institutions that erected these barriers to the poor.

Although proponents of community action agreed on this analysis of the poverty problem, they differed in their interpretation of the role the poor should play in bringing about change in the policies and programs of the pertinent institutions. Whereas some believed change could be brought about by obtaining the support of groups that already had considerable political influence, most argued it would come only if the poor were politically activated and involved. For this latter group, mobilization of the poor was a necessary first step toward creating a coalition with sufficient strength to bring about reform.[5]

Support for increased involvement of the poor in the political system was not limited to those whose primary concern was poverty. Those who initially promoted the community-action concept were soon joined by a second group whose central concern was the long-standing withdrawal of the poor from politics—as evidenced in their low voter-turnout for elections and in their general reluctance to engage in other types of political behavior. Such proponents saw the "maximum feasible participation" clause as one means of securing greater involvement of the poor in the political process.

For the most part, those taking this position came from high-status backgrounds; many were connected with the media, and not a few were directors of major foundations.[6] While it is impossible to know their motivations in holding this position, it is probable that their underlying concern was with dealing with the discontent prevalent among the large sector of the population that is poor. Unlike the initiators of the community-action idea, they saw the program not as a means of promoting social justice but as a strategy for controlling and regulating conflict, for dealing with discontent.

In any political system, those satisfied with the system's allocation of values (and resources) must also concern themselves with the problem of those less satisfied. Groups that are dissatisfied with public policies may resort to strategies that can result in disadvantages to those more satisfied with the political system. Such strategies can range from the use of violence, at one extreme, to the support of candidates promising a major reallocation of values and resources, at the other. Additionally, should discontent grow widespread, the implementation of government decisions will become increasingly difficult. Implementation always rests on the cooperation of various sectors of the population, though the particular groups involved will vary with the policy area; hence, for example, implementation of the tax laws requires the cooperation of many more citizens than the regulation of airline rates.

The ability of a government to obtain this cooperation is related to whether its citizens believe the government is concerned about their interests. People who trust their government are far more likely to obey or accept its laws, even those they perceive as harmful to their interests. In short, the effectiveness of a government, defined in terms of its ability to carry out its decisions, is dependent on the levels of content and discontent existent within the general population.[7]

One strategy for managing discontent is co-optation—the process of absorbing new elements into the workings of a system in order to undercut threats to its stability and continued existence. Co-optation offers a number of advantages for control purposes. It brings representatives of the dissident group into the system. Having gained some of the rewards membership in the system confers, these representatives also acquire a stake in maintaining the system, for the continuance and expansion of their own rewards is dependent upon the continuance of the system. Once inside the system, such representatives also become subject to control techniques not previously applicable: They become subject to the system's sanctions and can expect to be rewarded, if they show themselves agreeable to some degree of control, and to be denied additional rewards or lose existing ones should they not prove sufficiently amenable. Withal, co-optation does not simply operate as a control device. The involvement of representatives of discontented groups is likely to lead to increased influence by such groups on the decisions and policy outputs of the system.

By the mid-1960's, individuals and groups concerned with the maintenance of the American political system had good reason to be concerned about the apparent lack of trust most blacks in the large metropolitan centers had in the government. The decades of black political apathy had, by this point, been replaced by a growing political awareness and involvement in their communities, and most of this political activity was taking the form of open expressions of discontent with the political system.[8] Sit-ins, boycotts, and street demonstrations became daily activities of black activists. Eventually, the fears of many observers materialized as widespread violence broke out in scores of American cities. By 1967, New York, Philadelphia, Los Angeles, Newark, Chicago, Omaha, Cleveland, San Francisco, and Detroit were among the cities hit by major riots.

Yet, even before these riots began in 1964, concern over the rising levels of black discontent was manifested in support for the legislative passage and administrative implementation of the "maximum feasible participation" clause. Those intent on managing and controlling discontent and those involved with social reform joined forces to support the community-action program. Both groups promoted federal financing of local poverty groups that involved real participation of the poor. The reformers tended to view these poverty groups as the organized base from which the poor could express discontent and press for change; the "elitists" viewed them as a means of promoting the inclusion of representatives of the black community in the ongoing political system.

Once organized, these local poverty groups were to present serious political problems to the existing political forces—especially the mayors—of the large cities. Under the Economic Opportunity Act, such groups could undertake either social-service programs or political activities and expect funding. If they chose the latter alternative, they were bound to make political demands and attempt various strategies in support of such demands. The changes in government policy these groups were to seek would inevitably be at the expense of other elements in the community. Demands for integrated facilities or for increased government expenditures for ghetto projects would inevitably come to be resisted by groups threatened by such claims. No astute mayor could remain unaware that the activation of such political behavior among the poor might produce extremely difficult problems within his political constituency.

Despite such pitfalls, the mayors of most large cities had sufficient power to influence, to a large degree, the manner in which OEO administered the "maximum feasible participation" clause.[9] In most cities, the mayors had a fairly wide discretionary range in determining the direction and extent to which the clause was to be implemented. In New York, the city under consideration in this study, two Mayors have had responsibility for carrying out the community-action program: Robert F. Wagner, Jr., and, since 1965, John V. Lindsay. Each has followed a different policy in implementing the "maximum feasible participation" clause. One promoted the formation of new groups of ghetto residents and pressed for their inclusion into the political system; the other sought to thwart the development of such groups. The study that follows attempts not only to describe these divergent responses but also to explain them by reference to the electoral considerations underlying the policies followed by each mayor. It is, of course, presumed that, regardless of some idiosyncrasies peculiar to New York City per se, the analysis that follows will have relevance to the politics of race and poverty in most of our large urban centers today.

The Wagner Administration

Robert F. Wagner, Jr., was New York City's Mayor during the first year and a half of the community-action program's existence. During that time, the general policy of the Wagner Administration was to resist the involvement of the hitherto unorganized poor in the program. At certain points during his administration, it was necessary for Wagner to grant some concessions to those seeking increased participation of ghetto residents in the poverty program. On the whole, however, the community-action program under his direction was marked by the exercise of decisive influence by public officials and private welfare agencies. Analysis both of implementation at the city-wide and neighborhood level and of the content of the programs themselves will serve to support this conclusion.

CITY-WIDE LEVEL

In January, 1964, Lyndon Johnson declared his "unconditional war on poverty." During the months immediately following this declaration, Robert Wagner made it very clear that he wanted to retain control of the distribution of federal poverty monies within the city. In the spring of that year, in testimony before the House committee considering the Economic Opportunity Act, Wagner urged that local government officials should hold final power of approval over community-action projects. In so testifying, Wagner joined other large-city mayors in warning Congress against allowing groups of ghetto residents a controlling voice in determining the allocation of poverty funds.[10]

In June, 1964—two months before Congress was to pass the Economic Opportunity Act—Wagner established a Mayor's Council Against Poverty (CAP) and an Anti-Poverty Operations Board (APOB). Both were composed wholly of city officials, with Paul Screvane—President of the City Council—occupying a critical position on each: Screvane, later to become the key representative of the Mayor in the city's poverty program, was vice-chairman of CAP and chairman of APOB. According to the Mayor's plan, CAP was to make the final determinations regarding the allocation of community-action funds, while APOB would have operational control of the program. It was APOB that was to prepare the city's initial application for poverty funds, and, in the early months of the program, power gravitated toward APOB because of this strategic position in the application process.[11] APOB was made up of ten city officials whose functional responsibilities were related to the poverty area—for example, the commissioner of welfare, the executive director of the Youth Board, and so forth.

Meanwhile, New York City's private welfare community had begun to raise objections about this CAP- and APOB-dominated structure for administering the community-action program. For many years, private charities in the city had provided the poor with such services as day-care centers, family counseling, and recreational activities. On the basis of their experience, these charity institutions felt they should receive a large proportion of the funds to be distributed by the poverty program. This expectation was not new; these charities had been receiving public funds since the middle of the nineteenth century. Nonetheless, many of the strongest proponents of the "maximum feasible participation" clause had wanted the inclusion of the clause in the act in order to prevent just such a channeling of funds to these established private agencies rather than to indigenous ghetto groups.[12] Among the city's private charities, the dominant organizations were the sectarian federations: the Federation of Jewish

Philanthropies, the Federation of Protestant Welfare Agencies, Catholic Charities of the Archdiocese of New York, and Catholic Charities of the Diocese of Brooklyn. Privately, they informed the Mayor of their concern over their exclusion from the policy-making structure.[13] The Community Council of Greater New York, coordinating council for all private welfare agencies (with a board dominated by representatives of the sectarian agencies), publicly demanded the inclusion of the private agencies in determining the allocation of the city's poverty monies.[14]

In January, 1965, the Mayor responded to the demands of the private welfare community by initiating two changes in the organizational structure to administer the community-action program. CAP was enlarged to include representatives from the private sector, and more importantly, a Planning and Coordinating Committee (P&C) was formed. The P&C had the power to advise CAP and authority to act in CAP's name. The private charities were the dominant influence within the P&C committee, and, throughout the remaining year of Wagner's term, the P&C committee would serve as the spokesman of these interests.

At this point, no representatives of the poor were involved in the top-level boards and committees responsible for administering the community-action program. The dominance of public officials and representatives of the private welfare agencies was reflected in the city's proposal for funding, submitted to the OEO in March, 1965. This proposal stipulated that all community-action programs in the city were to be operated either by public agencies or by the large private agencies.[15]

In the face of these developments, pressure was building to force the city to include ghetto residents in the administration of the community-action programs. Most important, OEO refused to fund the city's proposal until the city agreed to the inclusion of the poor within the decision-making structure. In Washington, Congressman Adam Clayton Powell began hearings. During these, representatives of groups from the slum areas of a number of cities—including New York—complained that they had not been given a voice in the running of their local poverty programs. In the Senate, Jacob Javits had the minority staff of the Labor and Public Welfare Committee issue a report attacking the city's proposal for its exclusion of two ghetto groups from funding. (The two groups were the Puerto Rican Forum, a city-wide federation of Puerto Rican community groups, and Youth-in-Action, a grass-roots organization in Bedford-Stuyvesant). At about the same time, Congressman John V. Lindsay announced his candidacy for mayor and attacked the incumbent administration for its failure to involve the poor. And, in the city, Paul Screvane—Wagner's heir-apparent—was running into difficulty in his bid for the Democratic nomination for mayor in part because of this issue. Another mayoral candidate, Congressman William Fitts Ryan, was hammering at the issue of lack of involvement of the poor by the city, and his candidacy was siphoning off the support of Reform Democrats who might otherwise have backed Screvane.[16]

The combined pressure from OEO, from representatives of the ghetto, from the liberal wing of the Republican Party, and from the Reform Democrats forced Wagner to make concessions concerning the composition of CAP. Up to this point, representation on CAP had been limited to public officials and social-agency personnel. In early May, Wagner announced that CAP would be expanded to include community leaders (whom he would select), representatives of existing juvenile delinquency agencies, and representatives of the poor. The juvenile delinquency agencies had been established in several of the city's poverty areas as a result of the activities of the Ford Foundation and the President's Committee on Juvenile Delinquency. The best known of these agencies were Mobilization For Youth (MFY) and Haryou-Act. The representatives of the poor were to be selected in poverty areas not being serviced by these juvenile delinquency agencies. The membership of CAP was to number sixty-two, with public officials making up 30 per cent of the body, social agency personnel 25 per cent, community leaders 21 per cent, juvenile delinquency agency representatives 14 per cent and representatives of the poor 11 per cent.[17] More importantly, at its first meeting, the new council established an executive committee, which was to become its decision-making body. Membership on the executive committee was shared equally by three groups of participants—public officials, representatives of the private social agencies, and representatives of the juvenile delinquency agencies.

These concessions, however, still did not satisfy those who wanted to involve the poor. OEO continued to withhold funds; ghetto residents held mass meetings calling for increased representation; and liberal Republicans (and the press) continued their attacks.[18] With the mayoral primary drawing closer, Screvane's need for the votes of the Reform Democrats was becoming even more evident to the mayor. Thus, on the first day of June, Wagner again altered the membership of CAP, enlarging it to include a potential maximum of 100 members. He gave the juvenile delinquency agencies additional seats and increased the number of representatives of the poor to be selected by poverty areas not presently covered by the juvenile delinquency agencies. With this reorganization, the membership composition of CAP was to be: public officials, 18 per cent; representatives of social agencies, 15 per cent; community leaders, 13 per cent; juvenile delinquency agency representatives, 19 per cent; and representatives of the poor, 34 per cent.[19]

Despite these concessions concerning the membership of CAP, Wagner initiated a number of other changes that were effectively to maintain control of the community-action program in the hands of the city and the private agencies. He established the Economic Opportunity Committee (EOC), which was to replace APOB as the administrative arm of CAP. Its membership consisted of the eleven city officials who were the members of APOB and six laymen appointed by the mayor (two of whom were the directors of the Federation of Jewish Philanthropies and the Catholic Charities of the Archdiocese of New York) and it was thus under the effective control of city officials. The staff of EOC prepared the applications for federal community-action monies and was to administer the funds received from OEO. This early entrance into the application process by EOC and its total control over the implementation of the community-action program enabled the city to retain considerable influence over the program. Wagner had given merely the appearance of political power to the ghetto representatives on CAP; in fact, he continued to retain actual control over the poverty program.

Having established EOC, Wagner turned his attention to the question of giving APOB new responsibilities. Under the revised structure, it was to have sole authority for approving applications for anti-poverty programs financed entirely by the city as well as for applications for the matching funds that are required for all federal grants. APOB used the same staff as EOC, but this presented no problem since the eleven city officials who comprised APOB were in control of EOC. Wagner used APOB both to fund with money those projects that failed to get the approval of CAP or OEO and to veto those proposals for federal monies that the city did not want funded.[20]

Inside CAP, the representatives of the poor did not exercise much influence. While CAP's major responsibility was to pass on all proposals to be sent to OEO, such proposals were first processed by the staff of EOC and then sent to the P&C Committee, which represented the interests of the private sector. The P&C committee then sent their recommendations to CAP's executive committee, which, in fact, made most of CAP's decisions.[21] This executive committee (or CAP on those few occasions it met) accepted almost without exception the recommendations of the P&C Committee.[22]

The active involvement of the poor in the deliberations of CAP was also held up by the slow process by which they were chosen. In the designated poverty areas where no juvenile delinquency agency existed, community conventions were held to select the members of the local community committee. Delegates to these conventions were representatives of those area organizations that had been invited to attend. The resulting community committees then selected the delegates to CAP—two from each area. This procedure proved time-consuming, with the result that, of the thirty-two representatives of the poor provided for, only two had been selected by the end of October, 1965.[23] Thus, few representatives of the poor served on the council during the Wagner Administration.

In sum, an analysis of the community-action program on a citywide level during the Wagner Administration leads one to conclude that the involvement of the poor was minimal. While they achieved representation on CAP, this was more than offset by the combined influence of EOC, APOB, and the P&C committee, and by the slow selection procedure. During this period, city officials and private welfare agencies dominated city-wide decisions that were to determine the shape of the poverty program.

Neighborhood Level

The original centralized operation envisioned by the Wagner Administration was also subject to considerable debate, so that, in the end, changes were made in order to accommodate the demand for neighborhood involvement in administration and implementation. The final program put forth by the city called for the designation of sixteen neighborhoods as poverty areas. In three—the Lower East Side, Central Harlem, and Bedford-Stuyvesant—the established juvenile delinquency agency in each area was named the organizational representative of the neighborhood. Hence, in the Lower East Side, the organizational representative was MFY; in Central Harlem, Haryou-Act; and

in Bedford-Stuyvesant, Youth-in-Action. In the other thirteen
neighborhoods, community committees were to be selected by
conventions called by the city; representatives of established
organizations in these neighborhoods were to be invited by the
city to attend their area convention and select their committee.
In addition, in each of these thirteen neighborhoods, a Community Progress Center (CPC) was to be established. These
centers were to provide some social services for the residents
(for example, job training) and to refer those in need to existing
agencies providing services to the community. Besides selecting
the poverty area's representatives to CAP, the community committee was to act as an advisory board to the community CPC.

The Wagner Administration's opposition to the involvement
of the poor can be illustrated by examining the selection process
for these community committees and the degree of autonomy
allowed the CPC's. About half of the thirteen designated poverty
areas held their conventions while the Wagner Administration
was in power. Generally, each convention was dominated by
conflict between the representatives of the welfare and religious
institutions in the community on the one side and the representatives of organizations challenging these traditional social institutions on the other. The traditional institutions often included the
settlement houses, the Catholic Church, Protestant churches,
the YMCA, and members of the local business community.[24]
Their opponents were more likely to be poor and to be affiliated with organizations that had only recently emerged in the
ghetto community.

Most observers tend to agree that the traditional social-welfare
institutions were generally victorious in these conflicts.[25] The
selection process was biased in their favor because participation
was limited to the organized elements in the ghetto. As a result,
the conventions tended to select the middle-class representatives
of these institutions. The community committee produced by
this process then tended to select two like-minded members to
serve as representatives of the poverty area on CAP.[26]

Despite the dominance on these community committees of
traditional forces in the ghetto, the city administration insisted
on retaining significant control over the CPC's. The program
content of these centers was determined by the city,[27] and the
Wagner Administration appears to have exercised considerable
influence over their staffing.[28] At the neighborhood level, the
Wagner Administration could derive satisfaction from the fact

that the traditional welfare institutions were in control of the community committees and that the city exercised considerable influence over the operation of the CPC's.

PROGRAM CONTENT

The community-action programs funded by the Wagner Administration were set up and carried out by three different groups of agencies: public agencies, private welfare agencies, and community-based agencies. The preference of city hall was for service-oriented rather than political-action programs, and the administration was very successful in achieving this goal. Most of the programs funded were in such areas as job training, Head Start, recreation, home management, and tutorial programs for students.[29]

The only organizations that concerned themselves with social protest were the community-based agencies, but even these often found themselves hamstrung. For example, each of the CPC's had the funding to hire forty-five block workers who could, potentially, involve themselves in organizing the community. By and large, however, the city and the traditional welfare institutions that dominated the community committees kept such activities to a minimum.[30] Still, while few neighborhood-based groups engaged in political activities to any significant degree, they were nonetheless obtaining a constituency as a result of their service programs. Job training, Head Start, and the like made an organization known in the community; in time, such organizations could turn to the recipients of their services and obtain support for more action-oriented programs.

WAGNER'S POLITICAL STAKES

Mayor Wagner's opposition to the involvement and political activation of the poor in the community-action program apparently stemmed, in large part, from his need to please his electoral constituency. Like most large-city Democratic mayors, Wagner had been elected by an alliance of middle-income white ethnic groups and low-income nonwhite groups. Implementation of the "maximum feasible participation" clause would antagonize his middle-income supporters and undermine the traditional organized ghetto groups that had actively supported him. Only one important element of his constituency did favor the involvement of the poor in the poverty program: Reform Democrats. For the most part, the concessions the Mayor made concerning the composition of CAP were in response to the demands of this group.

Wagner had good reason to assume that the use of federal funds to finance the political activities of ghetto groups would lead them into conflict with his middle-class supporters. Low-income groups could be expected to pressure for a host of demands antagonistic to middle-class interests. They could, for example, be expected to demand additional city services, such as expansion of local hospital and public health services or increased recreational facilities in the ghetto. Such demands could be met only by increasing the tax load of middle-class residents. Similar effects would result from the demands of ghetto groups for the active recruitment to the welfare rolls of all those who qualified for welfare. Attacks on the educational system and the police would antagonize large and prestigious elements of his white constituency. Wagner had already gone through one experience that had warned him of these possible consequences: By the time the city's poverty program began in earnest, he had been forced by his middle-income constituents to put the brakes on the political activities of MFY. One of the juvenile delinquency programs promoted by the Ford Foundation and the President's Committee on Juvenile Delinquency, MFY had been set up on the Lower East Side. Its financial backing came from federal and private sources as well as from the city. In 1963 and 1964, MFY gave financial and staff assistance to low-income groups involved in attacks on several city departments as well as on the school system and police. MFY had also given active support to voter registration drives. In time, MFY came to encourage local residents to participate in two school boycotts and to engage in rent strikes.

The middle-class interests affected by these activities reacted strongly. Local school principals lodged a public complaint against MFY, and the police department indicated its displeasure over an MFY resolution favoring a civilian review board. Local Italian politicians on the Lower East Side opposed MFY's efforts to enroll Puerto Ricans as voters, while real estate interests attacked the use of MFY funds to promote rent strikes. Eventually, public charges were made that MFY was riddled with Communists. In time, the Mayor worked out a compromise concerning MFY, but not before he had learned of the dangers inherent in a program promoting the political activation of the poor.

Wagner's strongest ties in the black community were with its politicians and ministers. Both groups were threatened by any major changes in the slums. Black politicians, dependent on the continued existence of a lower-class segregated constituency, saw major social reform efforts undermining their sources of support. Black churchmen, ministering to lower-status churches, felt threatened by changes in the black community that might weaken their influence over their parishioners. Wagner was also friendly with the leaders of "moderate" civil rights organizations, and these men preferred quiet negotiation to mass demonstrations as a means of promoting their demands. In fact, the New York chapter of the NAACP supported Wagner's attempts to maintain control over the program.[31] All three groups of black leaders felt that the use of poverty funds to promote new groups in their community threatened their own leadership positions. In the past, this leadership structure in the black community had delivered its votes to the candidates of the Democratic Party, and Wagner had no stake in supporting the use of poverty funds to promote the establishment and maintenance of new ghetto groupings that might threaten his bases of support in the black community.

The only element in the Wagner constituency supporting increased involvement of the poor in the community-action program, the Reform Democrats, was by and large made up of young Jewish and Protestant "intelligentsia" who resided in Manhattan. In the 1961 primary, they had helped Wagner defeat Arthur Levitt, the organization choice. In 1965, Paul Screvane, Wagner's heir-apparent, was locked in a close primary fight with Abraham Beame, the candidate of many of the same organizational elements that had opposed Wagner in 1961. To win the primary, it was essential that Screvane gain the votes of most of the reformers. By 1965, the reformers—who had always been issue-oriented—had moved away from their traditional concern with "good government" issues and were speaking to such "liberal" issues as the Vietnam war and the poverty program.[32] Since their inception as a group, the reformers had supported attempts to democratize the Democratic Party. In 1965, their commitment to democratic norms was transferred to the poverty program and they supported attempts to involve the poor. It was Screvane's need for reform votes that eventually led Wagner to make concessions concerning the composition of CAP.

In sum, Wagner's attempt to maintain control over the poverty program and to limit the involvement of the poor was in accord with his political needs. Neither his middle-class constituency nor his supporters in the black community wanted the community-action program used to bring hitherto unorganized ghetto residents into the political system. The few concessions to increased participation of the poor to which Wagner agreed were made only to win critical electoral support for his candidate for mayor.

The Lindsay Administration

Since 1965, the community-action program has been operated under the direction of Mayor John V. Lindsay. During these years, his administration reversed most of the policies of his predecessor. Whereas the Wagner Administration resisted the involvement of the poor, the Lindsay era has been marked by the opening up of opportunities for newer groups in the ghetto. Ghetto representatives have, in large part, replaced white public officials and private welfare agencies as the most influential group of actors in this policy arena. The Lindsay Administration has, however, continued the Wagner policy of maintaining a considerable degree of control over the program. As in the previous section, analysis of developments at the city-wide and the neighborhood level, as well as of the content of the programs themselves, will serve to support this conclusion.

City-wide Level

During its first six months in office, the Lindsay Administration provided several indications that there would be major changes in the administration of the community-action program. Most importantly, the Mayor announced the appointment of a task force to survey the city's antipoverty program and all other official programs intended to aid the poor. This task force was headed by Mitchell Sviridoff who, as a result of his administration of New Haven's poverty program, had a national reputation. In appointing this study group, the Mayor made it clear that the existing structure would have only a short life span in his administration. There were other signs during these months of the new Mayor's policy preferences in this area. The private welfare community became increasingly unhappy about their relations with the Mayor. They found the staff of the P&C committee cut and the new Mayor seeking to diminish their proportionate share of the community-action funds for the fiscal year

1966-67.[33] By the third month of the Lindsay Administration, the chairman of the P&C committee had resigned, and, when no new chairman was appointed and no meetings of the committee held, it ceased to exist. At the same time, the executive committee of CAP—where the representatives of the poor and of the juvenile delinquency agencies were better represented—was increasing its influence in the shaping of the poverty program.

The report of the Sviridoff study group was released late in June, 1966. Its primary recommendation called for the establishment of a superagency—the Human Resources Administration (HRA), as it was to be called—which would coordinate all city activities in the areas of community action, manpower and career development, and social services and public assistance. In the area of community action, its primary proposal for the city-wide level was a call for a major change in the composition of CAP and for the abolition of APOB. The 100-member CAP was to be replaced by a 24-member council, and 12 of these members were to represent the poverty communities and to be appointed by the local coordinating organizations (called community corporations) in the poverty areas. Such corporations would be established in all of the poverty areas of the city and democratic procedures—generally, direct elections—were to be followed in selecting the boards of these corporations. Each board would, in turn, select a president, and the presidents of each of the corporations in a borough would meet and select the borough's representatives to CAP. The size of each borough's representation was related to the number of its residents on welfare, with a proviso that each borough be guaranteed one seat.

This recommendation provided the representatives of the poor with half of the seats on CAP, a proportionate share equivalent to that obtained from the previous administration (if the Wagner total is taken to include both those representatives selected in poverty areas and those coming from the juvenile delinquency agencies). Additionally, the report recommended provisions to insure representation for the poor while the corporations were being formed; this was done specifically to avoid the situation that had obtained under the Wagner Administration. (In fact, on the date the Sviridoff report was released, about two-fifths of the representatives of the poor had not yet been selected for the 100-member council created by Wagner.)

The remaining twelve CAP members were to be private citizens appointed by the mayor, with a maximum of four coming from the board or staff of any agency receiving funding from CAP. This recommendation gave Lindsay the opportunity to appoint allies of the poverty community, and it placed severe limits on the number of representatives of the private welfare community that could be appointed. Upon the release of the report, the private welfare agencies made no secret about their displeasure. The executive director of the Community Council of Greater New York publicly expressed concern over its recommendations, while other agencies expressed their apprehensions privately.[34]

The report also recommended that the reorganized CAP assume the functions of APOB. CAP would thereby have final authority not only over the allocation of federal community-action funds, but also over city poverty monies as well. There would no longer exist a board representing the city administration that could veto applications for federal funding (by denying them the city's share of the grant) and that could fund organizations and programs that failed to win the approval of the poverty representatives on CAP.

On the other hand, the Sviridoff task force recommended the continuation of the Wagner policy concerning the staff that was to prepare the funding requests and to implement the program. It recommended that the city administration retain control over these functions. The report called for the abolition of EOC. To replace EOC, it proposed the establishment of the Community Development Agency (CDA), and it went so far as to recommend that the executive staff of the commissioner of CDA also serve as the staff of CAP. This would enable the city administration to control the staff of CAP. The replacement of EOC by CDA was presumably done to enable the Lindsay Administration to appoint its own personnel to serve as the staff resource for CAP. In short, the Sviridoff report aided the poor in gaining access to CAP and significantly increased the authority of that body, but it continued to deny them control over crucial staff resources.

In August, 1966, the Mayor followed the recommendations of the Sviridoff report and issued an executive order establishing the Human Resources Administration. The executive order provided that CDA and a reorganized CAP would be component parts of HRA. Lindsay named Mitchell Sviridoff administrator of HRA. George Nicholau, then deputy director of the northeast regional headquarters of OEO, was named commissioner of CDA. In September, the Mayor announced the establishment of a 28-man CAP, whose members were equally divided among representatives of the poverty areas and private citizens appointed by the mayor. The poverty area representatives were generally to be selected by the community committees that had already been established under the Wagner program. These committees were to continue to name representatives until they were replaced by community corporations, which would then represent their areas. Most of the members named by the Mayor had close ties with the major private social agencies, but a few of his appointments could be expected to become the allies of the poverty area representatives.[35]

In the ensuing year, a major conflict arose. On one side were Sviridoff, Nicholau, and other top administrators at HRA; on the other, most members of CAP (with their allies in CDA), who represented newly emerging organizations in the ghetto. On one level, this dispute centered around the distribution of influence of these various officials and organizations. Both groups wanted to control the city's community-action program, but the Sviridoff report recommendations and the Mayor's executive order implementing them had provided the Sviridoff-Nicholau alliance with superior resources; these CAP was seeking to wrest away. Underlying this conflict, however, were fundamental divisions concerning the content of community-action programs and the groups that should be responsible for the administration of the poverty program. The Sviridoff-Nicholau group believed that the community-action program should be oriented in the direction of providing social services, while most CAP members championed organizing efforts and political activities. These CAP members also objected to the fact most of the top administrators in HRA and CDA were white, believing that the direction of the city's poverty program should be mainly in the hands of nonwhites.

Sviridoff's resignation in August, 1967, one year after he had assumed control of HRA, brought the conflict to a head. In the months that followed, the Lindsay Administration made a number of decisions intended to deal with these issues. The first concerned personnel changes at HRA and CDA. At HRA, top-level administrators and staff people who had come in with Sviridoff left. Their replacements assumed their new positions with the understanding that their involvement with the community-action program would be minimal.[36] In CDA, nonwhite personnel came to occupy the top-level positions. George Nicholau resigned and was replaced by a black man with previous experience with the community-action program at the neighborhood level—Major

Owens. Owens, in turn, appointed a Puerto Rican—Jack Agueros
—as his deputy commissioner.

At the same time, the Lindsay Administration made several
moves to insure that CDA would be responsive to its interests.
In appointing Owens, Mayor Lindsay rejected John L. Edmonds,
who had been deputy commissioner of CDA and was the candidate of "militant" black antipoverty workers who had staged
demonstrations on his behalf.[37] The same pattern repeated itself
several months later when Owens dismissed the man he had appointed as deputy commissioner and selected another, less "militant" Puerto Rican in his place.[38] Yet another example of this
pattern involved Thelma Johnson, reputed to be the leader of
the black staff members of CDA when Nicholau was commissioner.[39] Miss Johnson was director of the Education Action Division of CDA and had promoted community control of the
schools. In support of her position, her division had bypassed the
field staff of CDA and had communicated directly with various
ghetto groups. Despite the esteem in which she was held by
black coworkers and the popularity of her position within ghetto
communities, Owens instituted a reorganization within CDA that
abolished her division.[40] In short, the Lindsay Administration
"molded" CDA into an organization that would be responsive to
the Mayor and would not take independent actions of its own.

The Mayor, moreover, continued his policy of placing the
crucial staff resources for the review of proposals and the implementation of funded programs with CDA rather than with
CAP. In testimony before the City Council, Major Owens stated
that CDA had the primary responsibility in these areas.[41] At these
same hearings, the Chairman of CAP admitted that primary evaluation of all proposals was done by CDA.[42] CDA's staff for these
functions, in March, 1969, numbered 300 compared to the
Council's 8.

This situation has not led CAP into conflict with CDA. Instead,
their relations continue to appear quite amicable. CAP members
opposed to the Sviridoff-Nicholau policies have seen their interest
in having CDA dominated by nonwhites realized. Moreover, in
accord with their wishes, CDA has promoted the organization
and politicization of the poor rather than social service programs.[43] As a result, CAP has involved itself in policy issues in
the areas of education and public assistance and is presently, with
the support of CDA, pressuring the local community-action
agencies to make political activities their highest priority.[44]

Within CAP, the influence of the supporters of the newly organized groups in the ghetto has increased. Mayor Lindsay has not only not interfered with this shift in power within CAP, but he has resisted opportunities to abort this change. When, in 1967, Congress—reacting against the use of community-action programs for funding political activities of the poor—enacted the Green Amendment, the city's chief executive was thereby enabled to "pack" the top policy-making body in community action with public officials and deprive the poor of representation. Mayor Lindsay, however, refused to implement these provisions.[45] Instead, he limited the number of public officials on CAP to the minimum amount allowed by the Green Amendment—one-third. At the same time, the Mayor retained the initial arrangement of providing the representatives of the poor with half the seats on the council. Hence, the reorganized CAP contained twenty-five representatives of poor communities, seventeen public officials, and nine representatives of city-wide groups (some representing private social agencies, and others representing organizations "friendly" to the interests of the poor). Because they have a number of potential allies among the public officials and groups represented, the poor easily dominate this arrangement. Their potential allies among the public officials have included the Mayor and, at one time or another, such officials of his administration as the chairman of the City Planning Commission, the chairman of the Urban Action Task Force, the Economic Development Administrator, the Housing and Development Administrator, the Health Services Administrator, and the Social Services Commissioner. In addition, the representatives of the Urban Coalition, Citizen's Committee for Children, and the Puerto Rican Community Development Project have been potentially sympathetic to the poverty representatives. As a result of these actions, the poverty area representatives regularly attend CAP meetings while the public officials and the city-wide groups attend with less frequency, thereby leaving CAP in the hands of the poor.[46]

In short, on a city-wide level, the representatives of the poor (more specifically, those affiliated with newly emerging elements in the ghetto) have exercised more influence in the Lindsay Administration than during the Wagner years. During Lindsay's tenure, the poor came to dominate the deliberations of CAP, a goal they never achieved during his predecessor's administration. Moreover, while both mayors denied CAP the crucial resources necessary to determine the character of the community-action

program, the administrative arm of CAP under Lindsay (CDA)
has been made responsive to the dominant groups in CAP.

NEIGHBORHOOD LEVEL

There was also a significant difference between the Wagner
and Lindsay administrations on the neighborhood level of the
community-action program. Under Wagner, the representatives
of the poor in the poverty areas were selected in community conventions dominated by the areas' established social institutions.
Soon after Lindsay's election, the new Mayor leaked word to the
press that he preferred a procedure that would involve the unaffiliated poor.[47]

The release of the Sviridoff report in June, 1966, gave a clear
picture of the Mayor's goals concerning the selection of representatives of the poor. The report recommended establishment of
community corporations in all poverty areas of the city. These
corporations would review all proposals for funds from groups in
the area, and they would also coordinate all funded programs in
their communities. The boards of the corporations were to be
selected by democratic procedures, which generally meant some
form of direct election. There was to be no means-test for voters
or candidates. While the recommendations permitted some variation in the way different areas might select their boards, it insisted that the majority on each of the boards be selected by
some democratic election procedure. The Sviridoff study group
expressly criticized the Wagner convention system for not representing the unaffiliated poor and, hence, for giving "excessive
influence" to "established organizations."[48] In the words of the
report, "the process should make possible the selection of a board
which is broadly representative of the community. . . . the inclusion of unaffiliated persons is important so that the Corporation avoids domination by the representatives of existing
groups."[49]

Twenty-five neighborhoods in the city came to be selected as
poverty areas and, by March, 1969, seventeen of them had established community corporations. Although the selection process
for the board members of the corporations varied to some extent
in each area, there were certain common characteristics. Two-
thirds of all board members were directly elected. The CDA
played a prominent role in the formulation of election plans and
in efforts to get area residents to participate in the elections. Most

elected board members were chosen from smaller geographic areas within the poverty area represented by the corporation; the corporation's territory was divided into smaller districts to aid candidates who, having only minimal funds, nonetheless had a following in a concentrated area. Moreover, all the boards reserved a certain percentage of their seats for poor persons (those whose income fell below the federal government's official poverty level); these percentages varied from one-third to half the seats. One other common characteristic of these elections was the very small turnout of the eligible voters: Turnouts ranged from 1 to 7.7 per cent of the eligible voters.

The contestants in these elections represented a variety of interests. Some represented the traditional social agencies in the area; others, the juvenile delinquency agencies; still others represented the interests of recently organized groups. Finally, there were occasions when candidates primarily represented the interests of a particular ethnic group. Observers of the elections have tended to agree that the traditional institutions in the area did not do as well as they had under the Wagner convention system. Instead, the representatives of newly established groups often found themselves elected as board members of the corporation.[50] The election procedure appears to have identified and aided new local leadership in ghetto areas; yet, though Lindsay's community-action program has reached some elements of the previously unaffiliated, it is doubtful if it has reached those groups—such as the Black Panthers—who have been less likely to work within the system. (Responsibility for contact with such groups has fallen on the Urban Task Force headed by Barry Gottehrer.) Thus, at best, the community-action program has brought only some groupings in the ghetto into the political system.

If the Lindsay Administration promoted increased participation by ghetto residents at the neighborhood level, it nonetheless retained considerable control over the activities of local organizations.[51] In this respect, Lindsay policy has been similar to that followed by the previous administration. The instrument of control is CDA. CDA not only dominates the formulation of programs at the city-wide level, it also exercises the same kind of domination at the local level.[52] CDA's sources of influence include its knowledge of OEO and CAP guidelines and priorities (information either not passed on or ignored by the local agencies) as well as its commanding position in the final determinations made on the city-wide level. Thus, all local agencies know that their

funding is dependent upon CDA approval, and CDA maintains
control over program implementation through its fiscal reporting
systems.[53] The corporations do have a considerable degree of
autonomy in the personnel area, with authority to hire their own
staffs subject only to compliance with broad guidelines of CAP
and OEO. Despite this area of discretion for the corporations, the
trend appears to be toward greater control by CDA over the
activities of these agencies.[54]

PROGRAM CONTENT

The fundamental conflict in the Lindsay Administration has
been between those who wanted to emphasize social service programs and those who wished to use poverty monies for political
activities. Initially, with Sviridoff and Nicholau in commanding
positions, almost all of the programs were in the service area.
Sviridoff stated his policy preferences in his report. He desired
to see community-action monies spent on social service programs
—in areas such as employment, manpower training, educational
services, and child-development services—which would have max-
imal resident participation.[55] From a political point of view,
Sviridoff and his close aides believed that this usage of community action-funds would command support from both the poor and
the liberal communities. They believed that the funding of political activities would leave the program with no allies and less
support—except from noninfluential "militant" sources.[56]

With the resignation of Sviridoff and his allies, however, the
trend in recent years has been toward increased emphasis on
political activities. It is almost impossible to obtain any reliable
data as to the content of the various programs.[57] Yet, all of the
"soft" evidence points in the same direction. An analysis of the
program guidelines adopted by CAP in the past three years reveals a steady progression in the direction of increased support
for political activities. The guidelines for 1967–68, reflecting
Sviridoff's preferences, made educational services such as Head
Start the highest priority. By comparison, the guidelines for
1969–70 state that programs involving "advocacy planning and
action" are to receive the highest priority in funding. The 1969–
70 guidelines define such programs as having "the common aims
of inducing local citizens to exert pressure on institutions to alter
their policies and services in response to articulated community
goals."[58] Interviews with personnel in the program division of
CDA and at the corporation level support this conclusion.[59] Ad-

ditionally, all of the leading officials involved in administering the program, including the directors of HRA, CDA, and CAP, have issued statements in support of the use of poverty monies for political programs.[60]

There are numerous examples of political activities undertaken by the community-action agencies over the past few years. They have been most active in the educational arena. In the dispute over community control of the schools, CAP endorsed the Bundy Plan in November, 1967, and, at the height of the confrontation, proposed its own plan for community control of the school system. At the local level, community-action funds were used by numerous organizations in support of the Ocean Hill-Brownsville school district.[61] These activities apparently had the approval of the top echelon at CDA.[62] Finally, the local boards of the three demonstration school districts included a large number of individuals who were initially involved in the community-action program. Community-action agencies have also been involved in political activities in the areas of welfare and housing.[63] At the risk of over-generalizing on the basis of very limited and "soft" data, it appears that the community-action agencies have been most active in promoting the goal of community control in the policy areas that have concerned them.

LINDSAY'S POLITICAL STAKES

The community-action program under the Lindsay Administration was clearly different from the Wagner Administration's. Whereas Wagner had sought to discourage the involvement of previously unaffiliated elements in the ghetto and had opposed the use of the program for organizing and political purposes, Lindsay reversed both of these policies. Both mayors did, however, share a common concern for maintaining control over the program.

The position of Mayor Lindsay can be explained by comparing the political situation in which he found himself with that of Mayor Wagner. A fusion candidate, Lindsay was elected in 1965 as a reform Republican mayor. His electoral base was unstable. Because the Republican Party is a minority party in the city, Lindsay needed to expand his support beyond the regular Republican vote. In 1965, this support came largely from Reform Democrats. These Reform Democrats shared the antimachine bias of previous "good government" movements, but they were also much more "liberal" than their fusion predecessors. The heroes of the reform movement were Adlai Stevenson, Herbert Lehman, and Eleanor Roosevelt—all antiorganization *and* liberal Democrats. Thus, when the Democratic candidate in 1965 was an organization regular with no particularly outstanding liberal credentials, they supported Lindsay in large numbers. Even with the support of most of the regular Republicans (the Conservative Party candidate William Buckley attracted some of these votes), the Liberal Party, and a large share of the Reform Democratic vote, Lindsay won by only a small margin and with well less than a majority of the vote.

Looking toward 1969, Lindsay must have realized he would face difficulties. Lindsay was aware that he had been elected with the votes of two groupings who were in sharp opposition on most issues. As the Republican candidate, Lindsay had received the votes of many regular and conservative Republican voters; he also had the support of the most liberal wing of the Democratic Party. The probability of his retaining the support of both groups after four years as Mayor was small.

Thus Lindsay needed to obtain additional support from among the electorate. The poor were an obvious target. At the time, the most effective political structure in the ghetto was the Democratic Party organization, but the growing politicization of the poor threatened to undermine their traditional alliance with the white middle-class in that party. There were a significant number of issues on which the poor would find their demands opposed by their erstwhile allies. Lindsay could use the community-action funds to set up independent organizations in the ghetto, which could then compete with the Democratic clubs for support among the poor. By staffing these community-action groups with people from the community and by permitting them to engage in political activities, the Mayor increased the possibilities that these organizations would become centers of support for him against the candidate of the regular Democratic organization.

Such an alliance with the poor could not be expected to lessen his support among Reform Democrats. The reformers generally had a liberal stance on most issues, and, as they were, on the whole, upper-middle-class professions, their interests would not be directly affected by the entrance of the poor into the city's political system. The bureaucrats who manned the city agencies would be in the line of fire, not the reformers, who were generally employed by the city's large corporations or by the firms that service these corporations (for example, law, accounting, advertising).

This same analysis applies to the "moderate" wing of the Republican Party. Those voters who identified with that wing also tended to be engaged in the very same concerns that employed the Reform Democrats. Moreover, the large corporate community with which this group of voters has strongly identified had, in the late 1960's, given many indications that it desired the alleviation of many of the problems besetting the poor. Many of these companies were by then aware that their continued prosperity depended upon tranquility in our great cities.

The only element in the alliance that elected Lindsay in 1965 that would be disaffected by his move toward the poor would have been the conservative Republicans in his own party. Primarily middle-class private homeowners, often civil servants or in businesses of their own (or in firms or businesses that serviced these small businesses), they could be expected to oppose demands of the poor that would either require increased tax payments or some form of integration. Lindsay, however, could calculate that he would retain the votes of some of this group so long as he was the regular Republican candidate and that the votes of those who left him would more likely end up going to the Conservative Party candidate rather than to the Democratic candidate, who would be his major opponent.

Yet Lindsay must also have been aware of the risks contained in allowing the previously unaffiliated poor to run their own political organizations. These groups could make demands whose financial costs would alienate his upper-middle-income voters. These organizations could stir fights with bureaucratic groups that had a constituency among elements of the Lindsay alliance. Last, once the expectations of these newly organized ghetto residents began to rise, they might begin making demands that Lindsay couldn't possibly satisfy, and this could lead these groups to reject the Mayor. In order to avoid these situations, Lindsay moved to insure that CDA would be responsive to his demands and that it would be able to control the activities of the community-action agencies. In this way, Lindsay hoped to minimize the risks that accompanied his support for promoting participation of the poor in the poverty program.

Conclusion

There were significant differences in the policies followed by the Wagner and Lindsay administrations in administering the "maximum feasible participation" clause. The Wagner Administration sought to limit the involvement of the poor and to keep control over the community-action program. The Lindsay approach, while also concerned with retaining control over the program, did promote the involvement and participation of new groups of the poor. These differences in policy reflected different political needs. Wagner was concerned about maintaining the traditional Democratic middle-income–low-income alliance and saw the introduction of new elements of the poor into the political system as a threat to the alliance. Lindsay, seeking new sources of support in order to buttress an unstable minority alliance that had elected him, saw the community-action program as a means of increasing his support among the city's poor nonwhite voters.

Though the data are fragmentary, the two groups that supported the inclusion and implementation of the "maximum feasible participation" clause could find some satisfaction in its impact on the city's poverty program. The reformers had sought to involve the poor in order to bring about fundamental changes in the institutions that governed their lives. Clearly, these changes have not occurred in New York City (or in any other large city). The school system, the institutions involved in providing health and welfare services, the law-enforcement agencies—none of these have changed appreciably over the past five years. But could one have expected the community-action program alone to bring this about? In part, the problem lies in the program's meager funding (the city's total, including city funds, for non-earmarked programs has averaged about $35 million a year). But, in large part, the problem is that the support required to bring about such changes must come from both the black *and* the white communities and the community-action program was only intended to bring about changes among ghetto inhabitants.

Within the ghetto, the community-action program has helped the poor to build up their power base. It has involved new participants in the political process. The program has been a source of recruitment of new leaders of the poor. It has encouraged ghetto residents to believe they can obtain control over institutions and events within their community. Finally, its leaders have obtained important political skills, such as knowledge about running an organization, and an understanding of the larger political processes.

Those who, because of their concern for social control, supported the program could find satisfaction in newspaper reports during the summer of 1969, in which the program was credited with preventing major riots in our large cities.[64] These reports argued that the political activities inspired by the poverty program served as "safety valves" and diffused energies that might otherwise have gone into large-scale rioting. At the same time, there was universal recognition that the program had not reached those elements in the black community that might resort to guerrilla warfare. While large-scale rioting has apparently decreased in frequency, the number of shoot-outs between "militant" blacks and the police has, if anything, increased. It was in recognition of this limitation of the program that Mayor Lindsay established and used the Urban Task Force. However, to the extent that the community-action program has served to isolate the "militants" in the black community, the groups concerned with controlling and preventing violent conflict between the races can take some comfort.

Notes

1. The description of proponents of the community-action concept relies heavily on the excellent case study by Richard Blumenthal, "The Bureaucracy: Antipoverty and the Community Action Program," in ed. Alan P. Sindler, *American Political Institutions and Public Policy* (Boston: Little, Brown, 1969), pp. 128–80. Another excellent study, which describes the origin and initial implementation of the clause is Brian H. Smith, "The Role of the Poor in the Poverty Program: The Origin and Development of 'Maximum Feasible Participation'" (Master's thesis, Columbia University, 1966).
2. A first-rate study of the political difficulties these projects encountered can be found in Peter Marris and Martin Rein, *Dilemmas of Social Reform: Poverty and Community Action in the United States* (New York: Atherton, 1967).
3. This thesis was promoted in a book that had wide impact on the thinking of this group. See Richard A. Cloward and Lloyd E. Ohlin, *Delinquency and Opportunity: A Theory of Delinquent Gangs* (New York: The Free Press, 1960).
4. An excellent analysis of the psychological effects of ghetto life is to be found in Kenneth B. Clark, *Dark Ghetto: Dilemmas of Social Power* (New York: Harper & Row, 1965).

5. These disagreements among the group that was most active in promoting the community-action approach are very well described and analyzed in Blumenthal, *op. cit.* (note 1), pp. 137–42.

6. It is perhaps worth noting that one study of the first two years of the community-action program in New York, Philadelphia, and Chicago concluded that newspapers generally supported the political activation of the poor. See Paul E. Peterson, "City Politics and Community Action: The Implementation of the Community Action Program in Three American Cities" (doctoral dissertation, University of Chicago, 1967), pp. 345–53.

7. For a perceptive analysis of this function of government, see William A. Gamson, *Power and Discontent* (Homewood, Ill.: Dorsey Press, 1968).

8. See, for example, Lester W. Milbrath, *Political Participation* (Chicago: Rand McNally, 1965), pp. 138–41.

9. For an article describing the reaction of mayors in general to the clause and the strategies they followed, see Stephen David, "Leadership of the Poor in Poverty Programs," *Urban Riots: Violence and Social Change,* Proceedings of the Academy of Political Science XXIX (July, 1968).

10. The other large-city mayors who made similar requests were Richard J. Daley of Chicago, Jerome Cavanaugh of Detroit, and Raymond Tucker of St. Louis. In addition, the U.S. Conference of Mayors took a similar position. For a description of this testimony, see Smith, *op. cit.* (note 1), pp. 29–34.

11. Peterson, *op. cit.* (note 6), p. 134. The Peterson dissertation is, in the author's opinion, the finest work describing and analyzing the Wagner Administration policies in this area.

12. For a description of the objections to traditional private agency services by these proponents, see David, *op. cit.* (note 9), pp. 87–88.

13. Peterson, *op. cit.* (note 6), p. 136.

14. For a study of the distribution of influence among the city's charities within the Community Council, see Stephen David, "A History of the Internal Political Life of the Community Council of Greater New York" (Ph.D. dissertation, Department of Public Law and Government, Columbia University, 1967).

15. Howard W. Hallman, "Community Corporations in New York City" (draft paper written by a member of a study group formed by Mayor Lindsay, January, 1969), p. 2.

16. In the actual vote, this siphoning-off succeeded in denying Screvane the nomination. Ryan obtained 15 per cent of the vote, thereby enabling Abraham Beame to defeat Screvane in the primary.

17. Peterson, *op. cit.* (note 6), p. 141.

18. *The New York Times,* May 26, 1965; May 31, 1965.

19. Peterson, *op. cit.* (note 6), p. 141.

20. *The New York Times,* March 25, 1966; Bertram M. Beck, "Organizing

Community Action," in eds. Robert H. Connery and Demetrios Caraley, *Governing the City: Challenges and Options for New York* (New York: Praeger, 1969), pp. 163–64; Peterson, *op. cit.* (note 6), pp. 148–49.

21. Hallman, *op. cit.* (note 15), p. 3; Institute of Public Administration, *Developing New York's Human Resources, A Report of the Study Group Directed by Mitchell Sviridoff,* 2 vols. (New York: Institute of Public Administration, 1966), I, p. 14. Hereafter referred to as the Sviridoff report.

22. *Ibid.,* I, p. 14.

23. City of New York, "Facts on the Poverty Program in New York City" (Press release, October 26, 1965).

24. Peterson, *op. cit.* (note 6), p. 154.

25. Hallman, *op. cit.* (note 15), p. 31; Peterson, *op. cit.* (note 6), p. 68; *The New York Herald Tribune,* December 9, 1965.

26. Interview with Raleigh Davenport, Director, CAP, August, 1969.

27. Peterson, *op. cit.* (note 6), p. 170; Sviridoff report, *op. cit.* (note 21), I, p. 14.

28. The Sviridoff report charged that there was "dissatisfaction with the CPC approach because the Community Committees were required to accept a pre-packaged staffing pattern and because the staff are city employees." See Sviridoff report, *op. cit.* (note 21), I, p. 13. The conclusions of the Sviridoff report were supported by Hallman in his article and by Raleigh Davenport, CAP Director from the summer of 1966 through the summer of 1969. See Hallman, *op. cit.* (note 15), p. 7. Davenport's evaluation was made in an interview with the author, cited in note 26. Peterson, however, concluded that the community committees wrested much of the control over personnel from the city. See Peterson, *op. cit.* (note 6), pp. 170–71.

29. Beck, *op. cit.* (note 20), p. 164; interview with Henry Cohen, former first deputy administrator of HRA, August, 1969; interview with Raleigh Davenport, cited in note 26.

30. Peterson, *op. cit.* (note 6), p. 181.

31. *Ibid.,* p. 321.

32. Peterson reports that Reform clubs were most interested in these two issues in 1965. *Ibid.,* p. 230.

33. *The New York Times,* June 3, 1966; Peterson, *op. cit.* (note 6), pp. 150–51.

34. *The New York Times,* June 14, 1969; June 28, 1969; Hallman, *op. cit.* (note 15), p. 30.

35. The potential allies included the Reverend Milton A. Galamison; former State Assemblyman Frank Torres; Winslow Carlton of MFY; David W. Berry of the New York City Mission Society; and the Reverend H. Carl McCall of the Taconic Foundation. Peterson reached the same conclusion in his analysis of the representatives selected by the Mayor. *Op. cit.* (note 6), p. 151.

36. *The New York Times*, October 7, 1967. Two years later, the City Council study of HRA would conclude that the administrator of the agency—Mitchell Ginsberg—exercised little influence over CDA or CAP or over any of the other constituent parts of the superagency. Council of the City of New York, *Final Report of the In-Depth Study of the Human Resources Administration of the City of New York*, July 24, 1969, p. 6. Hereafter referred to as Council report.

37. *The New York Times*, April 16, 1968.

38. *Ibid.*, July 4, 1968; August 8, 1968.

39. At one point, black staff members who were loyal to Miss Johnson engaged in a fight with Puerto Rican staff members loyal to a competitor of Miss Johnson's. See *The New York Times*, June 23, 1967.

40. City of New York, "Proposed Reorganization Design for the Community Development Agency," summer, 1968.

41. City of New York, "Public Hearings Before the City Council Special Committee to Make an In-Depth Study of the Human Resources Administration," March 3, 1969, p. 426. Hereafter referred to as Council hearings.

42. *Ibid.*, testimony of Edwin Greenidge, Chairman, CAP, March 3, 1969, pp. 322–35. The Council committee studying HRA reached the same conclusion. See Council report, *op. cit.* (note 36), pp. 32–33.

43. Council hearings, *op. cit.* (note 41), testimony of Major Owens, March 3, 1969, pp. 420–26; Council report, *op. cit.* (note 36), p. 33. Also, interview with Lloyd Terry, Assistant Commissioner, Program Operations, CDA, August, 1969.

44. For a statement of CAP's program priorities for the fiscal year 1969–70, see City of New York, Council Against Poverty, "Versatile Program Guidelines: 1969–70," March, 1969.

45. For a discussion of the Green amendment and the factors that led to its passage, see David, *op. cit.* (note 9), pp. 97–100.

46. Council hearings, *op. cit.* (note 41), testimony of Edwin Greenidge, pp. 408–9.

47. *The New York Herald Tribune*, December 12, 1965.

48. Sviridoff report, *op. cit.* (note 21), II, p. 23.

49. *Ibid.*, p. 16.

50. Hallman, *op. cit.* (note 15), p. 31; Beck, *op. cit.* (note 20), pp. 172–78; interview with Henry Cohen, cited in note 29; interview with Bernice Lyons, Representative to CAP from the Long Island City Community Corporation, August, 1969; *The New York Times*, January 20, 1969; February 7, 1969.

51. In addition to the corporations at the local level, there are also what is known as delegate agencies. Both types of organizations operate community-action programs. At present, the programs operated by the corporations are more heavily funded than those of the delegate agencies. Thus, in fiscal 1968–69, more than twice as much money went to pro-

grams operated by the corporations as to activities performed by the delegate agencies. See Hallman, *op. cit.* (note 15), p. 34.

52. *Ibid.,* pp. 33–34; Council report, *op. cit.* (note 36), pp. 32–33.
53. Council hearings, *op. cit.* (note 41), testimony of Major Owens, pp. 150–57. In his testimony, Owens repeatedly stressed that his field staff was too small to undertake adequate monitoring of the local-level agency activities. See also pp. 488–93.
54. See the highly informative testimony of Henry Cohen, which provides a historical overview of the attempts made by the Lindsay Administration to exercise central control at this level. Council hearings, *op. cit.* (note 41), pp. 122–25.
55. Sviridoff report, *op. cit.* (note 21), I, pp. 14-17.
56. Interview with Henry Cohen, cited in note 54. For an insight into Sviridoff's political thinking, see the interview, given after he resigned from HRA, in *The New York Times,* February 25, 1968.
57. Two reasons for the lack of this data are the feelings of many people in the program that it could be used against them and the inexperience of many of those employed to administer the program. In his article on the New York community-action program, Bertram Beck indicates he ran into similar difficulties. *Op. cit.* (note 20), p. 174.
58. See the following documents of CAP and CDA: "Program Goals and Guidelines for New Areas (March 22, 1967)," "Community Action Program Proposal Submission Guidelines for Program Year 1968–69," and "Versatile Program Guidelines: 1969–70."
59. Interview with Richard Brown, Deputy Assistant Commissioner, Program Planning and Budget Review, August, 1969; Interview with Bernice Lyons, cited in note 50.
60. *The New York Times,* February 15, 1969. Council hearings, *op. cit.* (note 41), testimony of Mitchell Ginsberg, HRA Administrator, February 14, 1969, pp. 78–88; testimony of Edwin Greenidge, pp. 357–73, interview with Lloyd Terry, cited in note 43. In an analysis of Philadelphia's community-action program, which also elected its local representative, Paul Peterson concluded that the elected representatives sought "particularistic" goals (such as specific aid for constituents) rather than supporting programs intended to aid the poor as a group. Peterson attributes the selection of particularistic goals as a function of the election procedure used to select the local representatives. See Paul E. Peterson, "Forms of Representation: Participation of the Poor in the Community Action Program," *The American Political Science Review,* LXIV, 2, pp. 491–507. In light of Peterson's findings and the "softness" of the data available about the content of New York City's programs, there is a need for detailed studies of the programs at the corporation and delegate agency level.
61. Council hearings, *op. cit.* (note 41), testimony of Edwin Greenidge, pp. 390–94.

62. *The New York Times,* October 12, 1968.
63. In a recent *New York Times* article, a city official—annoyed over the constant political involvement of these agencies—labeled the personnel of the community-action agencies as "povertycrats." *The New York Times,* Nov. 9, 1969.
64. For example, see *The New York Times,* August 10, 1969, p. 61; *ibid.,* section IV, p. 9.

3. Police:
The Civilian
Review Board Controversy

EDWARD T. ROGOWSKY,

LOUIS H. GOLD, AND

DAVID W. ABBOTT

On May 2, 1966, Mayor John V. Lindsay fulfilled a campaign promise by issuing an executive order creating a new Civilian Review Board (CRB) to receive complaints against the police. The Mayor's announcement touched off one of the most bitterly fought electoral battles in New York City's history. It also signaled the emergence of what now may safely be termed a continuing crisis in New York City politics. At its core, this crisis involves the capacity of the city's political system to respond creatively to the stress generated when the civil rights movement

This chapter is a revised and updated version of the authors' study *Police, Politics and Race: The New York City Referendum on Civilian Review* (New York and Cambridge: The American Jewish Committee and the Joint Center for Urban Studies of the Massachusetts Institute of Technology and Harvard University, 1969). Used by permission of the authors and publisher.

59

moved north and assumed new forms. The central hypothesis of this chapter is that New York City has been governed by an institutional structure in which the loci of power reside in large autonomous bureaucracies, and it is the collision of this power structure with the race issue that has precipitated a crisis in the political life of the city.

As recently as 1960, when most observers confidently believed that New York's government was one of the most pluralistic and open in the nation, Sayre and Kaufman sounded a cautionary note in their otherwise optimistic study of the city. After demonstrating the multicentered nature of the city government and its ability to accommodate diverse values, they suggested that "one of the consequences of this ordering of [the] city's political relationships is that every proposal for change must run a gauntlet that is often fatal. The system is more favorable to the defenders of the status quo than to innovators."[1] A political system that must operate under these constraints faces the risk of *immobilisme* and irrelevance. The very structures of influence and associated rules of the game that contribute to its pluralism may limit its ability to manage conflict or to produce structural reforms appropriate to new political conditions. Under these circumstances, there exists a systemic strain leading toward expanded conflict: *status quo* groups seek to maintain the stability and autonomy of existing structures of influence, while advocates of change seek to undermine the values that support those structures.

Nowhere is this strain more evident than in the politics of race in large Northern urban centers. And, contrary to the earlier expectations of most liberal observers, it is now clear that neither the democratic ideology of equality of opportunity nor good-government notions concerning the public interest will automatically resolve the conflict generated by racial issues. The civil rights advocate in the North soon discovered he was not simply fighting against the attitude of racial prejudice—a battle that might be won easily by a traditional liberal coalition; he was also faced with the need to overcome official ideologies that serve to protect existing influence structures. Time-honored principles of municipal reform, such as "the separation of politics and administration," "promotion by merit," and the dictum that "administrative decisions should be made by professionals," present subtle and, therefore, more difficult obstacles to surmount. These values, which are, for many, the cornerstone of the openness and pluralism of the system, also secure bureaucratic autonomy and protect

patterns of institutional racism. The logic of advocacy leaves no
alternative other than escalating the conflict in the hope of mobilizing sufficient political support for social change. Recent political events in New York City, however, suggest that the escalation
of conflict may result in little more than a heightened sense of
frustration for the innovator in symbolic, rather than substantive,
politics.

The Civilian Review Board controversy contains all of these
elements. At its institutional core, the controversy revolved
around the tripartite relationship between city hall, the administrative leadership of the Police Department, and the organized
police bureaucracy—primarily, the Patrolman's Benevolent Association (PBA). Sayre and Kaufman provide the best formulation
of this relationship, which they find common to both the Police
and Fire departments:

> The leaders of the Police and Fire Associations focused their atten-
> tion most continuously upon their own agencies—the top command
> of the Police and Fire Departments. Here their first aim has been to
> reduce, as drastically as they can, the access of outsiders to the
> decision-making process and to absorb the supervisory and execu-
> tive ranks of the two Departments into their own bureaucratic sys-
> tem. . . . The two Departments are now closed in the most exact
> sense. The Police and Fire Bureaucracies are supervised and directed
> by officers and officials whom they recognize and regard as "their
> own." . . . In the Police Department, the closed system now extends
> by accepted custom up to and including the Commissioner, with
> only one or two secondary posts of limited assignment open to
> outsiders. . . . The leaders of the Police and Fire Associations are
> more than ordinarily secure in their own "citadels", their own de-
> partments into which fewer and fewer outsiders (whether Mayors,
> other officials, party leaders, or interest groups) are allowed to
> intrude except on terms of deference and a willingness to subscribe
> to established mores.[2]

In consequence, both the mayor and the police commissioner
have been cut off from those resources that might allow them to
affect leadership or direction over the police bureaucracy. Typi-
cally, the only outside institution capable of imposing change
upon the Police Department has been the court system, and its
effectiveness has been limited largely to ensuring constitutional
safeguards in pretrial proceedings.[3] Otherwise, the rules of the
game have prescribed that any alteration in enforcement policy
must be a product of decision-making wholly within the Depart-

ment, and few mayors (or commissioners) have had the temerity to challenge the power of the entrenched bureaucracy.

Civilian Review: Stages of Conflict

In the thirteen-year history of the struggle for civilian review, several political processes have been called upon in the attempt to resolve the controversy. At each stage, the outcome reflected an imperfect compromise among some of the participants and led others to search for a new battleground. Each decision was only temporarily binding. Conflict continued to grow until, by 1966, it had expanded to such proportions that an internal political, or bureaucratic, compromise was no longer possible. Instead, the problem was translated into an electoral question, when a public referendum on civilian review was forced by some of the participants.

The first round of the controversy occurred in the early 1950's. The precipitating event was the appearance of a story in the *New York World-Telegram and Sun*.[4] The writer, benefiting from a "leak," exposed what was an allegedly secret agreement made in 1952 between the New York City Police Department and U.S. Assistant Attorney General McInerney. According to the agreement, the New York City police were to be exempt from FBI queries in cases involving complaints of civil rights violations. Police Commissioner Monaghan's immediate response to the story was to deny such an accord existed, although his statement was subsequently contradicted by McInerney and others. At about the same time the story broke, a federal grand jury in New York City began hearings on charges of police brutality. These hearings, along with several other investigations sparked by the story, served to promote the visibility of the issue.

The range of participants in this initial stage of controversy was limited, despite the publicity given the issue. The NAACP and the New York Civil Liberties Union (NYCLU) were the most prominent organizations involved. As the several investigations continued, these two groups, joined by a smattering of "good-government" organizations, demanded some form of civilian review of the police, especially in the handling of complaints of alleged brutality by members of the force.

Incumbent Mayor Vincent Impellitteri played no active role in the controversy. Supporting his Police Commissioner, he rejected demands for Monaghan's ouster and otherwise refrained from any attempt to exercise mayoral leadership over the Police

Department. The PBA introduced its classic rejoinder to demands for civilian review by ascribing protests against brutality to Communists and other suspicious groups. Although a few local public officials—including Representatives Adam Clayton Powell and Jacob Javits—joined in the demand for investigations of brutality, the issue did not generate direct political impact. This was particularly evident in the deliberations of the City Council, where the matter narrowed to the question of what sort of investigating committee to create.

The strain between external demands and internal resistance was apparent in the temporary solution that was enacted. Commissioner Monaghan created an internal Civilian Complaints Review Board, composed of three Deputy Commissioners, and announced that the department would institute, for members of the force, a human-relations course designed to improve police-community relations. Outsiders viewed these changes as a smoke screen. Departmental turmoil was evidenced by a number of staff changes, including the appointment of the first Negro deputy inspector. In the November, 1953, mayoral election, civilian review was not an issue, but shortly after his victory, Robert Wagner announced he would replace Monaghan.

During the next several years, a constant demand for stronger review procedures was heard, and complaints against police brutality, especially in the black and Puerto Rican neighborhoods of the city, intensified. But, as a single issue, civilian review could not muster sufficient political strength to battle the established police bureaucracy. It was only with the intensification of the civil rights movement, especially in Northern cities, that the issue in New York escalated.

In April, 1964, James Farmer, National Director of the Congress of Racial Equality (CORE), stepped up his group's demand for an independent review board. The new Police Commissioner, Michael J. Murphy, responded with a defense of the department's internal board, scoring the drive by "irresponsible people" to undermine police effectiveness.[5] As the public debate mounted, additional groups joined the call for civilian review, including the Puerto Rican Committee for Civil Rights, the City Club, the Metropolitan Council on Housing, the executive committee of the New York County Democratic Party, and the Liberal Party. The PBA continued to spearhead antiboard forces and was joined by the Teamsters Union, the Commerce and Industry Association, and the New York City Transit Authority Policemen. Although

City Councilman Theodore Weiss (Democrat of Manhattan) introduced a bill to create an independent board, his continuing
leadership role in this issue in the Council was symptomatic of the
narrow party support in the matter. Weiss, a Reform Democrat
and one of the most ideologically oriented councilmen, could not
hope to attract much support among his more timid colleagues.
When the Council began hearings on the Weiss bill in June, 1964,
the PBA turned out 1,200 policemen to picket City Hall against
the measure.

In July, the issue exploded beyond the confines of City Hall.
Large-scale rioting broke out in the streets of Harlem and
Bedford-Stuyvesant following the shooting of a fifteen-year-old
black youth by a white policeman, and police efforts to restore
order gave rise to further charges of brutality. The outbreak of
rioting propelled Mayor Wagner into the center of the controversy. Wagner's role can best be described as that of the traditional political "broker." Although the constituency supporting
reform of police review procedures had grown and the need for
action was dramatically demonstrated by the riots, Wagner saw
no clear liberal–minority group coalition on which he could rely.
The police bureaucracy, on the other hand, particularly through
the PBA, had increased its opposition to any change in the internal review procedure. Among its other effects, the issue of a
review board apparently led to continuing efforts to protect the
department's internal prerogatives (especially over its promotion
system) from any outside interference, mayoral or otherwise.

Faced with these circumstances, Wagner chose to play a medi-
ating role. Among his moves, he held a series of conversations
with Dr. Martin Luther King, Jr., who had urged the creation of
an independent review board. In August, however, Wagner rejected this idea and offered instead a set of tangible benefits to
the black community. After repeating his caution to policemen
against the use of brutality, Wagner announced two moves aimed
at "cooling off" the situation. In addition to the assignment of
more black policemen in Harlem, the appointment of the first
black man to head the central Harlem precinct was made. Wagner also outlined a seven-point program designed to provide jobs
for unemployed young people. As a "Reform" Mayor, Wagner
was clearly obliged to act, in contrast to the noninvolvement of
his predecessor at an earlier stage of the controversy. His style,
however, dictated choosing accommodation in the face of conflicting demands, and this thereby guaranteed only temporary
resolution of the matter.

With this appointment, the PBA began to take steps to block the creation of an expanded Review Board with civilian members. In a television interview on February 20, Cassesse said the PBA was prepared to spend its whole treasury (estimated at $1.5 million) to fight the board. The PBA initiated a variety of legal moves to block an independent Review Board, including the introduction of legislation in Albany prohibiting such a body. Meanwhile, the failure of the City Council to produce enabling legislation left Lindsay with only one direct option. On May 2, he and Commissioner Leary jointly announced the creation, by *executive order,* of an independent review board with four civilian and three police members. (The board members were not appointed until July, when the Mayor named one black, one Puerto Rican, one Irish Catholic, and, as chairman, Algernon D. Black, senior leader of the New York Society for Ethical Culture. One of the three police members was black.)

In the days immediately following its creation, the board was criticized from all sides. Both the NAACP and CORE attacked it, believing that its powers were not extensive enough and that its inadequacies would prevent it from alleviating the "suspicion and hostility of minority-group communities toward police justice and policemen."[8] The PBA reacted by challenging the Mayor's legal right to create such a board. According to the PBA brief against the board, the City Charter reserved exclusive authority over police affairs, including review procedures, to the department. Thus, the Mayor could gain the authority for the creation of the board only by public referendum to amend the charter. The PBA had also been gathering the 45,000 petition signatures required to enter referendum of its own on the ballot; the PBA amendment to the City Charter proposed that Review Board membership be limited to the Police Department, which would thereby make the civilian board illegal. In a separate action, the Conservative Party had begun collecting signatures for a differently worded amendment also to be put to a referendum vote. In July, the PBA filed 51,852 signatures with the city clerk; the Conservative Party, 40,383. During this period, racial tensions ran high, and the NYCLU accused Cassesse of "injecting a thinly veiled racism" in his attacks on the board.

Through legal action, the Mayor tried to keep the issue off the ballot, believing that a city-wide fight on civilian review would be divisive. But, in September, the courts upheld the PBA petition. To avoid confusion in an already confused and overheated

situation, the Conservative Party then withdrew its petition, clearing the way for a direct electoral battle, which would bring
binding resolution.

The lines in the referendum campaign were sharply drawn.
The opponents of civilian review were organized into the Independent Citizens Committee Against Review Boards, with the
PBA as the dominant group. Other constituent groups included
the Conservative Party, various American Legion posts, parents,
taxpayers, and homeowners' organizations, the Brooklyn Bar
Association, the Businessmen's Citizens Committee, and the
Queens Civic Councils Federation. Support for the board came
from an impressive number of civil rights, civic, religious, and
labor groups organized in the Federated Associations for Impar-
tial Review (FAIR) and dominated largely by the NYCLU.
Among the groups that rallied under the FAIR banner were the
Guardian's Association (the organization of black policemen),
the American Jewish Committee, the B'nai B'rith Anti-Defamation
League, the Liberal Party, the Citizens Union, and several at-
torneys organizations.

The array of organizations on both sides obscured real differences in campaign effectiveness. FAIR's credentials were impressive, but its organization depended almost entirely on volunteers.
Although many prestigious groups freely announced their support
for the Review Board, the needed financial contributions were
slow to materialize. Moreover, many of the groups backing FAIR
were elite organizations and, as such, did not have the large
memberships that could amount to electoral strength. The PBA,
on the other hand, suffered no shortage of funds with which to
communicate its campaign message. As a mass-membership organization and with the benefit of newly developed experience in
gathering petition signatures and staging rallies, the PBA was
easily able to translate its resources into an effectively managed
city-wide campaign. While FAIR tried to integrate its many
spokesmen into a coherent campaign, the PBA, with its organizational skill and autonomy, was concentrating on direct voter
impact. The FAIR campaign suffered further from the fact that
its initial strategy was directed at keeping the referendum off the
November ballot. This matter was not resolved until September,
leaving FAIR's managers with very little time in which to combat
the PBA's ongoing efforts. The referendum outcome provided
additional evidence of the differential stakes in the campaign—
FAIR's basis was primarily ideological and its campaign cited the

intangibles of greater fairness and justice under the Review Board; the PBA, in contrast, was willing to risk its own organizational survival and was able to stress the alleged direct impact of the Review Board on police performance and safety in the streets.

The CRB Referendum: Patterns of Voting Behavior

For City voters in 1966, Question 1—the proposal to abolish the Review Board—vied for prominence with the New York State Gubernatorial contest. On the surface, the issues—both for and against the board—seemed simple. The PBA argued that the board would impair the morale and efficiency of the police force and, as a consequence, increase crime in the streets. Norman Frank, PBA General Counsel and antiboard campaign coordinator, claimed that policemen would hesitate in the line of duty, fearing the possibility of unjust censure. In contrast, FAIR, denied that the Civilian Review Board would impair police efficiency, citing Philadelphia as a city in which the crime rate had actually declined since the institution of such a board. FAIR also claimed that the presence of civilian members on the board would help restore public confidence in the Police Department and, by guaranteeing fair hearings for complaints of brutality, lessen discontent.

Withal, the issue beneath the surface, seldom articulated in public statements by either of the chief adversaries, was that of race. A Civilian Review Board was widely regarded as a means to satisfy the demands of blacks and Puerto Ricans for an independent channel for their complaints of police brutality. The ardent advocacy by black and civil rights groups of greater civilian review clearly identified the Review Board as a civil rights cause and obscured the fact most blacks were even more concerned with the problem of achieving adequate police protection in ghetto neighborhoods than with incidents of police brutality.[9] Because of the apparently inseparable association of civilian review with black militancy, the referendum clearly became a measure of the presence of "white backlash," of resentment and reprisal by white voters toward the demands of the black protest movement. Thus the issues of race and "crime in the streets" produced a highly charged campaign that linked two of the most troublesome domestic problems to the issue of civilian review.[10]

The verdict registered by the electorate was overwhelming in its rejection of the Review Board: 1,313,161 (approximately 63 per cent) voted "yes" (to abolish civilian review) and 765,468 (approximately 36 per cent) voted "no." As expected, in areas with heavy concentrations of blacks and Puerto Ricans, the vote favored by substantial margins the retention of the Review Board. Most of these districts were in Manhattan, the only one of New York's five boroughs to produce a majority in support of the board. The black and Puerto Rican areas of the city, together with a few scattered others, were lost islands in a sea of city-wide opposition.

The magnitude of the outcome was stunning. For years, the white electorate of New York City had been dominated by a coalition of liberal forces—a coalition that had been especially willing to support the demands of blacks and other minority groups. In addition to giving clear and consistent support to a string of liberal candidates for state and national offices, these electoral groupings had rallied behind the symbols of liberal reform in both the 1961 and the 1965 New York mayoral elections. Yet, in the 1966 referendum, the presumed liberalism of white voters could not be translated into support for the Review Board. For the first time in recent years, white New Yorkers turned their backs on a clearly articulated liberal cause, and civil rights forces suffered their worst defeat.

The marked departure from past voting patterns highlights the relationship between racial issues and the changing nature of electoral politics in New York City. The attitudes and perceptions of white voters and the ways in which they responded to the Review Board controversy are central to understanding this relationship. The analysis that follows is based on data gathered immediately after the election in a survey conducted among a random sample of voters in Brooklyn and aimed at probing public attitudes related to the referendum.[11]

IMPACT OF THE CAMPAIGN

Referenda, initiatives, and ballot propositions, unlike partisan elections in which candidates and political parties compete for public office, have seldom, until recently, aroused much public interest or controversy. Voter apathy combined with low levels of information on the nature of the issues have been generally reflected in a substantially smaller vote on referenda than in elections for public office. These phenomena, combined with the confusing wording of the CRB referendum—"yes" meant abolishing the Review Board and "no" retaining it[12]—suggest the possibility that the Review Board vote presented a distorted picture of the actual preferences of the total electorate. In other words, could the defeat of the Review Board be attributed to low voter turnout and/or confused voting?

All available evidence runs contrary to this hypothesis. The contest over the Civilian Complaint Review Board aroused un-usual and intense interest; nearly 85 per cent of those city residents who voted for governor voted on the issue of civilian review (see Table 1).

TABLE 1
Participation in the Gubernatorial Election
and in Lottery and CRB Referenda

Vote	New York City	Brooklyn
Gubernatorial	2,464,894	747,865
CRB referendum	2,078,629	618,417
Per cent of gubernatorial vote	84.3	82.7
Lottery referendum	1,395,888	455,112
Per cent of gubernatorial vote	56.6	60.9

In contrast, only 57 per cent of those city residents who voted for governor voted on the highly publicized proposal to create a state lottery, the proceeds of which were to be used for public educa-tion. In Brooklyn, nearly 83 per cent of those who voted for governor also voted on the Review Board referendum, but only 61 per cent voted on the lottery.

Respondents were asked whether they were more or less inter-ested in the issue of the Civilian Review Board (hereafter re-ferred to as CRB) than in the gubernatorial contest (see Table 2); nearly 30 per cent were more interested in the CRB referen-

TABLE 2
Interest in the CRB Referendum Compared with
Interest in the Gubernatorial Election

Interest	Number*	Per Cent
More interested in CRB referendum	109	29.7
More interested in gubernatorial	95	25.9
Equally interested in both	163	44.4
Total	367	100.0

*The difference between the sample total of 374 and the totals in this and other tables is explained by "don't know" answers or failures to respond to questions.

dum than in the gubernatorial contest, and 44.5 per cent expressed at least the same level of interest in both contests.

The reverse wording of the referendum probably posed the most severe test of the over-all awareness and interest of the electorate. Strategists for both sides feared that the voters would be confused on how to vote. The PBA circulated thousands of posters reading, "VOTE YES—STOP CIVILIAN REVIEW BOARDS," while FAIR distributed other thousands reading, "DON'T BE A YES MAN FOR BIGOTRY—VOTE NO." The results of the intensive educational campaign were clearly successful: Less than 2 per cent of the respondents in the Brooklyn survey appear to have mistakenly voted contrary to their actual preferences on the Review Board issue. By any measure, then, the New York electorate was extraordinarily aware of, and responsive to, the issues surrounding the CRB controversy.

BACKGROUND FACTORS AND THE VOTE

In New York, group values and interests have always played a significant role in the political life of the city. Partisan coalitions, as well as ideological cleavages, have usually found their roots in the basic socio-economic divisions of the city's diverse population. Within the white electorate, patterns of liberal and conservative political predispositions have been associated with differences in religion, ethnicity, education, income, occupation, and social class.[13] Past support for liberal measures has been drawn primarily from the ranks of the Jews, the better-educated, and those in higher-status occupations, while Catholics and those with working-class orientations have tended to espouse more conservative political preferences. It was expected that the CRB vote would reflect these general patterns (see Table 3).

The fact that barely 32 per cent of all respondents were in favor of civilian review indicates the extent to which the central tendency of the white electorate shifted toward a more conservative political stance. While socio-economic factors do account for some of the variance in Review Board support among white Brooklynites, it is also clear that no population grouping withstood the electoral tide of CRB opposition. Religious identification proved to be the group factor that most clearly distinguished CRB supporters and opponents. Too few Protestants were represented in the sample to justify generalizations about their preferences,[14] but Catholic-Jewish differences were distinctive.

TABLE 3
Position on CRB, by Religion, Education, Occupation
Income, and Social Class (Percentages)

Category	Number	For	Against	Don't Know/ No Answer
All respondents	(374)	31.9	64.6	3.5
Religion				
Protestant	(17)	23.5	70.6	5.9
Catholic	(130)	16.2	83.1	0.8
Jewish	(214)	40.2	55.1	4.7
Education				
Grade school	(83)	25.3	69.9	4.8
High school	(175)	23.4	72.6	4.0
College	(110)	50.0	50.0	–
Occupation				
Professional and technical	(62)	51.6	46.8	1.6
Business and managerial	(62)	45.2	53.2	1.6
Clerical and sales	(54)	20.4	77.8	1.9
Blue collar	(124)	20.2	75.8	4.0
Not in the work force	(72)	31.9	61.1	7.0
*Income**				
$ 0– 3,999	(38)	34.2	60.5	5.3
4,000– 7,499	(81)	24.7	70.4	4.9
7,500– 9,999	(70)	22.9	75.7	1.4
10,000–14,000	(68)	38.2	61.8	–
15,000 & over	(59)	39.0	59.3	1.7
Subjective Class Identification				
Working class	(225)	18.6	76.0	5.4
Middle class	(129)	37.8	60.4	1.8

*Nearly 16 per cent of respondents failed to reply to this question. Probably more among high-income respondents than among low-income ones did not answer. The former, as other social data suggest, tended to be somewhat more favorably inclined toward the CRB.

Catholic voters overwhelmingly opposed the CRB, by a ratio of five-to-one. Jewish voters were more evenly divided: 40 per cent supported it, and 55 per cent opposed it. The nearly monolithic Catholic consensus on the CRB (83 per cent in the Brooklyn sample) greatly exceeded the level of Catholic cohesion in support of John F. Kennedy in the 1960 Presidential election (73 per cent in the Brooklyn sample and 78 per cent nationally, according to Gallup), confirming the unusual group salience of the CRB issue for Catholics. Although Jewish support for the CRB exceeded that of other religious groups, the fact that only 40 per cent of the Jewish respondents voted for the board reveals a severe crack in the hitherto solid Jewish support for liberal measures in New York City. Whereas an extremely high level of group cohesion was obtained among Catholics, Jewish voting patterns reveal virtually complete dissensus.

Social class also accounted for variations in CRB sentiment. All of the standard indicators of class—education, income, occupation, and self-identification—showed that upper-class respondents were more likely to support the CRB than were lower-class respondents. Each class-related factor revealed a similar phenomenon consistent with the general electoral trend; categories from which liberal support might have been expected were badly split on the issue of civilian review, while conservative-leaning socio-economic groupings produced overwhelming opposition.

Education seemed to have a cumulative effect on attitudes toward the CRB. Only one-quarter of respondents with an elementary or high-school education favored the CRB as compared with 50 per cent of college-educated respondents (Table 3). Yet, even here, the Catholic-Jewish difference held fast. The proportion of college-educated Catholics who supported the board was half the proportion of the equivalent Jewish group (see Table 4). In general, the association between education and CRB attitude was more consistent among Jews than among Catholics, indicating that, in this respect, education appeared to have had a greater impact on Jews than on Catholics.

Occupational differences also affected attitudes toward the CRB. More than half the professionals favored the board, as com-

TABLE 4

Percentages of Catholics and Jews in Favor
of the CRB, by Education and Occupation

	Percentage in Favor of the CRB	
	Catholics	Jews
Education		
Grade school	17.6	30.4
High school	13.3	31.8
College	25.0	54.4
Total number	(129)	(201)
Occupation		
Blue collar	11.8	31.2
Clerical	22.2	20.0
Business	30.0	46.0
Professional	16.7	62.5
Total number	(108)	(166)

pared with only about 20 per cent each of clerical and blue-collar workers (Table 3). Once a control for religion was introduced, occupation appeared to be a very weak indicator of CRB sentiment among Catholics, whereas, among Jews, both occupation and education appeared to be equally potent and reinforced each other (Table 4). Thus, highly educated Jewish professionals supported the CRB, while poorly educated lower-class Jewish workers strongly opposed it.

In summary then, it is apparent that all population groupings, including those with a reputation for political liberalism, shifted in a more conservative direction on the question of civilian review. Within this general trend, striking contrasts between Catholics and Jews held true at virtually all educational, occupational, and income levels. However, social-class indicators had differing impacts on these major religious groupings. Catholic cohesion withstood the influences of education and occupational status, while these factors had a clear and consistent impact on Jewish preferences. Nevertheless, only college-educated and professional Jews managed to produce a majority in favor of the CRB, and, in the final analysis, the dissensus revealed within Jewish groups is more impressive than their support for the board.

PARTISAN POLITICS AND THE CRB

Although it was obvious from the beginning that the CRB referendum was a political issue of considerable importance, the political implications of the controversy were never cast in clear partisan terms. Neither of the major parties could be said to have taken a definite position on the question, and both leading candidates soft-pedaled the issue in their campaigns, apparently hoping to avoid attracting fire from either side of the controversy. The campaign behavior of the major-party candidates, combined with the separation of the ballot proposition from party labels, served to insulate the average voter from cues or guidelines that normally flow from his basic identification with one of the major political parties.

Identification with either major party did not clearly distinguish supporters from opponents of the CRB. More Democrats than Republicans were likely to favor the CRB, but, even so, these were a minority among Democrats (see Table 5). Similarly, Democratic voters in the 1965 mayoral and 1966 gubernatorial election did not differ appreciably from Republican voters in

TABLE 5
Party Identification and Position on the CRB (Percentages)

Party Identification	Position on the CRB		
	Number	For	Against
Democrat	(212)	30.2	69.8
Republican	(47)	14.9	85.1
Liberal	(15)	80.0	20.0
Conservative	(11)	0.0	100.0
Independent	(73)	47.9	52.1

their stand on the CRB (see Table 6). But support of New York's minor parties—Liberal and Conservative—was clearly associated with attitudes toward the CRB. Most Liberal Party supporters favored the CRB, while all Conservative Party supporters in the sample opposed it (Table 5). Similarly, voters for candidates endorsed by the Liberal Party were more likely to support CRB than voters for the other Democratic or Republican candidates (Table 6). But the strongest association appeared between voting

TABLE 6
Position on the CRB by Candidate Choice
in Recent Elections (Percentages)

Election	Position on the CRB		
	Number	For	Against
Gubernatorial election, 1966			
O'Connor (D)	(116)	31.0	69.0
Rockefeller (R)	(137)	35.0	65.0
Roosevelt (L)	(35)	54.3	45.7
Adams (C)	(28)	0.0	100.0
Mayoral election, 1965			
Beame (D)	(139)	33.1	66.9
Lindsay (R-L)	(149)	41.6	58.4
Buckley (C)	(33)	3.0	97.0
Presidential election, 1964			
Johnson (D-L)	(281)	38.8	61.2
Goldwater (R-C)	(60)	6.7	93.3

for a Conservative Party candidate and opposition to the CRB. Barry Goldwater had been endorsed by the Conservative party and had essentially attracted a right-wing Republican vote. Over

93 per cent of the people who voted for Goldwater and 97 per cent of those who voted for Conservative candidate William F. Buckley in the 1965 mayoralty also opposed the CRB.

The gubernatorial candidacies of Liberal Franklin D. Roosevelt, Jr., and Conservative Paul Adams offered clear-cut choices on civilian review: Roosevelt was firmly committed to the CRB, and Adams was even more firmly opposed. These options were all the more compelling for voters with strong sentiments on CRB, since neither the Democratic nor the Republican candidate was willing to campaign actively for or against the CRB. The two minor parties were not similarly inhibited; by making the CRB into an essential issue in their New York City campaigns, they activated and reinforced ideological predispositions and effectively emphasized the link between ideology and attitudes on the CRB.

The apparent salience of the CRB issue among conservative voters may explain the surprisingly strong showing of the Conservative Party in New York City, where it outpolled the Liberal Party by 234,590 to 218,840—in contrast to the rest of the state, where the Conservative Party ran behind the Liberal. Adams's unequivocal opposition to the CRB seems to have provided an unusually attractive cue for conservative voters, and the CRB referendum may have furnished the "coat tails" that carried the Conservative Party to Row C (reserved for the third-place party and previously assigned to the Liberal Party) on the election machines in the next elections.

Civilian review had not yet become a direct electoral issue when John Lindsay ran for mayor in 1965, and his support of it did not seem to affect his popularity at that time. After his election, however, when he determined to carry out the CRB proposals, he became intimately identified with it; in fact, the CRB was frequently referred to as "Lindsay's Review Board." When asked if they approved or disapproved of the job Mayor Lindsay was doing, more than 58 per cent of the respondents expressed their disapproval. Of this group, an overwhelming 80 per cent opposed the CRB. More than half of those who approved of the Mayor, on the other hand, also supported the board (see Table 7).

The patterns of the CRB vote across the several partisan factors discussed in this section reinforce the conclusions suggested by the previous analysis of socio-economic factors. The Civilian Review Board controversy clearly stimulated unusual unity

TABLE 7
Position on the CRB, by Respondents' Evaluation of
Mayor Lindsay's Performance in Office, November, 1966
(Percentages)

Evaluation of Mayor Lindsay's Performance	Position on the CRB		
	Number	For	Against
Approve	(102)	55.9	44.1
Disapprove	(204)	20.0	80.0
Don't know	(44)	38.6	61.4
Total	(350)	(114)	(236)

among conservative ranks and tore asunder the white liberal voting coalition. Whether ideological predisposition is measured in terms of party identification, past voting record, or evaluation of Mayor Lindsay's performance in office, conservative voters opposed the board in overwhelming numbers and liberals failed to resist the general swing to the right of the white electorate.[15]

"Crime in the Streets"

The major thrust of the PBA's campaign was the growing menace of crime in the streets and what the PBA saw as the CRB threat to deprive the police of the support and confidence they needed if they were to be effective. A much publicized advertisement showed a young white woman emerging from the subway, alone and apprehensive on a dark street. The caption read: "The Civilian Review Board must be stopped! Her life ... your life ... may depend on it." Given this general context of the campaign, did the average white Brooklynite perceive a threat to his personal safety and, if so, did those perceptions help explain the low level of support accorded to the CRB? The respondents were asked a series of questions related to their perception of personal safety. Four of the five questions had also been asked of a national sample of American adults in the summer of 1966. The Brooklyn response varied considerably from the national sample (see Table 8).

Brooklyn respondents registered greater levels of concern for their personal safety than did the respondents in the national sample. Although almost 90 per cent of the Brooklynites interviewed felt more or less safe about walking alone in their neighborhood during the daytime and almost three-quarters felt safe

TABLE 8
Perceptions of Personal Safety: A National
Sample and the Brooklyn Sample Compared (Percentages)

Perception of Safety	National Sample*	Brooklyn Sample
1. How safe when walking alone in the daytime?		
Very safe	85	65
Somewhat safe	10	23
Somewhat unsafe	3	8
Very unsafe	2	4
2. How safe when walking with a companion after dark?		
Very safe	†	44
Somewhat safe	—	33
Somewhat unsafe	—	13
Very unsafe	—	10
3. How safe when walking alone after dark?		
Very safe	44	27
Somewhat safe	23	25
Somewhat unsafe	18	24
Very unsafe	15	24
4. Stayed home because it was unsafe to go somewhere?		
Yes	16	40
No	84	60
5. Concerned about having home broken into?		
Very concerned	14	35
Somewhat concerned	37	39
Don't worry at all	49	26

*Data in this column were gathered by the National Opinion Research Center in July, 1966. *Cf.*, Philip H. Ennis, *Criminal Victimization . . .* , *op. cit.* Professor Peter H. Rossi kindly made the raw data available before publication.

†Question not asked.

with a companion at night, 40 per cent indicated that they stayed home out of fear instead of going where they wanted to, and nearly three-quarters were at least somewhat concerned about having their homes broken into. It would seem that fear of lawlessness may have been reinforced by, but did not originate with, the PBA campaign and apparently had a solid foundation in the respondents' perceptions of safety in Brooklyn.

When Brooklyn responses were fitted into a cumulative scale of perception of personal safety,[16] it becomes clear that the relationship between perceptions of safety and attitude toward the CRB was both weak and inconsistent (see Table 9). The average

TABLE 9
Perceptions of Personal Safety and
Respondents' Position on the CRB (Percentages)

	Perceptions of Personal Safety					
	Very Unsafe					Very Safe
Position on the CRB	0	1	2	3	4	5
For	21.7	37.0	30.8	34.8	36.9	30.2
Against	78.3	63.0	69.1	65.2	63.1	69.8
	100.0	100.0	99.9	100.0	100.0	100.0
Total number of respondents = 361	46	27	39	66	130	53

Mean Scale Scores: All respondents = 3.03
CRB supporters = 3.15
CRB opponents = 2.98

Brooklyn respondent indicated feelings of safety on three of the five items (mean = 3.03); opponents of the CRB felt somewhat less safe (2.98) than did supporters (3.15). Further analysis shows that the relationship between perceptions of personal safety and attitudes toward the CRB was more consistent among women and the elderly and that both these groups expressed especially high levels of concern. On the other hand, no consistent relationship was discovered among male respondents. On balance, it is clear that the Review Board controversy was waged in an atmosphere of substantial concern over the growing urban crime rate, but that the respondents' perceptions of their own personal safety failed to offer clear differentiation between CRB supporters and opponents.

ATTITUDES TOWARD THE POLICE

Most white Brooklynites viewed the Police Department quite favorably. They did not feel there was much police brutality: 23 per cent said there was none at all; 56 per cent said there was "just a little"; less than 5 per cent said there was a lot. Additionally, most respondents felt that, if they expressed their fears, the police would be responsive: Some 62 per cent said that if they did not like "the way the police were handling a problem in their neighborhood," they could do something about it. Apparently, FAIR's campaign had failed to convince these respondents that police brutality was a major problem.

When asked to explain why they opposed the CRB, Brooklyn respondents most frequently replied that the Review Board would hamper the police in providing the "strongest possible protection" (see Table 10). But almost two-thirds defended their stand for a

TABLE 10
Reasons Given for Opposing the CRB

Response	Number	Per Cent
A Civilian Review Board makes enforcement more difficult; it hampers the police. "We need the strongest possible protection."	89	37.2
The police should be judged by their peers. Civilians do not have expert knowledge and should not interfere.	62	25.9
The police are doing a good job; a Civilian Review Board is unnecessary	28	11.7
Anti–minority group references: "The board serves the interests of Negroes," etc.	15	6.3
The board hurts police morale; they might hesitate.	9	3.8
Antiadministration references: "Mayor Lindsay should not get everything he wants."	8	3.3
The police and politics should be kept separate.	6	2.6
The board serves the interests of criminal elements.	3	1.3
General: "The board does more harm than good."	19	7.9
	239	100.0

variety of reasons that had nothing to do with crime or protection. One-fourth of the CRB opponents thought that policemen should not be subjected to the judgment of nonexpert civilians, and 12 per cent simply gave the police a blanket vote of confidence. Many respondents seemed to be echoing PBA complaints against several measures that had been introduced by Mayor Lindsay, especially in the Police Department. In a department that was traditionally Irish, the Mayor, besides forcing out Commissioner Broderick and appointing a new commissioner from outside the department's ranks, had promoted Sanford D. Garelik, a Jew, to the post of chief inspector and Lloyd G. Sealy, a Negro, to assistant chief inspector. Furthermore, in another instance of "city hall meddling," Lindsay had appointed a black and a Puerto Rican to the CRB. Many voters were expressing support not only for law and order, the police function, and the need to make New York a safer city, but also for the Police Department per se.

In order to define more clearly public attitudes toward the police on issues such as effectiveness, courtesy, service, honesty, and meritoriousness, the respondents were asked five questions borrowed from the National Opinion Research Center national study (see Table 11). Their answers confirmed the impression of

TABLE 11

Attitudes Toward the Police: A National Sample and the Brooklyn Sample Compared (Percentages)

	National*	Brooklyn
1. How good a job do the police do in being respectful to people like yourself?		
Very good	59	50
Pretty good	26	32
Not so good	4	3
No opinion	11	15
2. How good a job do the police do in giving protection to the people in this neighborhood?		
Very good	42	33
Pretty good	35	38
Not so good	9	11
No opinion	14	18
3. How good a job do the police do in being prompt in answering calls?		
Very good	39	33
Pretty good	30	33
Not so good	10	13
No opinion	21	21
4. In general, do you think that the salaries of the police are too high, too low, or about right?	†	
Too low	—	28
About right	—	48
Too high	—	3
No opinion	—	21
5. Do you think that the police are almost all honest, mostly honest with a few who are corrupt, or are they almost all corrupt?		
Almost all honest	59	16
Mostly honest	30	70
Almost all corrupt	3	7
No opinion	8	7

*National Opinion Research Center data. See footnote to Table 8.
†Question not asked.

a generally favorable public attitude toward police. Comparisons made between the answers to three of the four questions that were asked of both groups uncovered only insignificant differences between Brooklyn respondents and the national sample. Somewhat fewer Brooklynites than respondents in the national sample thought the police were respectful enough to people like themselves, that they did a good job of neighborhood protection, or that they answered calls promptly. But an enormous gap separated the Brooklynites' conception of police honesty (16 per cent thought all police were honest) from that of the national sample (59 per cent thought all police were honest). The gap was closed when respondents who thought police were mostly honest were bracketed with those who thought they were all honest: 89 per cent of the national sample and 86 per cent of the Brooklyn sample. Few in either sample were willing to characterize their local police force as "mostly corrupt."

The scale of pro-police sentiments[17] among the Brooklyn respondents failed to show a consistently significant relationship with their position on the CRB issue except in the case of those with the strongest pro- or anti-police feelings (see Table 12).

TABLE 12
A Scale of Respondents' Attitudes Toward the
Police and Their Position on the CRB (Percentages)

	Scale of Attitudes Toward the Police					
	Least Favorable				Most Favorable	
Position on the CRB	0	1	2	3	4	5
For	44.9	34.2	32.4	30.7	31.1	25.0
Against	55.1	65.7	67.6	69.3	69.0	75.0
	100.0	99.9	100.0	100.0	100.1	100.0
Total number of respondents = 361	49	35	34	166	61	16

Mean Scale Scores: All respondents = 2.49
CRB supporters = 2.38
CRB opponents = 2.65

Respondents least favorable to the police were more likely to support the CRB than those who were most favorable toward them. Most respondents, however, came in the middle, and their feelings about the police had a negligible effect on their position toward the CRB. Anti-CRB respondents, as a group, were slightly more favorable toward the police than pro-CRB respondents.

A stronger correlation emerged when the respondents were asked if they had a relative or close friend on the police force (see Table 13). The strong Catholic cohesion on the issue of CRB,

TABLE 13

Respondents' Positions on the CRB, by Their Attitudes Toward, and Personal Relationships with, the Police (Percentages)

Position on the CRB	Scale of Pro-Police Attitudes (0–1)	(2–3)	(4–5)	Total
Respondents *without* personal ties with police				
For CRB	46.7	38.0	35.7	39.8
Against CRB	53.3	62.0	64.3	60.1
All	(60)	(129)	(42)	(231)
Respondents *with* personal ties with police				
For CRB	27.3	18.3	22.9	21.1
Against CRB	72.7	81.7	77.1	78.9
All	(22)	(71)	(35)	(128)

which has already been described, may be explained in part by the fact that some 54 per cent of the Catholic respondents had relatives or close friends on the police force whereas only 21 per cent of the Jewish respondents had such ties. At every level of pro-police sentiment, Catholic respondents with personal ties to the police were much less likely to support the CRB than were those who had no policemen in their family or among their friends. These respondents seemed to give more weight to evaluations of police performance when making their decisions on the CRB.

The substantial overlapping identification between the police force and Catholics may have contributed to the emergence, in the minds of individual Catholics, of a group position on this issue. However, the large pro-CRB vote among Puerto Ricans suggests that Catholicism, as such, was not the source of this behavior. The explanation is, rather, that the police are very much part of the historic group experience of Irish and Italian Catholics in New York[18] and most other large cities, and the Police Department has, consequently, become a strong positive reference symbol for these Catholics. This is further illustrated by the fact that ties of friendship and family had a much greater influence in shaping pro-police attitudes among Catholics than

TABLE 14
Mean Scores of Catholics and Jews on Pro-Police
Attitude Scale, by Personal Relationship with the Police

	Mean Scale Scores	
Personal Ties with Police	Catholics (Number = 129)	Jews (Number = 209)
Without personal ties with the police	2.41	2.44
With personal ties with the police	3.03	2.34

they did among Jews (see Table 14). In fact, Jews responded just the other way: Those who had a policeman among their family or friends took a slightly more negative view of the police than those without such ties.

THE IMPACT OF RACIAL ISSUES

Sympathy for the Negro in his pursuit of equality, according to national-opinion surveys, reached its high-water mark in 1963. It was probably even higher in March, 1965, when Alabama state troopers and local posses used riot guns, pistols, tear-gas bombs, and nightsticks to break up a voter-registration march from Selma to Montgomery. Thereafter, public opinion toward the black revolution began to cool.[19]

When the riots exploded in Watts in August, 1965, the image of the "Negro" as a victim assaulted by Bull Connor's cattle prods changed to that of blacks as aggressors. Confronted with the radicalization of the civil rights movement, the calls for black power, and the intensified pressure for integrated schools and housing in the North—sometimes accompanied by violence and threats of violence—whites became more critical of black demands. These attitude shifts signaled a change in politics. By 1966, it was evident that many candidates had been caught in some type of racial cross fire.[20]

New York City, also, was affected by racial strife fraught with political implications. The drive for the CRB was born during the riots in Harlem and Bedford-Stuyvesant in the summer of 1964, and the CRB as a political issue became identified with the civil rights movement. Mayor Lindsay cited the racial peace in New York in the summer of 1966 to justify his creation of the CRB. The reiterated argument that it would help redress the grievances of blacks and Puerto Ricans over police brutality and unfair police treatment probably convinced many New Yorkers that they were not being asked to endorse civilian review as a general principle but rather to create special procedural guarantees for blacks and Puerto Ricans.

It was to be expected, therefore, that attitudes toward the black revolution would have a bearing on the way white people voted on civilian review. The response of the Brooklyn sample reflected the widespread disillusionment with the civil rights movement. Although over 75 per cent said that they would still permit demonstrations, especially if peaceful, and nearly half felt that the civil rights situation was improving, 62 per cent felt that civil rights leaders had been pushing too fast, and 68 per cent perceived the actions of blacks as generally violent (see Table 15).

These responses, combined into a single scale,[21] indicate the respondents' evaluation of the civil rights movement (see Table 16). There could be little doubt that the attitudes tapped by these questions had some bearing on the civilian review issue. Those who were more hostile toward the civil rights movement were much more likely to oppose the CRB than were those who were more favorably disposed toward black actions. Indeed, among the several attitudinal measures employed in this study, this scale emerged as the best indicator of Review Board votes, suggesting that racial attitudes played a significant role in determining the outcome of the November referendum.

Because of the general context of the campaign, it is hardly surprising to find a relationship between race-related attitudes and the CRB vote. But what did this relationship reveal about public attitudes toward blacks and their struggle for equal rights? Did the defeat of the CRB represent a reversal of attitudes toward the goals of the civil rights movement or only toward its tactics? Did the electoral outcome reveal the true extent of racial bigotry among white New Yorkers, or were motivations more complex? In short, was the "liberal establishment" defeated by the voice of "white supremacy?"

There is little evidence that the Brooklyn respondents were expressing attitudes of blatant bigotry. Eighty-five per cent of them believed that "Negroes learn as well as whites"; three-quarters said that they "would not mind if a Negro with the same income and education" moved into their neighborhoods; and 62 per cent rejected the notion that "we have to teach children that all men are created equal, but everyone knows that some groups

TABLE 15
Attitudes Toward the Civil Rights Movement (Percentages)

Question	Response (Number=361)
1. There have been quite a number of political and civil rights demonstrations over the past five years. Do you think that such demonstrations should be allowed no matter what, should be allowed only if the demonstrators remain peaceful, or should not be allowed at all?	
Allow no matter what	5
Allow if peaceful	73
Not allow at all	19
No opinion	3
2. In the past few years, we have heard a lot about civil rights activity. Do you think the civil rights situation is generally better, generally worse, or about the same?	
Better	49
Same	20
Worse	26
No opinion	5
3. Some people say that the civil rights people have been trying to push too fast. Others feel they haven't pushed fast enough. How about you?	
Too slow	5
About right	25
Too fast	62
No opinion	8
4. During the past year or so, would you say that the actions Negroes have taken to get the things they want have been generally violent, or generally peaceful?	
Generally peaceful	21
Generally violent	68
No opinion	11

are better than others." On the other hand, the respondents did express concern stemming from their image of the blacks. For example, 63 per cent agreed with the statement, "The trouble with letting certain minority groups into a nice neighborhood is that they gradually give it their own atmosphere," and nearly 80 per cent felt that it was fairly likely that "there would be more Negro rioting in New York City." The picture of white attitudes is one of substantial ambivalence; Brooklyn respondents were quick to reject the most extreme stereotypes of racial prejudice, but they voiced substantial concern about problems they associated with blacks.

TABLE 16

Respondents' Position on the CRB, by Their Attitudes
Toward the Civil Rights Movement (Percentages)

| | Attitudes Toward the Civil Rights Movement | | | | |
| | Least Favorable | | | Most Favorable | |
Position on the CRB	0	1	2	3	4
For	22.8	22.9	33.3	45.6	51.2
Against	77.2	77.1	66.7	54.4	48.8
	100.0	100.0	100.0	100.0	100.0
Total number of respondents =361	(79)	(96)	(66)	(79)	(41)

Mean Scale Scores: All respondents = 1.74
CRB supporters = 2.17
CRB opponents = 1.53

White ambivalence toward urban blacks suggests that the outcome of the Review Board controversy may have been related to the changing nature of the civil rights movement as it moved to the urban North. For nearly ten years, progress, slow but rather steady, has been confined to legislative and judicial breakthroughs that established the legal right to equal opportunity. But, by the mid-1960's, the limitations of legislative and judicial gains became all too obvious. The realities of life in urban slums dashed many of the expectations born of the promise of equal opportunity. Yet many whites found it difficult to accept the fact that black leaders in the North were demanding more than a removal of the formal barriers of *de jure* discrimination. Instances of Southern bigotry and brutality were easier to understand as obstacles to equal opportunity than was the "culture of poverty," with its concomitant handicaps and deprivations. Many whites consider their achievements to be the product largely of their own efforts, and they have internalized the values of individual achievement within a system governed by the rule of equal opportunity for all. Yet, despite their individual self-perceptions, their private accomplishments have been as much a consequence of group cohesion and their position in the social structure as of their own efforts. These values, and the enormous social distance between the white middle-class life style and conditions in the black urban slums, have prevented many whites from seeing that the rules for individual achievement have not operated in the

same way for all people. It was likely, therefore, that many whites
were caught in a conflict between the values of equality and of
achievement.

To probe for the tension between the goal of equal opportunity
and the demand for individual achievement, two questions were
put to the respondents:

1. Generally speaking, do you think that Negroes have had the same
   opportunities for advancement as other groups?
2. Do you think that Negroes have used their opportunities for
   advancement as well as other groups?

The first question was designed to measure awareness of, or
willingness to admit to, the reality of discrimination against
blacks; the second to determine whether the respondents applied
the same standards of achievement to blacks as they did to
members of other groups.

Over 55 per cent of the respondents felt that blacks had been
denied equal opportunities for advancement, but most of these
nevertheless thought blacks had not used their opportunities as
well as other groups had (see Table 17). Such evaluations of
achievement had a clear impact on support for the CRB: Respondents who said blacks had been denied equal opportunity
but had made good use of what opportunities they did have supported the CRB in much larger proportions than those who rec-

TABLE 17

Respondents' Position on the CRB and Their
Attitudes Toward Negro Opportunities (Percentages)

Those who say:	All Respondents (Number = 320)	Position on CRB		
		Number	For	Against
Negroes have same opportunities; haven't used them as well.		34.4	(111)	18.0	82.0
Negroes have same opportunities; have used them as well.	44.4	10.0	(32)	18.7	81.3
Negroes denied equal opportunities; haven't used them as well.		40.3	(128)	39.8	60.2
Negroes denied equal opportunities; have used them as well.	55.6	15.3	(49)	57.1	42.9

ognized the existence of discrimination but felt blacks had nonetheless not used their opportunities well. Those who implicitly denied the existence of discrimination—whether or not they thought blacks used their opportunities well—overwhelmingly opposed the CRB.

Many respondents appeared to have been cross-pressured by their perceptions of the reality of racial discrimination and their evaluations of black performance. Respondents who were Jewish, well educated, or in high-status occupations were much more likely to feel that blacks had been denied equal opportunities than respondents who were Catholic, poorly educated, or in low-status occupations (see Table 18).

TABLE 18

Attitudes Toward Negro Opportunities, by Religion, Education, and Occupational Status

	1 Respondents who say that Negroes have *not* had the same opportunity for advancement as other groups.	2 Respondents who say that Negroes have used their opportunities for advancement as well as other groups.	3 Cross-Pressure 3 = 1 − 2
Category	Per Cent	Per Cent	Per Cent
All respondents	54.7	26.5	28.2
Religious group			
Catholic	40.0	27.8	12.2
Jewish	62.6	23.0	39.6
Educational level			
Grade school	35.4	33.3	2.1
High school	47.6	23.4	24.2
College	79.8	25.7	54.1
Occupational status			
Low*	47.7	27.0	20.7
High†	66.7	21.7	45.0

*Includes clerical, sales, and blue-collar workers.

†Includes professionals, technical workers, businessmen, and managers.

There was, however, very little variation among these groups when they were asked to evaluate black performance; only 26.5 per cent of all respondents felt that blacks had used their opportunities as well as other groups. Paradoxically, the groups that were most aware of discrimination were least favorable in their evaluation of black performance. By comparing the spread between the responses to these questions, a rough measure of the extent to which respondents were cross-pressured may be obtained. Clearly, cross-pressure was most extreme among members of those groups usually associated with the white liberal coalition.

Did the existence of cross-pressure explain why liberals failed to give the CRB as much support as might otherwise have been expected? Among Jews, the college-educated, and those in high-status occupations, there was a clear difference in Review Board support offered by those respondents who were cross-pressured and those who were not (see Table 19).

TABLE 19

Impact of Cross-Pressures on Support for the CRB Among
Subgroups Showing Greater Awareness of Anti-Negro
Discrimination

| | Support for the CRB Among Those Who Say Negroes Have Not Had the Same Opportunities as Whites and Who Say: | | | |
| | Negroes *have not* used their opportunities as well as other groups (cross-pressured) | | Negroes *have* used their opportunities as well as other groups (not cross-pressured) | |
Subgroups of Respondents Showing Greater Awareness of Discrimination Among:	Number	Per Cent	Number	Per Cent
Jews	(86)	48.8	(29)	65.5
College-educated	(59)	54.3	(24)	62.5
High occupational status	(57)	52.6	(19)	79.0

Cross-pressured groups were evenly split on the CRB, while those who escaped this attitudinal conflict gave much more support to the board. Evidently, many liberals failed to provide the expected level of support to the CRB because of their conflicting attitudes toward blacks.

On balance, race was the most significant factor in the CRB contest.[22] Although the civil rights movement has increased people's awareness of the plight of blacks in America, many whites remain unconvinced that blacks are taking advantage of their hard-won, but limited, victories in the area of equal opportunity. As the focus of civil rights activity has shifted to the urban North, many whites apparently have associated blacks with the

social pathologies of urban slum life. The Review Board controversy crystallized these images, thereby solidifying the opposition
of conservative voters and splitting the white liberal coalition.

Conclusion

The CRB referendum proved to be a rout for civil rights forces.
For the first time in years, New York City's electorate rejected a
liberal position on the ballot. The referendum appeared to inten-
sify basic intergroup cleavages—a phenomenon often manifested
in nonpartisan elections in Northern cities that have large electoral minorities.[23] Blacks voted overwhelmingly for the board.
Irish and Italian Catholics, apparently because of their group
identification with the police force and their large representation
in the working and lower-middle classes, opposed the board by
a huge majority. Jews were divided roughly according to their
attitudes toward the direction of the civil rights movement.

The survey of Brooklyn voters also revealed a differential in
the ideological salience of the CRB issue. Conservatives were
united in their opposition to the board, while liberals were quite
divided. In large part, the ideological and ethnic divisions were
related to, and grew out of, the fact that no clear "liberal" position was ever well staked out in the campaign. Lacking sufficient
reasons to the contrary, many liberals therefore voted along other
attitudinal—especially racial—lines.

At first glance, the defeat of the Civilian Review Board might
be ascribed to the peculiarities of a referendum itself.[24] In the
absence of the moderating and modulating effects of political
parties, so the argument goes, the voters were free to cast an
easy and, perhaps, psychologically satisfying symbolic vote. Without the normal party cues to galvanize it, the familiar liberal
consensus simply fell apart and traditional political coalitions
gave way to other alliances—ethnic, religious, or ideological.
However attractive such an explanation might be, its limitations
are evident in the light of subsequent events. It appears, rather,
that the CRB referendum was something of a critical election in
the over-all pattern of New York City's politics. The concept of a
critical election has usually meant a fundamental change in basic
party loyalties signaling the emergence of a new electoral majority.[25] The critical element in the CRB election did not have to do
with basic party loyalties, since the referendum campaign was
conducted without the involvement of party labels. Instead, it
can be argued that the CRB referendum was a critical election in

that it provided a *legitimate* means for the direct expression by voters of race-related attitudes on a matter of public policy. As Glazer and Moynihan have observed in their re-examination of *Beyond the Melting Pot,* "the etiquette of race relations has changed" in the course of the 1960's.[26] Thus, the CRB election was the confirming event in the appearance of a new electoral etiquette that allowed for the open discussion of racial issues. In addition, the critical nature of the CRB election included the emergence of new symbols or power aggregations that have the capacity of enlisting voter support or opposition. The interesting thing is that these new symbols are the bureaucracies that have come to dominate life in New York—organizations such as the school system, the police, the teachers' union, the welfare agencies, the sanitationmen—and around which so much of the urban crisis revolves.

The first development that lends credence to this interpretation of the critical nature of the CRB election was the series of school strikes that erupted in the fall of 1968 and grew into a city-wide crisis. The confrontation over community control in the Ocean Hill–Brownsville experimental district generated deeply divisive attitudes. One study of this event documents the widening gaps between two major groups—blacks and Jews—and the extent to which both are beginning to reject the basic principles of accommodation.[27] With the school strike as the triggering event, several subsequent episodes of alleged black anti-Semitism may have contributed to a turn-around in the traditionally liberal attitudes of New York Jews, particularly toward programs aimed at helping blacks. As Nathan Glazer puts it, "Jews have become far more aware of the virtue of conservative working-class and middle-class values, which they always practiced but refused to celebrate."[28] The support of many Jews for the UFT position, coupled with the fact many teachers are themselves Jewish, is a functional equivalent of Catholic association with the Police Department and their strong opposition to the CRB.

John Lindsay's re-election as Mayor, in November, 1969, was the final step in a series of electoral clashes that evidenced the disarray in usual party voting patterns. The confusion of an incumbent Republican-Liberal Mayor's being denied renomination by Republican voters in the primary was added to by the chaos in the Democratic Party. No less than four "liberal" Democratic candidates divided the majority of primary votes, enabling conservative Mario Procaccino to gain the nomination with just over

30 per cent of the vote. Lindsay, with the Liberal Party endorsement and the benefit of an added fusion party line, was also challenged by Republican-Conservative John J. Marchi. His victory in the general election was based on a considerably different coalition than had elected him in 1965. Many Democrats returned to their party, perhaps as much in protest against the Mayor's record as in support of Procaccino. In the campaign, Lindsay worked very hard to hold down the expected rush of defectors among Jewish Democrats who had voted for him four years earlier. His success in stemming this tide was somewhat earned by "apologizing," in large part, for certain errors and by stressing the relative success of his administration during the rising urban crisis across the nation.

The electoral events of 1969, and especially Lindsay's victory, are particularly revealing of the patterns initially indicated in the CRB referendum. One analysis of post-referendum voting in the city's assembly districts has shown the extent to which CRB sentiment has been a powerful predictor of subsequent voting patterns.[29] For example, the assembly district correlation between pro-CRB votes and 1969 Lindsay votes was .977. Conversely, the correlation between pro-CRB votes and Procaccino votes in the June Democratic primary was −.924. The strength of this correlation only fell to −.723 when pro-CRB votes were related to Procaccino votes in the November election, a factor explained by the candidacy of Republican-Conservative Marchi. These data support the idea of the CRB referendum as a critical election, the first indicator of the new nerve centers among the city's voters.

Analysis of the CRB referendum and subsequent elections suggests the decline of political parties as the major expressive institutions in urban politics. In fact, attitudinal and group differences cut within and across party lines to rearrange the usual liberal and conservative coalitions. The stress on the political system created by the demands of blacks and other groups is revealed in these recent voting patterns. In this climate, the issues related to the problem of race have a widespread effect on elections in general. Indeed, in a way, the race issue has set the stage for the expression of other group differences. The recent local school board elections not only revealed significant differences over community control, but, in many areas, also indicated a deep split between Catholics and others over the question of public aid for private and parochial schools.

A decade ago, the sanguine view of the pluralists held that the openness of New York City's political system, with its overlapping and fragmented decision-making structures, permitted a high capacity of responsiveness. In the face of growing militancy for social change, it appears that this very same quality of openness is now what prevents the system as a whole from responding with sufficient effectiveness to create meaningful change while maintaining the social order.[30] With the decline of traditional party politics, the "new machine" in city politics consists of the constellation of organized bureaucracies and their supportive constituencies, which dominate in separate aspects of the city's life.[31] While demands for change are focused on these separate systems —demands for police review, decentralization or community control in the school system, and so on—the city as a whole is without the capacity to coordinate change in several sectors at once or to respond with over-all effectiveness. At best, this means the continuation of a crisis climate wherein those who seek change can achieve only partial satisfaction. At the same time, the expression of demands has itself engendered a departure on the part of many voters from the liberal values that were formerly taken for granted by a majority of the electorate. Many of the progressive values that underlie the call for urban reform and aid to blacks and other minority groups still hold the allegiance of city voters. Nonetheless a more narrowly defined "politics of interest" has come to have an influence greater than the traditional politics of liberal values.

Notes

1. Wallace Sayre and Herbert Kaufman, *Governing New York City* (New York: W. W. Norton, 1965), p. 716.
2. *Ibid.*, p. 429.
3. The limitations of court-imposed conceptions of justice as a constraint on police behavior have been perceptively explored by James Q. Wilson. See his *Varieties of Police Behavior* (Cambridge, Mass.: Harvard University Press, 1968), ch. 2, *passim*.
4. See Aryeh Neier, "Civilian Review Boards—Another View," *Criminal Law Bulletin* (October, 1966), pp. 10–18, for a history of the civilian review issue.

5. *The New York Times,* April 29, 1964.

6. *Ibid.,* May 20, 1965.

7. *Ibid.,* June 21, 1965.

8. *Ibid.,* May 4, 1966.

9. These findings of a poll conducted by John F. Kraft, Inc., among Negroes in Harlem and Watts were released by Senator Abraham A. Ribicoff (Democrat, Connecticut) and reported in *The New York Times,* September 4, 1966.

10. Crime and race were found to be the top domestic problems to which Americans were giving their attention in 1966. Philip H. Ennis, *Criminal Victimization in the United States: A Report of a National Survey,* submitted by the National Opinion Research Center to the President's Commission on Law Enforcement and Administration of Justice, Field Survey II (Washington, D.C., 1967); referred to hereinafter as the NORC study.

11. See Abbott, Gold, and Rogowsky, *Police, Politics, and Race: The New York City Referendum on Civilian Review* (New York and Cambridge, Mass.: American Jewish Committee and Joint Center for Urban Studies of MIT and Harvard, 1969), for a discussion of sample selection procedures and the questionnaire, pp. 47–58.

12. New York law requires that referenda be stated in the affirmative, and so the PBA-initiated measure called for the abolition of the board.

13. The persistence of these factors in New York City politics is treated in depth in Nathan Glazer and Daniel Moynihan, *Beyond the Melting Pot* (Cambridge, Mass.: MIT Press and Harvard University Press, 1963). For a recent review of the literature, see Edgar Litt, *Ethnic Politics in America* (Glenview, Ill.: Scott, Foresman, 1970).

14. Because of the small number of Protestants in the sample, they will not be considered beyond this point.

15. An analysis of several ideological items included in the survey revealed a similar pattern. Voters with conservative leanings staunchly opposed the board, and liberals, while maintaining their attachment to traditional liberal beliefs, failed to translate these beliefs into a pro-CRB vote. See Abbott, Gold, and Rogowsky, *op. cit.* (note 11), pp. 31–33.

16. All respondents were given a score equivalent to the number of consistent responses they made (from 0 to 5). These scores were combined into a Guttman scale, which has the property that a person who rejects a given item will also, nine times out of ten, reject all items of a more "difficult" nature. Hence, it was highly unlikely that a person who was afraid to walk alone during the daytime would feel safer at night. Conversely, the few who felt no concern about household security were very likely to have felt safe on the other items. For the technically minded, the coefficient of reproducibility is .94 and of chance reproducibility, .69.

17. The coefficient of reproducibility was .93; of chance reproducibility, .75.

18. The Holy Name Society, the Catholic fraternal organization in the New York Police Department, has a membership of about 17,000, nearly two-thirds of the whole police force.

19. See William Brink and Louis Harris, *Black and White* (New York: Simon and Schuster, 1967), pp. 16–17.

20. For a description of backlash as a factor in the 1966 elections, see *ibid.*, pp. 108–16.

21. Coefficient of reproducibility is .91; of chance reproducibility, .69.

22. For another interpretation, see Daniel P. Moynihan's foreword to our original report. Abbott, Gold, and Rogowsky, *op. cit.* (note 11), especially p. 4.

23. See J. Leiper Freeman, "Local Party Systems: Theoretical Considerations and a Case Analysis," *American Journal of Sociology*, 64 (1958), pp. 282–89, and Gerald Pomper, "Ethnic and Group Voting in Nonpartisan Municipal Elections," *Public Opinion Quarterly*, 30 (1966), pp. 79–97.

24. See Abbott, Gold, and Rogowsky, *op. cit.* (note 11), pp. 42–44, for our earlier interpretation of the referendum.

25. See V. O. Key, "A Theory of Critical Elections," *The Journal of Politics*, 17 (1955), pp. 5–18.

26. Nathan Glazer and Daniel P. Moynihan, "How the Catholics Lost Out to the Jews in New York Politics," *New York* (August 10, 1970), p. 49.

27. "Black and Jewish Attitudes in New York City, July 1969," draft of study #1925, mimeograph, Louis Harris and Associates, New York, 1969.

28. Nathan Glazer, "A New Look at the Melting Pot," *The Public Interest* (Summer, 1969), p. 181.

29. These data are part of a larger study of New York City and its politics being prepared by Professor Andrew Hacker. He kindly made these data available to us prior to publication of his study.

30. See David Rogers, "Obstacles to School Desegregation in New York City: A Benchmark Case," in Marilyn Gittell, ed., *Educating an Urban Population* (Beverly Hills, Calif.: Sage Publications, 1967), pp. 155–84, and Rogers, *110 Livingston Street* (New York: Random House, 1969) for a discussion of the *immobilisme* of the school bureaucracy and the inability to achieve change.

31. Theodore Lowi, "Machine Politics, Old and New," *The Public Interest* (Fall, 1967), pp. 83–92.

4. Housing: The Scattered-Site Controversy

JEWEL BELLUSH

Assuming office as Mayor in 1965, John Lindsay determined to move rapidly to launch innovative programs not only to fulfill campaign promises, but also to ensure that his administration would stand distinct from all previous ones. Doubtless, additional impetus lay in the fact that Lindsay, even at that early date, was already considered an attractive aspirant for the Presidency; hence, an active and creative city administration also offered a greater chance for national exposure. As a young and energetic Republican Congressman from New York's "silk stocking" district, Lindsay had developed a reputation as a liberal, pressing expansion of governmental activities in social and economic affairs, opposing infringements of civil liberties, and urging equality of human rights. As Mayor, his decision to press on with the city's public housing program (the largest and, in many ways, one of the more innovative in the nation) dovetailed neatly with his plans to project himself as the city's progressive programmer and held out the additional lure of enhancing his national reputation.

This chapter will focus on the most important and most controversial parts of his initial program in public housing. In terms of public housing, Lindsay was determined to make real an ideal suggested by the city's Department of Planning in a study that had appeared in 1962: "Racial and ethnic considerations are an integral part of any sound planning approach in this city. A color-blind government policy carried out in a color-conscious housing market can only entrench and aggravate the segregation of racial and ethnic groups, with all its enervating and corrosive consequences."[1] Fully committed to creating a planned integrated residential pattern of living in the city, Lindsay intended to attain this end by means of selecting vacant land scattered in middle-class white areas for new public housing sites.

Whatever his intentions, his decision to push this program in the early months of his administration provoked extraordinary difficulties and antagonisms, enervating the new administration's energies and subjecting the new Mayor to bitter conflict with community groups. This study seeks to focus, first, on the factors that influenced his choice and the major participants who helped shape it; second, on the public response and its impact on the program; and finally, on consequences of the conflict that ensued as these pertain to the Mayor's leadership in general and to public housing and integration in particular.

The Pre-Lindsay Situation

By 1965, New York faced a desperate housing situation, particularly among the city's low-income population: a tight housing market, low vacancy rates, scarcity of good sites, traumatic experiences with relocation, rising rents, a bureaucratic maze in housing construction, and, increasingly, negative public attitudes toward low-rent projects. Additionally, over the years, federal support for housing programs had been seriously trimmed, and, in a 1965 voter referendum, state assistance had suffered a disastrous setback.

THE HOUSING PICTURE

The city's housing problem had reached ominous proportions when Lindsay took office. Some 359,000 families continued to live in substandard or overcrowded dwellings, thousands occupying old-law tenements that lacked toilet facilities and decent ventilation and served as a threat to daily human existence.* Over a

---

* "Old-law tenements" are units built before the 1901 law prohibiting additional construction of housing of such structural design. Post-1901 tenements were to conform to the then improved standards of ventilation, light, safety, plumbing, wiring, and so forth.

sixty-four year period, the city had managed to replace only half of these illegal units, yet they provided the lowest-income families with the only housing available. A poverty-stricken population larger in size than the total populations of the average American city lived in deteriorating housing pressed within slum neighborhoods.[2] Ironically, these tenants carried a heavier burden than most of the city's population, for 80 per cent of those earning under $3,000 paid approximately a third or more of their income for rent. Thus, the poorest families of the city were trapped in desperate housing conditions, paying more rent or occupying less space than they should. At a minimum, half of the 80,000 families on welfare lacked decent housing.[3] Increasingly, the poor (and among these were the bulk of the city's black and Puerto Rican populations) found themselves in cramped quarters within compact islands of despair. While households with incomes of $6,000 or more constituted nearly 43 per cent of the city's population, only 20 per cent of the black and Puerto Rican households fell into this category. In 1960, 75 per cent of the largest households, containing five or more people, had incomes under $3,000, and the highest proportion of these families were black and Puerto Rican.[4]

Since the beginning of this century, New York has suffered a grave housing shortage, particularly for its low-income populations, a situation from which the city has never extricated itself: Construction dwindled in the face of wars, depression, inflated prices, high land-values, and spiraling building costs. Adding to the shortage was the persistent deterioration of aging accommodations. In the early 1960's, the U.S. Census Bureau estimated that over a half-million units in the city were inadequate and required rehabilitation or replacement. Housing experts suggested that the potential renewal market was over 800,000 units.[5] Pressure for residential space had not eased since 1960. The rental vacancy rate was 3.19 in the beginning of 1965, one of the lowest among the nation's cities. For approximately the bottom third of the city's population, subsidized housing was the only source available. By 1965, over 100,000 families were on the Housing Authority's waiting list for low-income dwellings.

Lindsay came into office correctly charging the city with a slowdown in the construction of low-income housing. Yet part of the reason for that slowdown lay in the timid response of the federal government. President Eisenhower reluctantly pursued a minor effort that was to provide approximately 20,000 units annually for the entire nation, which constituted the minimal need of New York City alone.[6] The conservative political context of the 1950's, reflected in Congressional obstruction, kept funds for public housing, along with health and welfare, seriously depleted. Neither the New Frontier nor the Great Society ever came up with the initiative or boldness essential for projecting a successful public-housing program.

Some 5 million families with incomes of less than $4,000—about 10 per cent of the nation—still lived in substandard dwellings in 1965. Such large and important cities as Baltimore, Cleveland, Detroit, and Boston, with sizable low-income populations, launched no construction starts between 1962 and 1965. The "decent home" for every American family, projected in 1949 by federal legislation, has yet to be realized: Even the 810,000 units promised in that legislation have not been built. Despite some expansion of the welfare state, public housing has remained America's stepchild, a program forever on the defensive and, in many ways, intentionally "meant to fail."[7] Despite the many innovations hailed in the 1965 Housing Act—leasing, rehabilitation, and rent-subsidization schemes—it constituted little more than tinkering, providing no genuine substitute for a much needed massive public effort to house the third of urban America that is in the low-income group. By 1966, federal housing provided accommodations across the land for 2,290,000 people, but some 11 million more had incomes below the minimal admission requirements set by public housing authorities.[8]

The stunning political successes of the real estate lobby contributed to the bareness of federal expenditures, as did grass-roots campaigns in many communities that killed even timid housing efforts.[9] Many of these grass-roots campaigns were initiated by the real estate lobby. So successful was this lobby in pursuing the "neighborhood strategy" that a group of Democratic senators, generally supportive of public housing, felt impelled to approve Johnson's diminished program, acknowledging: "We are all disappointed that the local public housing authorities have been unable to build the number of public housing units Congress has allocated. In the face of this fact, it is difficult to argue for an increase."

Real estate groups were inadvertently given an assist from a number of reformers and crusading journalists who played upon the failures of public housing to solve the problems of the cities. The attack on the federal government for its "cataclysmic money" and the laments of the city-beautiful enthusiasts criticizing the public housing design for producing slabs of cement and mammoth creatures of inhumanity contributed to the negative public attitudes toward public housing.[10] These aesthetic failures were, to a large extent, the handiwork of the real estate alliance, which had placed public housing bureaucrats under intense surveillance —limiting, circumscribing, and harassing, so that creative proposals that could have produced acceptable design while satisfying housing needs were killed by unit costs and restrictions on design. Given the rigidity of the unit cost allocation and faced with soaring prices due to increased labor and building costs, New York's Housing Authority was compelled at times to abandon projects. Pressed by an ever growing waiting list and caught in a cost squeeze, the Authority found itself forced to shoot projects forever upward, exposing itself to the critics' cries of high-rise "jungles."[11]

The federal urban renewal program, highlighted by empty promises and spongy actions, itself contributed a debilitating share to the city's housing woes. Aiming at just those urban areas with the largest number of low-rent units, it made inroads into available low-income housing, causing relocation to become a nightmare and creating more rigidly segregated communities.[12] As recently as the mid-1960's, for example, 57 per cent of families displaced from the Bronx Park South and 85 per cent from the Seward Park urban renewal projects were identified as low income, yet, on the former site, there was little provision for rehousing the displaced and, on the latter, no accommodations at all for the low income. Nor did the program reveal specific dwellings for the displaced elsewhere in the city.[13]

Despite the City Housing Authority's claim that it had the capacity to build 25,000 public housing units annually, between 1963 and 1966 there were, either under construction or about to commence construction, only some 12,000 units. The "magnanimity" of the federal government was displayed in the 1965 Housing Act, which provided, over a four-year period, for only 7,000 low-rent dwellings per year for New York. To create the impression that this impoverished effort constituted a sizable amount, government documents dramatized the fact the city was about to be awarded 28,000 units of public housing but played down the four-year spread. New York State offered even less solace to the city. Concurrent with Lindsay's election in November, 1965, state voters rejected two housing propositions that vitally affected the city. One would have authorized an additional $200 million state bond for low-rent housing projects and a $9 million annual increase in subsidy payments to maintain low rents in projects; a second would have increased subsidies to enable New York City and other localities to enlarge the borrowing capacity of their Housing Authorities.[14]

By the closing years of the Wagner Administration, housing spokesmen projected an output for 1966 of 3,500 units; for 1967, 2,800 units; and for 1968, 6,900 units. "The reasons," claimed a top staff member at the Authority, "is the lack of funds to support a greater effort."[15] Such, then, was Lindsay's legacy.

THE POLITICAL PROCESS AND PUBLIC HOUSING[16]

In addition to inadequate funding, Lindsay inherited from his predecessor a challenging, if not threatening political and bureaucratic system through which public housing had to be processed. Within the fragmented and disparate municipal government, there were at least four sets of actors in the life history of low-rent dwellings. One was the Housing Authority: composed of three members appointed by the mayor, two for overlapping five year terms, and the third, the chairman, serving at his call. The second was the City Planning Commission, with all seven of its members designated by the mayor for staggered terms of eight years each. Majorities of both agencies were required for approval of public-housing projects, with the latter directed by law to hold public hearings. These agencies, "served" by staffs largely recruited from the Civil Service, were not necessarily united in analysis or viewpoint. The Board of Estimate constituted a third cast of characters. It included the mayor, the City Council president, and the comptroller—all elected by a city-wide vote— and the five borough presidents, each chosen by voters on a borough (county) basis. A fourth identifiable group of actors involved in the processing of projects included the mayor and his personal staff. Their role and influence depended upon the chief executive's philosophy and attitude toward public housing as well as on his political interest and acumen. In a city as fragmented in structure as New York, the mayor's performance and leadership has always been of crucial importance in the development and character of the public-housing program. Because of the complex interrelationships of these four groups, the nature of the authority of each set of city actors in processing low-income housing programs and the informal methods evolved by the earlier Wagner Administration will be briefly reviewed.

Stage I: Initiation of the Program

Brief Overview.   The brief overview took place within the Housing Authority's Division of Program Planning; staff members would identify vacant or other suitable sites, inspect them informally, and review their possibilities in a cursory fashion. Should the project seem promising, a commissioner on the Authority might join a staff member in surveying the site. An energetic commissioner could seek sites out on his own and suggest them to staff members for initial examination.

Data Collection.   If the site seemed to have serious possibilities, the staff began to collect material and pertinent data such as apartment distribution, property-value estimates, design plans, zoning feasibility, available social and community services, and programs necessary to fill capital needs.

Political Considerations.   Over the years, the staff of the Division of Program Planning had acquired a sensitivity to political considerations that influenced their behavior and procedure. As a result, before any site was publicized or formally presented to the commissioners of the Housing Authority, or to any agency of government, the staff would be in close touch with Mayor Wagner's aides. The latter then handled the delicate negotiations with the borough president in whose bailiwick the site was located. Only on rare occasions would a site be further processed following negative reactions by a borough president. This early involvement of elected officials was understandable since, under the city's charter, the Board of Estimate plays a critical and decisive role in housing; its approval is required for all projects. The borough presidency, at one time an important administrative post, has fallen to near oblivion under the ax of successive waves of reformers who believed that only through centralized bureaucracy, under the leadership of the mayor, could good government come to New York. By the time of Lindsay's election, the most important substantive power remaining with the borough presidents was their membership on the Board of Estimate, a legislative body that overshadows the City Council. As a collective body, it has decisive authority over the expense and capital budgets. Each borough president has two votes while the mayor, president of the City Council, and comptroller have four each. Moreover, because each borough is coterminous with a county, which also serve as the core of the city's political system, most borough presidents became key figures in political party activity closely allied to the county and district party leaders within their boroughs. The city has been predominantly Democratic, and, with the exception of Richmond, the borough presidents have generally been of the same party. Despite much party factionalism over the years, borough presidents traditionally have acted together, for they have been aware that their voting power evolved out of collective effort. As each borough president was aware that he could exert maximum effectiveness when he joined with his fellow borough executives on the Board of Estimate, each became sensitive to the others needs, interests, and political pressures; together, they operated according to a politics of borough courtesy. Sayre and Kaufman have accurately highlighted the political strategy adopted by the county executives when they pointed out that, in their common cause as a group in the Board, they "maintain together a practice of 'borough courtesy' which they often succeed in persuading the city-wide members to observe, while in addition they seek to join with the Comptroller in a bargaining alliance which can guide the Board in the majority of its decisions."[17] The president of the City Council and the comptroller, while more oriented toward a city-wide view, owe much of their power base to the county party units. Hence, they have responded to county pressures and acted with acute sensitivity to the needs and problems of the borough presidents.

Traditionally, the Board has been controlled by Democrats. But, even when the mayor is of the same party, he is hampered by the fact that he has only four votes and that he must often labor mightily to muster a majority by an extensive system of political exchanges and payoffs. If he refuses to work within this political arrangement, the Board's collegial system could easily veto his program. In such a situation, the mayor can enhance his position only to the degree that he maintains these Board of Estimate participants as allies through personal negotiations, patronage, favors, and other arrangements. Given the factional quality of Democratic Party politics in the city and the city's fragmented type of governmental system, even a mayor of the same political party that has a majority on the Board of Estimate has had to devise a means of building enough unity to achieve whatever goals he sought. Public housing proved particularly sensitive to this problem.

Mayor Lindsay, who came to office through a loosely formed coalition of Republicans, Liberals, and dissident Democrats and independents, faced the forbidding task of representing a very different political alliance on a Board predominantly Democratic. The lone Republican on the Board (from Richmond) was no asset to a Republican-Fusion Mayor whose backing was liberal. Representing the conservative wing of the GOP, the Borough President of Richmond firmly rejected the Mayor's liberal attitudes—particularly his aims in public housing. Unless the new chief executive could evolve some new political approach, the decision-making apparatus invited only trouble.

Financial Feasibility. If the project received the necessary political blessings, a more detailed fiscal analysis would be made to determine the cost, particularly the question of meeting the circumscribed statutory and administrative limitations, federal or state. Once these preliminary negotiations and studies seemed to indicate smooth sailing ahead, the Housing Authority staff prepared for the next stage of discussions.

Stage II: Tentative Federal Approval

During this stage of negotiations, federal staff members at the Public Housing Administration (during the Lindsay years, known as the Housing Assistance Administration), city bureaucrats, and the Mayor's aides attempted to reach agreement on the proposed program in order to arrive at tentative approval. At times, this entailed lengthy and heated discussions over costs, design, and size. Additionally, tentative approval was not necessarily a guarantee of subsequent federal funding, especially if costs went beyond the prior amount originally approved.

Stage III: Approval of "Plan and Project" by the City Planning Commission

Once the Housing Authority had formally prepared a "Plan and Project," it was sent on to the City Planning Commission. There, the staff reviewed and discussed the contents in detail.[18] Conferences, attended by the staffs and Commissioners of both the Authority and the Commission, were then held with aides from the Mayor's office. Prior to Lindsay's Administration, most of these sessions were *pro forma*, since key decisions had already been determined. The date for public hearing before the Board of Estimate would then be set. At such hearings, community groups and civic organizations presented their views. Again, this form of consultation was of relatively little importance under Mayor Wagner because of the extensive political consultation with borough presidents that had taken place early in the decision-making process. Should a borough executive anticipate a sizable, well-organized community protest, he would usually oppose the project in the initial stage.

Stage IV: Approval of "Plan and Project" by the Board of Estimate

If a project received approval at the Planning Commission, it went to the Board of Estimate for review. When a particular project had provoked the anger of an alert community group, hearings at the Board of Estimate were usually heated. In fact, even after the Board's approval of a project, should a map or zoning change be necessary to accommodate the project on a particular site, these technicalities could easily become the means through which more protests were organized. For example, a member of the Authority staff noted one case in which a map change provided a neighborhood group opposed to a project with another chance to defeat it: "The same group who opposed the project in 1959 have now [1965] seized upon the map change for the opportunity to reinitiate their objections. Borough President Periconi, who had previously favored erection of the housing project has now turned about face and has opposed approval of the map change."[19]

Stage V: Federal or State Approval of the Development Plan

At this stage, the final plan was submitted to the federal (or state) agency. By no means automatic, this process involved serious review by federal staff members and could lead to rejection or to interminable delay of city projects. Federal delays were particularly serious at a time when land values continued to spiral and new labor contracts inevitably increased costs, especially in a union town like New York. In fact, pressure groups opposed to a particular project could use this stage in the political process to kill a program by delaying its acceptance—allowing enough time to elapse so that costs would rise to the point of making construction prohibitive.

SEGREGATED CITY

The intensification of the city's segregated residential patterns, depicted by scholars in the 1950's, continued unabated into the 1960's. The growth of the New York metropolitan region contributed to a worsening racial problem, with whites moving to the suburbs and blacks and Puerto Ricans trapped in the city by factors of race and class. Between 1940 and 1960, figures show that 1,698,200 whites left the city, with nonwhites pouring in: 393,700 black and 376,500 Puerto Rican newcomers.[20] And, during the following four years, the net outmigration of whites and immigration of nonwhites to the central city accelerated. Additional important shifts of population had been facilitated by those whites who could not afford or did not choose to move to suburbia and who selected the mini-suburban environments in the outer boroughs—Queens and Richmond—or peripheral areas on vacant lands in Brooklyn, the Bronx, and northern Manhattan. As a result of these population movements, new residential areas formerly barred to blacks and Puerto Ricans were pried open, but the accommodations provided were already on the decline— seriously neglected by property owners and plagued by inadequate public services. Real estate brokers often rushed in with their block-busting techniques, hastening the transition. Although varied ethnic and class groups have always tended to cluster in discrete areas in New York, the pressure imposed by prejudice deepened and intensified the racial ghettoization process.[21]

Despite the city's comprehensive antibias law, a model for the nation, racial segregation in housing continued unabated into the 1960's.[22] The distances separating people increased sharply, and, as Morton Grodzins has suggested, "Social isolation of the Northern urban Negro was more complete than it ever was for the Negro rural resident in the South!"[23] According to one staff study done by the Housing Authority's Planning Department, ghettoization had, by 1965, reached a point of sealing off "large segments of human opportunity from those who dwell within them."[24] Residential segregation automatically ensured the segregation of a host of social institutions: education, recreation, health and welfare services, and shopping facilities. Exacerbating racial concentration were the segregation patterns emerging in the city's public housing projects. Pressure from blacks and Puerto Ricans for decent housing, white fears that led to suburban flight, a mandated income cutoff for public housing, and the sheer lack of adequate accommodations, public or private, had led to this pattern. Whatever the reasons, public housing was increasingly segregated.

Intensification of the ghettos reached such proportions that, by 1960, almost two-thirds of the city's black population lived in areas with 50 per cent or more black concentrations. The heaviest concentration—50 per cent or more—were in Manhattan's Harlem, Morrisania in the Bronx, Corona and Jamaica–St. Albans in Queens, and Bedford-Stuyvesant in Brooklyn. Of the city's non-white population, 80 per cent lived in these four areas. In turn, these sections were surrounded by black populations estimated to reach between 10 and 49 per cent; and each of these segregated islands seemed destined for additional expansion. Three additional segregated concentrations appeared to be developing rapidly in the Bronx, Queens, and Brooklyn. In sum, the city's population changes accelerated and intensified already pronounced patterns of segregation.[25] In 1966, the newcomers to power were aware of these trends and confident that they could control their direction.

Lindsay's Team: Amateur Democrats in Power

In the history of reform in New York City, no Republican Mayor could win office without wooing independent and dissident Democrats in the form of a fusion-type coalition. Lindsay was no exception; immediately upon assuming office, he began to fill the various governmental posts with men and women representing this loosely contrived combination. A key man assigned to housing, urban renewal, and planning was Donald Elliott, a youthful activist from a Reform Democratic Club on Manhattan's West Side and a one-time law associate of the Mayor's. Responsible for the development of key issues during the campaign, Elliott had also worked closely with the task forces headed by Edward Logue and Mitchell Sviridoff that were set up to study housing and welfare administration in the city, and he was also in communication with those studying city reorganization. These early contacts with Lindsay's instant "royal commissions" first introduced Elliott to the city's pressing problems, the serious bureaucratic tensions and the fragmented decision-making character of its governmental and political systems.[26] At the start of the Lindsay Administration in January, 1966, Elliott was appointed Counsel to the Mayor and Chairman of his Housing Executive Committee. Selected to assist him were Eugenia Flatow and Edward Robin, friends who had also been active in Reform Democratic politics. Through these appointments, the Mayor indicated that the reform wing of the Democratic Party in his coalition would select the strategies for housing and planning. It was this trio, led by Donald Elliott, that constituted the leading actors in the development of the Mayor's first set of public housing policies.[27]

The group shared a set of common ideas and attitudes that helped shape the program. In the first place, they agreed that Lindsay, as chief executive, should be the key figure in initiating and developing policy. It was not merely a matter of formal authorization by the City Charter but a conceptual view that, as a city-wide elected official, the Mayor expressed the "true" community needs of the population; only through the Mayor could the general, more broadly conceived public interest be discovered and projected. By means of bold and vigorous leadership, it would be his responsibility to press the interests of the entire city.[28] Second, these reformers not only rejected the old political style of extended bargaining, but were critical of the overcompromising of "true" community goals and of the tendency to allow government to muddle through. They were particularly appalled by what they characterized as the wheeler-dealer tactics of the previous administration and their corrosive effects on the city's public housing program.[29] As they saw it, planning, in general, and location of public housing sites, in particular, required a city-wide view of public needs that only the Mayor could set in proper focus. The site-selection process, which they inherited from the Wagner Administration, was put forward as an example of the overextended political bargaining and incremental planning. When a Housing Authority staff member was asked to brief them on the decision-making process, his detailed account of the negative role played by borough presidents confirmed their bias:

The extent to which the Borough President's reaction to public housing has hampered the Authority's building program may best be illustrated by actual experience during the past two years. Within that time frame the Queens Borough President has rejected (1) a 500 unit vacant land site in the Pomonok-Flushing section, (2) a predominantly vacant land site adjacent to the 5800 unit middle-income Rochdale Village, (3) a 215 unit vacant land site opposite the Worlds Fair groups, and has deferred action on a 430 unit site in Flushing. Site 1 was rejected on the basis that the adjacent middle-income housing project might desire additional land for expansion. Sites 2 and 3 were originally approved by the BP, such approval being withdrawn after that official yielded to pressure groups. . . . The Richmond BP has looked with disfavor on any attempt to provide additional public housing in his borough.

Our main problem in Manhattan is the high cost of land, even in deep slum areas. . . . The Bronx BP has rejected two slum sites in Bronx Park West that would accommodate about 400 units, also, a 300 unit site in the West Farms section, and a 1000 unit vacant city-owned site in the Schuyler Village section. He has frustrated our efforts to proceed with a 538 unit development in the Boston-Secor section.[30]

These Lindsay-Democratic reformers learned that a long list of projects had been abandoned, or indefinitely deferred, by borough presidents who were much too sensitive to community pressure. One site in the Bronx—Monterey—had been approved by the Housing Authority, the City Planning Commission, and even the federal Public Housing Administration, but was dropped on the request of Bronx Borough President Joseph Periconi (Republican-Liberal) after the Housing and Redevelopment Board indicated it wanted to process the area for middle-income subsidized housing. A vacant site near the World's Fair parking grounds had received the approval of all agencies concerned, up to and including the state Division of Housing and Community Renewal, but was belatedly deferred on the request of Queens Borough President Mario Cariello (Democrat-Republican-Liberal), allegedly to ensure expansion of the county's Hall of Science. Brooklyn Borough President Abraham Stark withdrew earlier approval for a site, reportedly because of the "pressures from the sponsors of the Mitchell-Lama developments."[31]

It was not difficult for Elliott and his colleagues to conclude that the *bête noir* in decision-making was the borough president —the weak link in ensuring an efficient and enlightened public housing program in New York City. From the viewpoint of reformers, the borough president represented only a segment of the city; he was therefore more parochial in outlook, easy prey to the narrower, more selfish interests opposed to public housing. They were also well-aware that the Board of Estimate was, at that time, made up of four Democratic Borough Presidents, a Republican from Richmond who was antagonistic to Lindsay's liberalism, and a Comptroller and City Council President who were regular, organization Democrats closely allied to political bases similar to that of the Borough Presidents. As a result of the negative role of borough presidents and Democratic control of the Board of Estimate, Elliott quickly sought changes in the decision-making process.

A third factor that influenced the strategy of Elliott and his colleagues was their firm conviction, bordering on missionary zeal, that only through their deep personal involvement on behalf of the Mayor, could a more honest and successful effort be made for public housing. They shared a mutual disdain for the Wagner legacy of "ineptness and bungling" and for the "incompetency" of the civil servants manning those city agencies involved in low-income housing who were too closely tied to the old disreputable way of doing things. Old-style politics, it seemed to these reformers, contributed to the failings of public housing in New York, particularly to its shoddy character and dismal design. Donald Elliott was affronted by the repetitive monumental slabs of block developments that had been built throughout the city. Influenced by critics who deplored the high rise, the dull design, and the piled-up mortar, he was attracted to the need for a radical change in physical form to ensure success.[32] Elliott concluded that only by breaking the huge projects into smaller and more attractively designed creations spread throughout the city could the public housing program become a success.

Decision-Making: Procedural Changes

In the early months of the Lindsay Administration, strategies were devised to implement the group's major objectives: to make the Mayor's role central, to eliminate "politicking" with borough presidents, to surmount the "ineptness" of the former administrations, and to launch a new integrated public housing program. Representing the Mayor, at the center of the newly designed decision-making apparatus, was Elliott. As chairman of the Housing Executive Committee and strategically placed in the office of the Mayor, Elliott assigned Edward Robin and Eugenia Flatow the task of collating ideas and instituting procedural changes that would speed up public-housing construction.[33] Suspicious of the Democratic legacy and lacking background and practical experience in dealing with New York's housing-and-planning jungle, the new administration, in its transitional period, produced its quota of difficulties.[34] Festering suspicion between the youthful, exuberant Lindsay aides and the older, experienced civil servants created acute tensions and anxiety.

Within weeks after assuming office, Lindsay aides were able to pinpoint a small group of men working in the various, far-flung agencies that handled public housing who were able, knowledgeable, and trustworthy. Under Robin's aegis, these men were organized on an ad hoc basis into the Working Group on Housing Sites; members were drawn from the staffs of the Housing Authority, City Planning Department (the staff arm of the City Planning Commission), and the Housing and Redevelopment Board.[35] As a body, the group constituted the city's most informed experts on its housing programs and system of operation, but their participation in decision-making was, to a large extent, to be limited to technical areas. The more political aspects of housing policy were determined by Elliott, Robin, and Flatow. In one case, for example, staff members at the Housing Authority were asked to review a particular site only in terms of its economic and geographical feasibility; other questions connected with broader policy were left to the Mayor's immediate staff.[36] A number of the working group's members, uneasy with the program objectives and style of the new Republican-Fusion team, preferred this arrangement; however, several staff participants, more anxious to share in the making of policy, felt constrained in this role and eventually left city government.[37]

Staff members of the respective agencies concerned with the various aspects of housing decision-making were directed to report to this specially constituted working group. Additionally, Robin instructed them to halt the practice of contacting other agencies on matters concerned with site selection—yet another attempt to give central direction to the city's cumbersome bureaucracy. Within four months, however, Robin realized that informal communications among staffs in various divisions of the city bureaucracy produced essential information and data for sites under consideration, and he, therefore, shelved this directive. Thereafter, to facilitate access to information and to augment its influence, the Mayor's staff used the interdepartmental working group as a funnel between the bureaucratic apparatus in the city and Donald Elliott in the Mayor's office. Additionally, it was hoped that this method would speed the flow of ideas, enhance efficiency, and protect the identity of the program as a *Lindsay* program.

Of all the Elliott goals, the most important was the elimination of the veto power by borough presidents. Elliott sought to achieve this by decree, declaring that, henceforth, there would be no consultation or bargaining in the initial stage of processing projects. Lindsay aides hoped to circumvent those particular officials they believed had in the past been most instrumental in whittling away effective low-income housing programs. Thus, in the opening months of the administration, Robin, pressed by staff members as to when site "consultations" between the administration and the borough presidents would take place, responded that this would not occur until *after* the Mayor had presented his program to the public in March.[38] Believing in the efficacy of strong executive leadership, the Lindsay team felt that, merely by asserting the Mayor's prerogatives and publicizing what they conceived to be "the public interest," they could overcome the restraints imposed by governmental fragmentation and "nefarious" political pressures. The essence of these structural alterations in the decision-making system involved an important change in the nature and character of the political process, a change that Elliott and his colleagues may not have anticipated. A definite shift in political style was instituted: from negotiation marked by extensive bargaining and compromise within a private, if not secret, context, to a politics of open struggle, intense conflict, and public confrontation.

Decision-Making: Policy Changes—Image or Reality?

Under tremendous pressure to produce a list of suitable sites, the newly created working group was told that "the Mayor wants to start out with a workable, rational plan to move projects ahead, looking to a marked increase in the pace of construction."[39] Within two months, Lindsay's aides excitedly agreed upon a policy that was eventually to be formalized as the scattered-site program. It provided that approximately half of all future low-income projects were to be built on vacant land in outlying areas of the city, within stable middle-income white communities; compared to previous projects, these would be smaller in size, more discrete in shape, and designed to blend more harmoniously with the surrounding neighborhood. In short, this was more than a housing program; it was a deliberate policy aimed at producing a community integrated along racial, as well as economic, lines.[40] Eventually, twelve scattered sites were selected, and the working group decided to present them in a single package, hoping by this means to circumvent the whittling down process of the borough presidents.[41]

There were certain advantages in designing the public-housing
program along all these lines. First, because of the serious financial limitations imposed on the city by the federal and state governments, the skimpy allocations for public housing, and the
rising costs in construction, packaging the proposed sites in one
bundle would make them appear an enlargement of Lindsay's
housing endeavors. Second, though previous administrations had
built a limited number of scattered-site projects, Lindsay's presentation of the program in package form would likely make it
appear innovative; the announcement of a program to integrate
public housing by means of site selection could well elicit recognition of the Mayor's unique leadership in planning. In fact, his
aides wanted to project the Mayor as a courageous figure, dedicated to pursuing policies that, while politically hazardous, were
morally sound. The housing program fitted this aim, for sites were
to be selected "not simply to find locations where public housing
would not be opposed or vetoed."[42] And, of course, from an
ideological point of view, the reformers were completely devoted
to this liberal effort. With its success, they hoped to slow down,
and perhaps halt, the expansion of the city's ghettos; by enabling
low-income black and Puerto Rican families to improve their life
styles, they hoped to end the brutalized impact of those ghettos.
Less stigma would be attached, they thought, to inconspicuous
public-housing projects, especially when these were located in
stable white communities. Lesser numbers of low-income families
might find it much easier to be accepted and assimilated in
middle-class neighborhoods. And, by building on vacant land,
the city could eliminate the horrendous consequences of relocation from which its minority-group populations had long suffered
in the wake of the "progress" of urban renewal. Furthermore,
without the need for demolition, construction could begin
quickly, if not immediately. In light of the severity of the low-
income housing shortage, using vacant land would be far preferable to a slum-clearance program that, in the end, usually
ensured a decline in available housing. Finally, it was hoped that
scattering sites would compel the Borough Presidents to follow
the Mayor's lead, since each was to share a part of the "burden"
of providing sites within their respective counties.

Should the Mayor have worked to eliminate the Borough Presidents entirely from the decision-making process as members of
the Board of Estimate? Such a step would have necessitated
changes in the City Charter; but the fastest route for such modi-

fication of power was not through a charter commission but by
means of legislation in Albany. Although both chambers of the
state legislature were then in Republican hands, the Mayor's
liberalism was much too extreme for most upstate lawmakers.
Besides, upstate Republicans were traditionally indifferent, if not
hostile, to the city. Lindsay clearly could not turn to the city's
Democratic legislative contingent to curtail the authority of their
party colleagues on the Board of Estimate, nor could he solicit
the help of the Republican Governor, for, between both men,
tensions were already growing. Thus, whether he liked it or not,
the Mayor had to negotiate with the Board of Estimate.

Could the Mayor have handled the obstructionism of the
Borough Presidents with a more effective alternative than his
scattered-site package? Through the scatter package, he thought
he placed the burden of compromise on the Borough Presidents.
What his aides did not adequately appreciate, however, was the
depth of feeling the sites would stir up in the affected communities. The explosions that were produced by many of the selections were to have the effect of giving added support to the
Borough Presidents, who became the "protectors" and "defenders" of their neighborhoods. Conversely, responsibility for the
program was placed squarely on the Mayor. As will be subsequently discussed, the would-be supporters of the Mayor's policy
were unable to produce the political thrust necessary to bolster
the position of the chief executive. Thus, the Mayor's aides had
moved into a highly sensitive arena in which their desire for
quick change, their inadequate knowledge and somewhat limited
reform perspectives, and, in the end, their naïveté about their
ability to provide alternative sources of support prevented them
from providing a more careful and balanced analysis of the economic, social, and political realities operating at the time.

Part of the problem lay in the reformers' objective. The creation of racially balanced communities within the city was a
concept built on abstract notions about democracy and social
justice. Acceptable as a normative position, these notions were
unsupported by the perceptive reasoning and empirical data so
necessary to effective implementation. The reformers entered a
field in which they had little background or experience, and their
lack of understanding or appreciation of the delicacy and complexity of achieving their goal was unfortunate. No matter the
high-minded motivation of reform zealots, enough concrete evidence was available to the Mayor's housing aides to demonstrate

that groups unequal in class and status generally pull apart into separate enclaves, creating permanent community and even street divisions. "Every status level," sociologist Suzanne Keller has written, "has its own distinctive ways of manifesting its status concerns, and, differently though these may be expressed, expressed they are."[43] Despite the moral tone of reformers dedicated to constructing balanced communities, mixing individuals and groups of different social classes with different conceptions of family life, child rearing, social relationships, and community had not in the past proved successful. On the contrary, material on new towns and housing estates in many parts of the world has indicated that the planned mixing of groups may contribute to tension and outright conflict. Evaluating a desegregation policy very similar in intent and objective to the Lindsay scattered-site plan, Dr. Keller warned: "This flies in the face of considerable evidence accumulated over at least two decades in a variety of communities where such mixing has in fact been attempted."[44] Perhaps most important to the Lindsay program, of all the criteria employed in creating heterogeneous communities, the mix of families with different incomes or occupations has proved to be the one least likely to produce success under current social conditions.[45] The problem, of course, is that low-income housing in New York—as in most of the nation's urban centers—is inextricably tied up with the question of race. After the experience of school integration in the South, a body of opinion grew up around the belief that the middle class—better educated and less economically threatened—was a better target for integration efforts. This may well have entered into the decision of Lindsay's aides to combine class and race integration in housing. Unfortunately, the added burden of class differences may also have been the deciding factor in the program's failure. Given our stratified society, people have consistently sought different living areas as natural reflections of their objective economic situations and distinct life styles, as much as of their ethnic or racial backgrounds.

If the race and class conundrum is predictably explosive, perhaps the most crucial question is whether public low-income housing is the best means for building balanced communities. Increasingly, in the public's mind, low-income housing has been equated with black housing; regardless of the reasons, the association is with poverty, ghettos, crime, delinquency, and slums. With so little money available for public housing, was it fair to burden an already meager program with a publicized crusade for integration? The waiting list for public housing has mounted annually; by 1966, well over 100,000 families were on it. For a maximum of 3,500 units, was the hostility the program aroused worth the cost? If, on the one hand, the reformers thought that the moral objective was more important than quantity, one must question their choice of strategy. If, moreover, they did not antic- ipate hostility from the community and chose their strategy accordingly, one must conclude they were naïve or uninformed about the politics of locating public housing in the city and around the country. In any event, the double burden imposed on the city's low-income housing program proved too much, result- ing in a marked decline in public-housing starts throughout Lindsay's term of office. While he had initially promised to build 160,000 units for middle- and low-income populations, by June, 1969, only 34,167 units had been started. Of these, 8,920 dwell- ings were constructed for low-income families.[46] The lowest annual figure of completed units since 1947 was 1,593; that was in 1968. Scheduled starts for that year were only 2,504.[47] During 1969, six scattered sites were finally approved by federal and state agencies; these amounted to 1,383 units, and a large share were allocated to the aged. The actual start of construction for these 1,383 units was still far off, because most bids were not to be taken before the end of the year.[48] While many factors contribu- ted to this poor record—spiraling costs, shrinking land sites, in- adequate federal and state support—the scattered-site program apparently put the final touches to the administration's failure to keep its promise of an enlarged and innovative housing program.[49]

Ironically, despite their limited knowledge of the sensitive work demanded for the task of creating integrated housing, the reformers neglected to fulfill their promise "to develop positive criteria for the selection of public housing sites." A pragmatic, rather informal, and loosely conceived strategy was employed to get the package together as quickly as possible.[50] With vacant land at a premium, it was no wonder a number of sites were of such poor terrain that expenses would be prohibitive for land fill, special piles, and construction techniques. While many areas of the city have often lacked such basic facilities as sewers, streets, and schools, a good number of the proposed sites were in an even more critical condition. For a number of sites, increased expenditures of city funds and a lengthy construction period would be required in order to bring the sites up to the minimal level essential to creating good communities. For the city to provide such basic amenities in the outlying vacant areas at a time of tremendous fiscal strain, bordering on crisis, constituted vague if not unrealizable hopes. Another practical consideration was the distance of sites from transportation; many would necessitate double fares, and bus service would have to be attracted to the area. The year before Lindsay took office, the Planning Department conducted a special study of vacant sites in peripheral areas for possible construction of public housing and concluded with a warning that:

> The vacant sites on the fringe of the City present problems of accessibility for those who commute daily to the Central Business District. If they were used to rehouse large numbers of residents, particularly those with low income and low skills, it would be necessary to provide improved access to jobs in the core of the City. These outer areas have greater promise for housing families whose breadwinners work in neighboring industrial sections or who are able to take a car or railroad train to work.[51].

Of the scattered sites, the Riverdale locations, set aside largely for the elderly, had such steep slopes that the essential improvement of grades would be both difficult and expensive. Although the Waldo site in the Bronx was put in the package, Lindsay's housing strategists soon found that it constituted an impossible location, and held on to it only as a means of bargaining with the Borough President for a replacement. In the case of the Flushing site, the project would go up close to a unique residential community of middle-class black homeowners already located in a white area. Many of Lindsay's own people saw this as a questionable selection. Roger Starr, Executive Director of the Citizens Housing and Planning Council and a warm supporter of Lindsay's scatter program, opposed the site,[52] and several staff members in the Planning Department urged the Lindsay team to reconsider its selection. One of them explained that her reservations stemmed from "the apparently successful integration which is being achieved by the community."[53] Were the aides more interested in having a site to augment the package, or were they really interested in creating balanced communities? Where indeed were the "positive criteria?"

In retrospect, the Mayor admitted that the scatter program resulted in "a political bloodbath."[54] Had his advisers intention-

ally chosen to disregard the political consequences the proposed
strategy might provoke, or had they simply misjudged it? The
answer is a matter of conjecture. Looking ahead to Lindsay's
political future, his aides were undoubtedly anxious to strengthen
and enlarge his political following. Having won as a candidate of
a loosely-conceived coalition of Republicans, Reform Democrats,
Liberals, and independents, Lindsay did not have the old-style
political support his predecessor had enjoyed. The scatter program may have been part of an over-all strategy for developing a
new political coalition in the city. The Mayor was, perhaps, trying to assure himself of the continued support of two important
groups: the upper-class professionals, amateur Democrats, liberal Republicans, and sundry independents on the one side, and
the black and Puerto Rican lower-class populations of the inner
city on the other. Most of the locations of the scattered sites were
in outlying areas of the outer boroughs of the city—largely in
Queens, a few in Staten Island and in the northern section of the
Bronx. These were communities of voters who were viewed as
cool to the Mayor's brand of liberalism and whose opposition to
public housing and other reforms could be anticipated. It may be
that the Lindsay people believed these communities were lost to
them anyway. It is difficult to know to what extent this reasoning
constituted the political considerations of the Lindsay reformers,
but if it did enter into their reckoning of the political implications
of the scatter program, they seriously misjudged the intensity of
the opposition and its political importance in the city's decision-
making process. They may also have misjudged both the composition of the opposition and the sources of their own support,
for, if the Italian voters of Corona constituted an already hostile
enclave, the same was not necessarily true of the equally affected
middle-class Jewish populations in the outer boroughs. In the
1965 mayoral election, Jews had been a significant source of
Lindsay support, despite their predominant traditional affiliation
with the Democratic Party and the fact that the Democratic candidate, Abraham Beame (himself a Jew), was a popular figure
among Jewish voters. Generally, on those city issues with a liberal
thrust—such as expanding services for low-income populations in
areas such as housing, education, and welfare—Jewish citizens
had been supportive. But their ideological leanings did not mean
that their support could be taken for granted, for, as subsequently
proven, their response often hinged on the character of the
issues, how they were raised, and how they affected Jewish pop-

ulations in a more personal and direct way.[55] In any event, once the policy was announced and acclaimed as an integrated housing program, it was inevitable that the white middle-class groups in the outer boroughs would be concerned, particularly as, by 1966, there were increasing tensions in the city over *de facto* segregation of schools, police protection, law and order, block-busting; and changing neighborhoods.

Ethnic Flack

Despite exaggerations that big cities primarily produce anomie and alienation among their populations, parts of New York contain discrete subcommunities boasting qualities of neighborhood life and people who warmly identify with their locale. Political scientists Wallace Sayre and Herbert Kaufman have written that "the diversity of New York is geographical as well as social; the city contains hundreds of neighborhoods, each with unique characteristics as distinctive as those of separate cities. Neighborhoods develop individually, because people of the same background tend to congregate and thus give each area, each subcommunity, its special flavor."[56] People of similar ethnic, religious, and class backgrounds have, over the years, huddled together in distinct areas of the city. While the melting-pot theory continues to attract many, research in ethnic studies has shown that the easy assimilation of these groups into the mainstream is more myth than reality. Competition and conflict have often dominated the social and political life of newcomers, and ethnic minorities have generally had to work hard to share the opportunities of American life; as one scholar has suggested, this struggle produced in the process, "status rivalries among the ethnic minorities, which, when combined with economic rivalries, invited abiding conflict."[57]

In the case of the Lindsay housing program, a number of the sites were plunked down in these ethnic islands of middle-class Italians, Jews, and blacks. The Italians of Corona, Queens, formed one major and effective opposition group. In 1966, Corona's basic population was Italian small-home-owners whose economic status could best be described as working class and lower middle class. Its blue-collar workers were largely semiskilled, employed in construction and manufacturing. Those designated as members of the white-collar class largely held clerical and lower-skilled office jobs, and they maintained their middle-class status through enormous physical effort. Their median income was approximately $5,700, below that of most white middle-class areas of the city. A number of these residents, recent arrivals from a lower economic class and social status, could recall their flight from deteriorating residential areas of the city. As one analyst has portrayed them: "They are an ethnocentric and highly status-conscious second generation, proud of the way they rose from a proletarian existence through their own efforts."[58] The intense hostility of these Italians to the program was perhaps in part due to the fact that, while labeled middle class, they were not that far distant economically or socially from the newcomers destined to inhabit the housing project. One sociologist has suggested that "the danger here is that the nearer people are, the more competitive."[59]

Life in Corona focused on the family, and some of the residents had been born in the house in which they lived, their offspring often finding homes nearby when they married. One local resident expressed the neighborliness and community spirit this way:

> Corona is a unique institution in the City of New York. It is the last remaining neighborhood community in the entire city. It is the only remaining community where you can still walk through the streets and greet every other person as a friend or neighbor. Numerous attempts have been made to destroy us as a community. . . . We have been considered a second-class community. The residents of Corona grew closer together, took pride in accomplishment and made a community which today is envied by any and all persons who are exposed to its atmosphere.[60]

It was this community pride and local identification with their neighborhood that influenced Corona's residents to fight for their locality against what they saw as the invasion of a lower class and a different race.

A local ad hoc neighborhood group was organized with the help of a former state assemblyman from the district. Supporting the group were the residents of nearby Lefrak City and Sherwood Village, postwar high-risers inhabited by a middle-income Jewish population. While those major city-wide Jewish organizations affiliated with prominent national groups had for years warmly supported integrated communities (and, as will be discussed below, approved Lindsay's program), a large segment of the Jewish residential population near the proposed project—which included members of some of these organizations—strongly opposed its proximity. Through their tenants' organizations, the

Jewish residents joined the fight; not only did they give numerical support, but they helped mobilize local Jewish political leaders and elected officials in the Democratic Party. Another source of aid came from more conservative pressure groups—organizations of homeowners and civic improvement and taxpayer associations. Real-estate interests also joined in and were led by Samuel Lefrak, who saw his middle-income projects located near the Corona site threatened. With far-flung property interests throughout Queens, Lefrak not only supported the community opposition (some have alleged with financial contributions), but also personally, persistently, and at times quite effectively pressured key figures in the administration to eliminate or change several of the Queens sites.[61] By fall, 1966, the Corona site was dropped on the grounds that the location could be better used for a much-needed new high school.[62]

The new location of the project—only a few blocks from the old site—was in Forest Hills, largely a Jewish enclave. Local politicians, close allies of the area's homeowners as well as of the tenants from the surrounding apartment houses, intensified their opposition; several alleged that the new location was chosen because Jews formed the one ethnic group that was split over low-income housing and thus their "liberalism" or, as one of the campaigners called it, "bleeding hearts," would constitute a base of support for the Lindsay program. More specifically, a very active politician suggested that "when the Germans squawked in Ridgewood they got their way with Lindsay, and the Italians in Corona won, too. The Jews, though, were the only ones to fail. Lindsay knew the sentiment was split in Forest Hills. The other ethnic groups got their way, but the Jews were used."[63] He may have been right; yet one of the unanticipated consequences of packaging the sites in a bundle was that, by bringing them together in this fashion, the disparate, hostile groups scattered throughout various parts of the city were also brought together. Somewhat typical was the formation of a coalition of local community groups near the Lindenwood site; these included such diverse organizations as the Rockwood Park Association, the Howard Beach Association, the Lindenwood Community Civic Association, the Lindenwood Community Youth Council, the Parents Association of P.S. 232, and Temple Judea.[64]

Another such example occurred in the Bronx community of Riverdale. Although a large share of the dwelling units within the five proposed projects for this area were to be set aside for the aged, local hostility was sharp and effective. The Riverdale area, located in the northern section of the Bronx, was one of the fastest growing postwar high-rise developments in the city, attracting large numbers of young, middle-class Jewish families. Because of inadequate planning by the city and the speed of its development, Riverdale experienced the formation of dozens of local community groups organized to fight for basic facilities and services—traffic lights, roads, schools, and better access to transportation. Riverdale's Jewish population was reflected in the make-up of the leadership of the local Democratic Party organizations and the majority of elected officials to both the state legislature and the City Council. These Jewish Democratic leaders joined their constituents to fight the battle against integrated low-income housing. Among them was State Senator Harrison J. Goldin, identified with the reform wing of the party. In testifying against one of the projects, Goldin explained that the area was the most neglected in the city and facilities were overcrowded. The site, he suggested, would better be used for middle-income residents, and the proposed low-income project should be located elsewhere. Besides, Goldin added, the Bronx neighborhood was already "ethnically balanced."[65]

The most interesting aspect of attack on the scattered-site program was the ethnic solidarity of the Jews and Italians who joined to fight it. Their organized efforts showed the power and effectiveness of minority groups when feelings are aroused in New York. Attention focused on those access points in the political and governmental systems that seemed particularly useful for mounting an effective campaign. Busloads of residents jammed the public hearings before the Planning Commission and the Board of Estimate in May, June, September, and November, 1966. Over 1,000 angry participants (many with children brought intentionally to dramatize their cause) crowded one of the hearings, staying long hours to testify. Arguments were generally phrased in economic and class terms; that is, that public housing threatened property values and the community's economic and social stability. "We don't object," claimed one resident, "to this low-income project on a racial basis but only on the economic level and the type of people that inhabit these projects regardless of the color."[66] The involvement in the protest of black homeowners was cheered as evidence that class, rather than race, was the basis of opposition to the package. Fearful that the proposed project would hasten the decline of their property, the black homeowners pointed to the experience of a nearby publicly aided middle-income project where the percentage of nonwhites had been increasing in recent years; by adding another project, they argued, the tipping would be complete, producing yet another "segregated ghetto." The undertone of race was nonetheless evident at times: "People being in general what they are," warned the representative of one of the civic associations, "integration is a broad and most controversial subject"; others echoed the fear that the community would in short order become a ghetto, "that another element would invade the area," that "another filthy slum would be established," that "we anticipate incidents," and that "juvenile delinquency will overrun us."[67] Withal, according to a survey (the only one known to have been taken at that time) of middle-class Jewish families residing in an apartment complex near one of the proposed scattered sites in Queens, racial dimensions did not appear as salient as class. Most respondents, while opposed to the construction of low-income units in their neighborhoods, supported the entry of middle-class nonwhites to their *own* developments.[68]

In addition to the hearings, neighborhood delegations visited commissioners and staff members concerned with housing, and a barrage of mail and telephone calls kept officials busy. The heart of their strategy—and given the American belief in grass-roots democracy, the most effective—was the appeal to "protecting their neighborhoods." While the Lindsay package was city-wide in scope and purpose, these various ethnic-organized subcommunities forced the policy into a more local context, a tactic that gave them an advantage in the fragmented local politics of the city. Every locally elected representative, from councilman to state legislator and congressman, and leaders from both political parties in their respective assembly districts, were called on to join their cause. At the grass-roots level, where party power begins to emerge in New York, these neighborhood groups invoked party intervention—particularly intervention from the dominant Democratic Party. Other researchers have found that ethnic groups are generally quite effective when seeking the support of party leaders, and this issue proved no exception.[69] The district leaders responsible for those bailiwicks in which community resistance emerged actually participated as active members of the ad hoc pressure groups. Their political stakes were considerable, for, not only were their constituents concerned and aroused, but their tenure was threatened by a low-income project that would cause population changes—the entering ethnic groups probably displacing the existing electorate. These threats to survival were viewed the same way by both regular and reform factions within the Democratic Party. District leaders testified in person at the public hearings and arranged private meetings with elected officials who, in turn, joined the opponents in presenting testimony. Local leaders also smoothed the way for discussions between the communities and the Borough Presidents, who were, in the city's fragmented governmental system, in key positions in regard to public housing programs. Local officials also interceded on behalf of their aroused constituents by raising all sorts of technical matters, questioning the advisability of particular sites, demanding explanations—or, more precisely, by harassing city and federal staff members responsible for reviewing the program. Neighborhood leaders in one Queens community urged their local congressman to assist them; in a lengthy letter on their behalf, he complained to the regional federal official, Herman Hillman, that the city's planning was "arbitrary and capricious" and that false information concerning community facilities had been offered by the authorities. This sort of intervention received prompt and serious attention in the regional office. Hillman passed the letter on to the city asking that a response be directed to him: "Your prompt and detailed reply to the points raised in the letter are requested."[70] Despite HUD Secretary Robert Weaver's open support for construction of public housing on vacant land outside the ghettos, effecting such a policy was another matter, and, in fact, the Lindsay package, once having produced the emotional outburst of neighborhood groups, had the effect of influencing federal strategy vis-à-vis the city.

Where were the Mayor's allies? The groups supporting his program could not match the political effectiveness of these neighborhood-based groups. Behind Lindsay were the city-wide groups concerned with civil rights and a number of housing reform organizations: the NAACP, the Urban League, the American Jewish Congress, B'nai Brith, the Catholic Inter-Racial Council, the Protestant Council, the Metropolitan Housing Council, the Citizens Planning and Housing Council, and the Community Service Society. These organizations were committed to the twin goals of public housing and integrated communities, but their support tended to have an impact more symbolic than real, most often taking the form of reading a statement of support at public hearings. Beyond such presentations, they appeared to exercise little effort. They neglected to develop an alliance among themselves; nor did any individual group pursue a strategy for gaining grass-roots support. Their activities were thus limited to a more generalized form of approval, more vague rhetoric than practical political influence. And, while city, state, and federal housing officials were being bombarded with mail and visitations from neighborhood groups, these city-wide organizations did little lobbying.

Perhaps one reason some of these groups did not mobilize effectively was because of their multidimensional character; that is, they were drained by competing priorities other than integrated housing that demanded their attention. In 1966, civil rights organizations were involved in many important issues—schools, police, jobs. Consequently, they couldn't muster the staying power of the locals, who kept up a barrage of attack whenever a crucial point of decision-making was reached. The city-wide Jewish organizations faced the added problem that their effectiveness was strained by internal tensions between city-wide leaders supporting Lindsay and the grass roots opposition coming from the districts where the projects were to be located.

Thus, the organizational weakness of his supporters on the one hand and the political effectiveness of neighborhood opposition on the other constituted serious obstacles to the Mayor's plan. In addition, the fragmented character of the city's governmental system afforded locally based groups adequate opportunities to frustrate the Mayor's executive authority. When his program finally reached the Board of Estimate, the Borough Presidents, the President of the City Council, and the Comptroller had all the votes necessary to defeat the bulk of it.[71] It will be recalled that the reformers thought that, by presenting public housing as a package of sites, the Borough Presidents would have to negotiate among themselves or else carry the onus of opposing the Mayor's program. What they did not appreciate was the political reality: that the hostility and public outcry from the affected communities would effectively protect the members of the Board and, in fact, project them as the "true" representatives of the community.

Notes

1. City of New York, City Planning Commission, Department of City Planning, *Urban Renewal Study Program, 1962–1963.* June 1962, page 1.

2.   CRITICAL RENTER HOUSEHOLDS

Critical Renter Households		*Persons in Household*	*Gross Annual Household Income*		
			Less than $3,000	$3,000-5,999	$6,000-9,999
Group I	Largest and lowest-income households	5 or More	39,532	104,259	
		3 or 4	96,400		
Group II	Other low-income households	3 or 4		261,646	
		1 or 2	419,383		
Group III	Large moderate-income households	5 or More			77,323

SOURCE: City of New York, Community Research Program, *New York City's Renewal Strategy, 1965.* December, 1965, page 36. Hereafter this report will be cited as *Renewal Strategy, 1965.*

The population of critical renter needs reached almost 1 million in 1965. *The Municipal Yearbook, 1965* lists the size of American cities, averaging about 200,000. See also, *The New York Times,* October 2, 1966.

3. *Renewal Strategy, 1965, op. cit.* (note 2), pp. 35–36; City of New York, Department of City Planning, Community Renewal Program, *Between Promise and Performance,* December 1968, p. 60.

4. *Ibid.,* p. 12.

5. Chase Manhattan Bank, "Business in Brief," April, 1969. Issued on a bi-monthly basis by the bank's Economic Research Division.

6. City of New York, Committee on Housing Statistics, *Housing Statistics Handbook,* August, 1966, pp. 80 ff. Hereafter referred to as *Housing Statistics Handbook.*

7. Jewel Bellush and Murray Hausknecht, *Urban Renewal: People, Politics and Planning* (New York: Doubleday Anchor, 1967), pp. 451–61.

8. Jeanne Lowe, *Cities in a Race with Time* (New York: Random House, 1967), p. 235.

9. Bellush and Hausknecht, *op. cit.* (note 7), pp. 457 ff.

10. Jane Jacobs, *The Death and Life of Great American Cities* (New York: Random House, 1961), chs. 15, 16, and 20; editors of *Fortune, The Exploding Metropolis* (New York: Doubleday Anchor, 1958), chs. 1 and 4.

11. New York City, Housing Authority, Central Files. Correspondence between the Housing Authority and the Housing and Home Finance Administration, Regional Office in New York City. Interviews with

Joseph Christian, Director, Program Planning, Housing Authority, June 23, 1969, and with Harry Fialkin, Director, Research and Statistics, Housing Authority, June 25, 1969. It should be noted that the New York Housing Authority itself can and should be criticized for the quality of public housing projects over the years; certainly the gigantic and monotonous high-risers spread over the cityscape do not evoke a sense of imaginative planning.

12. U.S. Housing and Home Finance Agency, *Relocation from Urban Renewal Project Areas* (through December, 1962) (Washington, D.C.: Government Printing Office, 1962).

13. *The New York Times,* June 5, 1966.

14. *Ibid.,* November 3, 1965.

15. Letter, Joseph Christian to Gerald Carey, General Manager, Housing Authority.

16. The information collected for this section is based on the following sources: Wallace Sayre and Herbert Kaufman, *Governing New York City* (New York: Russell Sage Foundation, 1965); Joseph Christian: memoranda on "Site Selection Procedure" (February 15, 1966), and "Site Selection and New Programs" (November 15, 1965), "Fact vs Myth: The Story of Public Housing," "Memo to Gerald Carey re: Housing Needs and Problems" (November 22, 1965), Central Files, Housing Authority; interviews with Joseph Christian; Ira Robbins, Commissioner, Housing Authority, June, 1969; and Julius Edelstein, top administrative aide to Mayor Robert Wagner and member of the Executive Committee on Housing, July 17, 969.

17. Sayre and Kaufman, *op. cit.* (note 16), p. 638.

18. The "Plan" is an undertaking (1) for the clearance, replanning, and reconstruction of the substandard and unsanitary sites upon which public housing projects are now being, or will be, developed, the clearance of which has been or will be impeded by the housing shortage and (2) for the erection of a public housing project on the particular site which, when completed, will aid in clearing the sites and areas. The "Project" is a specific improvement to effectuate the plan and to provide safe and sanitary housing accommodations on the site specifically designed in the plan.

19. Memorandum of Joseph Christian, November 11, 1965, Central Files, Housing Authority.

20. *Housing Statistics Handbook, op. cit.* (note 6), 1967, p. 46; Morton Grodzins, *The Metropolitan Area as a Racial Problem* (Pittsburgh, Pa.: University of Pittsburgh Press, 1958), pamphlet.

21. Karl and Alma Taeuber, *Negroes in Cities: Residential Segregation and Neighborhood Change* (Chicago: Aldine Company, 1965), p. 94; Karl Taeuber, "The Effect of Income Redistribution on Racial Residential Segregation," *Urban Quarterly,* IV (September, 1968), pp. 5–14.

22. City of New York, "Report of Housing and Urban Renewal Task Force to Mayor John Lindsay." Charles Abrams, Chairman. January 10, 1966, p. 6.

23. Grodzins, *op. cit.* (note 20), p. 11.

24. *Renewal Strategy, 1965, op. cit.* (note 2), p. 28.

25. Thomas Dye, "Urban School Segregation: A Comparative Analysis," in Marilyn Gittell and Alan Hevesi, eds., *The Politics of Urban Education* (New York: Praeger, 1969), p. 89.

26. Interview, Philip Finkelstein, Deputy City Administrator, July 17, 1969; Mimeographed materials from the office of Donald Elliott, Chairman, City Planning Commission; New York City, Department of City Planning, *Newsletter,* November-December, 1966.

27. The major portion of research materials used in this study concerning the strategy of the Mayor's staff was found in the central files of the Housing Authority and will hereafter be referred to as "H. A. Files."

28. The problem of interviewing the key actors on the Lindsay staff was perhaps due to the fact that a very heated campaign was under way at the time of research, and public housing was obviously one of the weak links in the Mayor's program. Edward Banfield and James Wilson, *City Politics* (Cambridge, Mass.: Harvard University Press and MIT Press, 1963), chs. 2 and 11; James Wilson, *The Amateur Democrat* (Chicago: University of Chicago Press, 1962), chs. 2, 6, on this idea; see, for example, interview with Edward Robbins, Director Community Renewal Program, June 26, 1969.

29. This does not imply that, once in power, they refused to negotiate or bargain, but their preconceived view was to have the Mayor on top, not a pawn of the system.

30. H. A. Files, Joseph Christian, memorandum, November 22, 1965.

31. *Ibid.,* Ira Robbins, Vice-Chairman, Housing Authority, Memorandum, February 24, 1966.

32. Donald Elliott, "An Interview: Can Planning Save our Cities?," Mimeographed files of Donald Elliott; Interview, Edward Friedman, former staff member, New York City Planning Department, May 29 and June 18, 1969.

33. H. A. Files, memorandum, January-March, 1966.

34. Interview with Julius Edelstein, former top staff aide to Mayor Wagner, assigned to housing program; he served as Vice-Chairman, Mayor's Executive Committee for Housing, July 17, 1969. Mr. Edelstein said that a special transitional group for housing was established by Mayor Wagner for the new administration, but it was not used.

35. H. A. Files, memorandum. The working group included: Edward Robin, Chairman; Richard Bernstein and Morton Isler, Department of City Planning; A. Benjamin and Frank Kristof, Housing Redevelopment Board; and Joseph Christian and Harry Fialkin, staff members, Housing Authority.

36. H. A. Files, memorandum.

37. Anonymous interviews.

38. H. A. Files, letters, Ira Robbins to Joseph Christian, March 7 and 8, 1966.

39. H. A. Files, memorandum by Edward Robin, February 15, 1966.
40. The scattered-site package was part of a larger housing program. Half of all the public housing units were to be built as vest pocket units on sites in inner core areas of the city. Under the 1965 National Housing Act, some low-income units were permitted through leasing, and the new administration hoped for approximately 500 such accommodations. However, the focus of this study is on scattered sites, because they evoked the controversy that affected the whole of the public housing program—inner core sites and leasing—subsequently causing a slowing down of the entire low-income housing effort.
41. The number of estimated sites vary from twelve to fifteen. One of the reasons for this discrepancy was that several of the selections were poorly located but remained on the list until the Borough President substituted another in its place. In other words, the Mayor's aides helped to use some of the sites as a basis for bargaining with the Borough Presidents.
42. City of New York, City Planning Commission Files, folder: "Approval of Site #19377," June 21, 1966.
43. Suzanne Keller, "Social Class in Physical Planning," *International Social Science Journal*, XVIII (1966), p. 505.
44. *Ibid.*
45. *Ibid.*, p. 507.
46. The writer must admit that there was great difficulty in getting data on housing construction during the Lindsay years. However, David Shipler in an article in *The New York Times*, June 5, 1969, did extract some important data, which Commissioner Albert Walsh, Chairman of the Housing Authority acknowledged as factually accurate in an interview with the author of this article, June 19, 1969.
47. *Citizens Housing and Planning Council Newsletter*, April–May, 1969.
48. H. A. Files, City of New York, Housing Authority, "Statement of December 31, 1968," mimeo.; Office of Director of Construction, "(Tentative) Planning and Bidding Schedule, Revised April 15, 1969."

Project & Location	Number Dwelling Units	Take Bids
3033 Middletown Road (F) Roberts Avenue, Jarvis Avenue Middletown Road, Hobart Avenue Bronx	182	6/17/69
2440 Boston Road (F) Boston Road, Holland Avenue Waring Avenue, Cruger Avenue Bronx	235	7/1/69
Bailey Avenue–West 193 Street Area (F) Bailey Avenue–West 193 Street Area and Heath Avenue Bronx	233	10/69

Project & Location	Number Dwelling Units	Take Bids
157th Avenue–79th Street (F) 156th Avenue, 80th Street Shore Parkway, 77th Street Queens	576	11/69
108th Street–62nd Drive Area (F) Horace Harding Expressway, Colonial Avenue, 62nd Drive, 108th Street Queens	848	1/70
East 180 Street–Monterey Avenue (F) Quarry Road, East 181 Street, LaFontaine Avenue, East 180th Street, Third Avenue, Bronx	236	1/70

49. *Under Construction*

		*Pending Construction**
1966	5,900	8,000
1967	5,800	9,700
1968	6,200	12,800

*"Pending Construction" constitutes vague hopes, not concrete realities, since federal or state approval has not been given. Inevitably, long delays meant increased costs, which, in turn, often caused the city to drop many of the proposed projects.

SOURCE: *Housing Statistics Handbook, op. cit.* (note 6), 1966, 1967, 1968.

50. This is amply documented by the materials in H. A. Files.

51. *Renewal Strategy,* 1965, p. 53.

52. City Planning Commission, "Hearings," June 15, 1966, on tape #49.

53. City Planning Commission Files, letters: Sylvia Wolosoff to Richard Bernstein, July 14 and 15, 1966; folder: "71/161 Street."

54. *The New York Times,* June 5, 1969.

55. Lawrence Fuchs, *The Political Behavior of American Jews* (Glencoe, Ill.: Free Press, 1956); Wilson, *op. cit.* (note 28), ch. 9; David Abbott, Louis Gold, and Edward Rogowsky, *Police, Politics and Race* (New York and Cambridge, Mass.: American Jewish Committee and Joint Center for Urban Studies of MIT and Harvard, 1969). Term paper, Miss Roth, student of Professor Marilyn Gittell, Queens College, "Analysis of Attitudes of a Jewish Middle Class Population in Fresh Meadows."

56. Sayre and Kaufman, *op. cit.* (note 16), p. 28.

57. Hugh Graham and Ted Gurr, eds., *The History of Violence in America* (New York: Praeger, 1969), p. 749.

58. United States, Bureau of the Census, *General Characteristics of the Population, by Census Tracts:* 1960; David Rogers, "Obstacles to School Desegration in New York City," in Gittell and Hevesi, *op. cit.* (note 25), p. 127.

59. Keller, *op. cit.* (note 43), p. 508.

60. City Planning Commission, "Hearings," June 16, 1966, Tape #20.

61. H. A. Files; see especially folders: "Lewis Avenue" and "108 Street and 62 Drive."

62. *Ibid.*

63. Interviews: Martin Psaty, former Assemblyman of the area and Martin Cohen, former Assembly District leader, September 1, 1969. These sentiments were also expressed by others, who wish to remain anonymous.

64. H. A. Files, folder: "157 Avenue and 79 Street."

65. City Planning Commission Files, #19343.

66. *Ibid.*

67. H. A. Files, City Planning Commission "Hearings," June 15 and 16, 1966; folders: "Lewis Avenue," "58 Lane," "157 Avenue," "71 Avenue," "Waldo," "Bailey," "Middletown-Jarvis," "Fort Independence," "Emmons Avenue."

68. Roth, *op. cit.* (note 55). Emphasis added by author of this chapter.

69. Sayre and Kaufman, *op. cit.* (note 16), p. 494.

70. H. A. Files; see especially memorandum written by Joseph Christian, "Areas of Persistent Difficulty with PHA," June 30, 1966; letter, Herman Hillman to New York City Housing Authority, Attention Walter Washington, June 13, 1967; letter, Donald Elliott to Walter Washington, August 18, 1967; "Memorandum to D. Elliott, Areas of Difficulty with PHA;" June 29, 1966. Folder: "157/79." Federal Agents reviewed the package of sites for several months, then sent it back specifying three conditions for approval: 1) Sites had to be located in the same geographical area in order to be considered grouped as a package; 2) each project had to be presented in such a way as to prove it could stand on its own financially; and 3) all jobs in the package would have to be bid at the same time. From the perspective of the city administration, this order was viewed as "sheer nonsense," since one of the reasons for the package arrangements was to overcome federal restrictions on costs by averaging out the expenditures among various projects. Thus several of the steep-incline and boggy-type sites, obviously more costly, would be balanced by those on less expensive city-owned vacant land.

71. H. A. Files. Manhattan Borough President Constance Motley supported the Lindsay program, and so did Percy Sutton, her successor. Hostility was so great from certain neighborhood groups, however, that, despite President Sutton's sympathy for the scattered-site program, he appreciated the difficulty his colleague experienced in Queens, and subsequently became a participant in the negotiations that changed the Corona site. Additionally, Bronx Borough President Herman Badillo had also publicly supported the Mayor's program, but, in private negotiations, again perhaps due to community opposition, raised a good many problems about particular sites. In fact, one of the better locations, sought for Mitchell-Lama (middle-income) housing, eventually was withdrawn from Badillo's program on his insistence.

5. Education:
The Decentralization-
Community Control
Controversy

MARILYN GITTELL

City institutions have yet to adjust to the changing character of the city population. Pressing needs have been met with limited responses. Although, over the last three decades, cities have increased their services—and, as one result, city bureaucracies have doubled in size—such expansion has not been paralleled by any fundamental change in structure and environment. Urban school systems are typical of this situation.

Throughout this century, and particularly since World War II, economy and efficiency, civil service reform, professionalism, and centralization have characterized the major movements in urban government. All these factors have contributed to the development of a remote, static bureaucratic structure, ill equipped to handle the demands of the new population that has flowed into most of the nation's urban centers. The old mechanism for immigrant entry to the city's political structure is gone: The political party no longer serves as the community welfare agency, as a major channel for achieving status or power. Today, government jobs are restricted by professional standards and examination procedures; the poor nonwhite, newly arrived and badly educated, is shut out of the system.

With the expansion of the nonwhite population in the cities, segregation in housing has intensified. The increased isolation produced by this pattern has made communication and meaningful contact between black and white less possible now than during previous periods.[1] And, while black and white grow further apart, the expectations and demands of the deprived now far exceed what present programs, set up to correct past inequities, can offer. The result is that the already existing feelings of isolation, neglect, and political impotence are exacerbated. As with other ethnic minorities in earlier times, the only source of power for the black ghetto community is racial solidarity, but, because of the changes in city administration, voting provides only a minor outlet for the effective use of such solidarity. Within the ghetto, there is increasing belief that only the kind of redistribution of power that assures the ghetto community a greater role in the policy process will be acceptable. The survival of America's urban communities will depend upon their ability to respond to these pressures; somehow they must make the adjustments necessary to accommodate these demands.

One of the first areas of attack has been the city school system because it represents so esssential a part of the total structure and so important a link to mobility in American society. Moreover, the movements of middle-class whites to the suburbs and lower-class nonwhites to the cities have effected radical changes in the school population; in many of our large cities, a majority of the lower-school population is now nonwhite.[2]

Of the nonwhite school children, many are first-generation urban dwellers and a large proportion of these are still rurally oriented; their cultural traditions differ significantly from the standard middle-class values embedded in the city school system and professed by teachers and school administrators. It is understandable, therefore, that the rate of failure of these children within the system is high. In the ghetto communities, parents are now asking whether it is the children or the system that is failing. One can take the position that the school system should subtract out black and Puerto Rican children—in New York City, over 51 per cent of the student population—from the standard measurements of performance, since the socio-economic background of these students is the cause of their failure.[3] Placing responsibility on the larger society may appear realistic; yet it also leads to a deterministic position in regard to failure. Thus, such children will fail until society does something about their socio-economic status, but their very failure will keep them in that status. This position not only locks these children into a rigid pattern of lifetime failure; it also shifts responsibility from the school system. If one assumes, however, that the test of an educational system is its ability to educate all its children, analysis must necessarily turn to the institution itself rather than to the clientele or the larger society. For one, this might make it possible to take the first realistic steps in breaking the deterministic pattern. From this latter perspective, it is clear that the New York City school system, and urban school systems generally, have failed to meet their responsibility.[4] Though the American public school system was founded on reform—the public school was seen by school reformers as a utilitarian tool to combat poverty, much as it is viewed by such reformers today—it is questionable whether this egalitarian ideal was ever really accomplished. No hard evidence is available on how competently the public school system educated its clients—in particular, those from immigrant families—fifty years ago. Even in regard to the record of the poor in the two most education-minded immigrant groups—Jews and Chinese—there are no dropout statistics and testing data proving their performance in the public schools was as good fifty years ago as that of their middle-class counterparts today. The suspicion is that the public school system never fully succeeded in educating its poor.[5]

If vast changes in population are integral to this failure, it is the lack of institutional adjustment to those changes that must be the subject of concern. Using New York as a case in point, we may ask what then the nature of power is in the school system and how it influences the decisions that are or are not made to accomplish educational goals.

The findings of this author's 1967 study of power distribution in urban school systems emphasized that, in the previous two decades, education in New York City had become amazingly insulated from public controls.[6] What is described is an abandonment of public education by key forces of potential power within the city. Bureaucratization and professionalization were contributing factors: Weber's theory of the emergence of a specialized bureaucracy, monopolizing power through its control of expertise, accurately described the role of the education bureaucracy in New York City. The claim that only the professionals can make competent judgments had been accepted, and contributing to, and perhaps growing out of, this attitude was the change in the mayor's role to one of noninvolvement. Civic and interest groups —other than the specialized education groups such as the United Parents Association (UPA) and the Public Education Association (PEA)—responded ambivalently to education issues; on the one hand, they accepted the notion of the professional competence of the bureaucracy, and, on the other, they recognized the need for reform but expressed a hopelessness regarding their ability to change the system. The result was narrow or closed participation in large areas of decision-making. Effective influence in these areas was restricted to an inside core of top supervisory personnel in the headquarters staff of the Board of Education and the United Federation of Teachers. Together, these two groups of professionals were responsible for major policy decisions affecting education in New York City. Policy alternatives were rarely discussed or offered, and the inclination to support the *status quo* was reinforced.

The circumstances surrounding the school decentralization movement in New York City from 1966 through 1969 provides a meaningful basis for reanalysis of the power structure as defined in that 1967 study. With some few additions brought in because the policy decision was taken to the state level, the actors are the same.

The Actors

Within any school system, the potential participants in the policy-making process are essentially the same. Legal power is usually divided between a board of education and a superintendent. The bureaucracy breaks down into a central administrative corps, field administrators, top supervisory staff, and middle management. Organizations representing supervisors are common in the larger school districts. Teachers, parents, and their respective organizations are also potential participants. Specialized education-interest groups may also be active and, at times, vitally effective. In the general community, there are other potential participants—local, state, and federal officials, civic groups, the press, business organizations, and individual entrepreneurs seeking the rewards of the school system.

THE BOARD OF EDUCATION

The Board of Education in New York City is the official policy-making body for the school system, and its members are responsible for long-range educational planning. Prior to 1961, the mayor directly appointed the members, and his appointments traditionally reflected careful consideration of local interests. A screening-panel procedure instituted in 1961 strengthened the role of the civic groups (who obtained representation on the screening panel), thereby reducing the influence of the mayor.*

The Board's role has largely been one of balancing conflicting pressures and interests. Essentially, it is a mediator rather than an initiator of policy. As the spokesman for official policy, the Board nominally participates in all major decisions. Though it spends a great deal of its time on sensitive issues, the balance of power in the Board generally fails to produce the consensus necessary for it to act in concert. These issues, though sensitive, are not necessarily major areas of policy; boards have rarely been involved in long-range planning. A major problem for the Board is its lack of an independent staff. This has greatly limited the level and character of Board decision-making. Without such a staff, the Board cannot realistically challenge or review the programs of the administrative bureaucracy.

THE SUPERINTENDENT

The highest ranking schoolman in New York City is the superintendent of schools. Appointed by the Board of Education for a six-year term, the superintendent lacks the most essential power of a strong executive—the power of appointment and removal. The system's supervisory staff is developed completely through promotion from the ranks, allowing the superintendent little flexibility in appointments. For example, all assistant superintendents receive tenure after a three-year probationary period. The super-

---

*From 1961 to 1968, the Board of Education had nine appointed members; in April, 1968, the Board size was increased under state law to fourteen. The 1969 decentralization law completely revised the selection procedures for Board members. An interim board of five appointed by the borough presidents was to hold office until July, 1970. They were to be replaced by a seven-man Board, five of whom were to be elected on a borough-wide basis with two additional members appointed by the mayor. In 1970, the interim board was given another year of life.

intendent's position is further weakened by his dependency on the
Board of Examiners, which sets up and administers the machinery
for promotions. It is not uncommon for the Board of Examiners
to delay examination and approval of candidates for assistant
superintendent whom the superintendent may wish to appoint
to his own staff. Because he cannot freely develop his own advisory staff and is encumbered by the appointments and promotions made by his predecessors, no superintendent can rely on
having his own team of trusted advisers. No superintendent can
expect to avoid having to cope with the potentially competing
interests of his own supervisory bureaucracy. No superintendent
can be sure that directives and policy statements he issues on key
policies won't in fact be attacked by his own supervisory staff,
both by that staff's external professional organizations, and, internally, by the organized committees on which the staff members
sit.

THE BUREAUCRACY

The education bureaucracy in New York City breaks down into
two separate categories: (1) the headquarters staff and (2) the
operational field staff. A precise figure on the size of the headquarters staff is difficult to determine, but it is estimated to be
somewhere around 4,000. At least 400 to 500 people working at
the headquarters do not appear in its budget; although serving as
full-time headquarters personnel, they are paid out of local school
budgets. The operational field staff includes some 2,200 principals
and assistant principals, 31 district superintendents, and 740
department chairmen.

A core supervisory group that holds much of the decision-
making power includes some thirty headquarters–staff–members,
among them, the executive deputy superintendent, the deputy
superintendent in charge of instruction and curriculum, the
Board of Examiners, twenty of the thirty assistant superintendents, and a few active directors of special bureaus.

With rare exceptions, members of the core supervisory group
come from within the New York City school system—many as
principals, almost all with long experience at headquarters. A
review of the background of the twenty-six top supervisory staff
members in 1965 revealed that their careers followed a general
pattern. Having served as principals or assistant principals, they
were brought into headquarters on special assignment and/or had
served on special committees (usually as a result of contacts

already established at headquarters). A recent study of school principals verified their general commitment to the *status quo* and their resistance to innovation in the system.[7] (As of 1970, there were six permanent black principals and one black district superintendent in the city.)

SUPERVISORY PERSONNEL ASSOCIATIONS

The Council of Supervisory Associations (CSA), organized in 1962, is a professional organization made up of the various individual supervisory associations, including those for high school principals, junior high school principals, elementary school principals, assistant principals, high school department chairmen, the Board of Examiners, assistant superintendents, and associate superintendents. The council has more than 3,000 members. Through the individual associations and, jointly, through the council (even though it has no formal position in the school system), the vested interests of the supervisory staff exert a strong influence in forming education policy. The council has openly opposed decentralization, a 1969 change in the student suspension policy, students rights proposals, school busing, the comprehensive high school plan, school pairing, and the dropping of IQ examinations—*after* these were adopted as official policy by the Board of Education and by the superintendent.

THE TEACHERS AND THE UNION

Because of its base of power in collective bargaining, the United Federation of Teachers is one of the school system's major policy-makers. The UFT, whose membership in New York City totals more than 40,000, is the official bargaining agent for the city's teachers, and the union contract determines an ever widening area of school policy. To a great extent, it determines the allocation of all education resources, because salaries and teachers' benefits represent close to half the total education budget; as a result, the union is of necessity directly involved in matters of over-all fiscal policy. In the last few years, the union has laid claim to other policy areas, such as those affecting school organization and governance, personnel practices, student behavior, and curriculum. Establishing the More Effective Schools (MES) program in their 1967 contract was the union's first major thrust into broad educational policy; the 1969 contract made further inroads into this area. In addition to the power exercised through the contract, the union wields considerable influence through the city-wide labor federation, the Central Labor Council. The UFT conducts extensive city and state lobbying activity through its own representatives and in association with this general labor lobby.[8]

LOCAL SPECIALIZED EDUCATION INTEREST GROUPS

Two specialized interest groups in New York City have traditionally shared the responsibility for overseeing public education policy: the United Parents Association and the Public Education Association. For many years, board memberships in both organizations overlapped, and their professional staffs worked closely together. Lately, because the PEA has supported stronger decentralization legislation, some disagreement has been evident.

The UPA is a central, city-wide organization made up of delegates elected by local-school parent associations that have chosen to join the central city agency. Its leadership has generally been drawn from the Jewish community. Its general membership is largely made up of middle-class white parents, who are primarily concerned with local school problems and facilities. Accordingly, the UPA has directed much of its attention to individual school matters. In recent years, site-selection controversies and school integration problems have occupied much of its time. The UPA speaks for parents and concerns itself with the immediate effects of policy on local school situations, although it has at times taken general policy positions on key issues. When possible, it makes use of direct influence on Board of Education members: Over the years, members of the city Board were often officers of the association; for example, the association's former executive director is now secretary to the Board. The association has at times supported appointments of supervisory staff, and it continues to maintain viable contacts within the bureaucracy. Although it is unlikely that the UPA could stimulate city-wide support for certain policies, it has effectively used this threat to influence staff and Board decisions. By and large, however, the association supports current school policy and offers little in the way of alternatives.

The PEA is a composite organization; its board is composed of the representatives of other interest groups and organizations active in the city. Its membership is generally drawn from the upper-middle class, although an effort has been made to attract the leadership of black and Puerto Rican groups to the organization. PEA's activities have centered on the broader and more long-range educational aspects of school policy. Its strategy has been to study special problems and to make public recommendations based on its analyses.

THE MAYOR

In almost every New York City administration since the 1940's, complaints of undue "political interference" have resulted in the delegation of increased responsibility to the Board of Education and the reduction of the role of the mayor. Mayoral noninvolvement is in part a result of public deference to professionalism. The institution of a strict merit system and internal controls over promotions and transfers has further limited the role of the mayor. Mayor Lindsay, however, chose to use educational reform to promote his image as a reformer. Lacking a base of support in the major-party structure, minor-party mayors are more likely to gamble on such issues to build their own constituencies, especially if they intend to move up the political ladder. Lindsay's experience on the decentralization–school-reform issue may well reinforce the view that mayors are not likely to gain political advantage from school issues.

CIVIL RIGHTS GROUPS AND THE DEMONSTRATION DISTRICTS

Primarily as a result of the 1954 Supreme Court decision on school desegregation, civil rights groups became involved in school issues in most large cities. In New York City, the NAACP, CORE, and EQUAL were the leading organizations in the struggle for school integration. Some local groups were organized in individual schools and neighborhoods around specific controversies, but they were short-lived. Unsuccessful in achieving school integration, these groups became the basis of a public challenge to the governance of large city school systems. All they had learned about the failure of city schools was rechanneled into an effort to achieve fundamental reform of a system that was incapable of reforming itself.[9]

The three demonstration school districts in New York City— IS (Intermediate School) 201, Ocean Hill–Brownsville, and Two Bridges—were an outgrowth of that civil rights–school integration movement. In each of the three districts selected for the experimentation with greater community involvement, demands for local control had already been made. In Brooklyn's Ocean

Hill–Brownsville, a rump local school board had been established; in the IS 201 area in Harlem, a ten-day parent boycott had overturned the appointment of a principal; and, in the Two Bridges area on the Lower East Side, local groups had named their own district superintendent. In establishing the three districts, the Board of Education was responding to the continuing pressure from areas that included what were probably the most actively engaged communities in New York City. The districts, their elected parent- and community-resident boards, administrators and their organizations were to become important participants (as well as political targets) in the city-wide struggle over school decentralization.

The plan for the creation of the districts was a product of meetings between the union, the Superintendent of Schools, and community groups. Ford Foundation representatives, who had been called in by Mayor Lindsay when difficulties first developed in IS 201, were also involved in the negotiations over the establishment of the districts. This was Ford's first involvement with the New York City school system; eventually, it agreed to fund the summer planning phase of the experiment.

In the poverty area known as Ocean Hill–Brownsville, public education had been failing at an alarming rate. By the fall of 1966, an aroused Ocean Hill–Brownsville community formed its own local school board. (The particular issue that sparked this action concerned the selection of personnel to staff a new intermediate school—IS 55—in the community.) By April, 1967, the Board of Education designated Ocean Hill–Brownsville, consisting of eight schools, as one of the three experimental demonstration districts.

The IS 201 complex in Harlem, made up of five schools, also had its seeds in a controversy over a new intermediate school— IS 201—in the area. At issue, however, was the site selected: The community saw the official site as a means of continuing *de facto* school segregation. When efforts to gain a site that could aid in integration failed, the community responded by demanding that a black principal be brought in and eventually by advocating total community control of the school within an experimental school district. The 201 complex was so designated in April, 1967.

Located on the Lower East Side of Manhattan and made up of five schools, the Two Bridges district emerged through the community's Parent Development Program, which had been designed to involve the poor in the education of their children. In the spring of 1967, a committee composed of representatives from the program, from the Two Bridges Neighborhood Council, and from one of the community's churches approached the Ford Foundation for a grant. (The Foundation had already granted planning funds to the IS 201 district.) Ford's selection of Two Bridges was based on its belief that the area had a substantial enough middle-class population to make it a test of decentralization in a middle-class community.

By spring, 1967, these three communities were officially designated by the Board of Education as demonstration school districts. Each had its special problems and each had somewhat different beginnings; yet all three had the same goal of demonstrating that a decentralized school district responsible to the community would improve the quality of education being offered to the children in the public schools of New York.

The districts moved quickly, electing their own local boards, appointing district administrators and staff, and setting out to take over education in their communities. But, from the outset, they faced enormous ambiguities concerning the limits and extent of their authority. This ambiguity was, in large part, the result of the fact that the motives and objectives of those who created the districts were in conflict: The Superintendent sought a relaxation of tensions in troublesome areas; the union hoped to get additional MES schools in each of the districts; and community leaders aimed at obtaining a power base for achieving change in the system.

The challenge the community presented to the entrenched power interests in education was immediate; so were the responses. Clearly, a community district that sought independent status would not be satisfied to have decisions made for it by the central staff, and these districts moved immediately to appoint their own administration and principals. By the fall of 1967, the UFT and the CSA, recognizing the threat, had entered into a joint court action to enjoin local appointment of demonstration school principals. At the same time, the UFT called a strike action to support its contract negotiations, which centered on salaries, the "disruptive child" issue, and the MES program. The demonstration districts, in part responding to the "disruptive child" issue, which many considered racially instigated, and, in part, seeing the union demands for a more direct role in educational policy-making via the contract as contrary to their own interests, refused support. In the three demonstration districts, all schools remained open during the strike, and relations between the communities and the union polarized further.*

THE STATE LEVEL

The decentralization controversy was ultimately to hit the state level before a settlement would be reached. On that level, two sets of actors were involved: the professional set, centered in the State Board of Regents and the State Commissioner of Education; and the political set, ranging from the Governor's office to the State Legislature.

Of the first, the State Board of Regents is the governing body for all public education in the state. The state commissioner of education is appointed by the Regents with the approval of the governor. Normally, the state department of education does not directly intervene in the city's educational affairs. Of course, legal and discrete relationships exist between the state and local school districts, resulting from the fact that education is a state function. The state education department did become involved in the decentralization controversy, since city education authorities seemed unable to resolve the issues. Because state officials were removed from the local warfare, it was hoped that some constructive resolution would be possible on the state level. In addition, Commissioner James E. Allen had indicated support for decentralization and worked diligently with the Regents to come up with a viable bill.

The second set of actors on the state level was led by the Governor's office and the leadership of the State Legislature. Here the power and influence of the UFT-CSA were apparent. Despite the fact that the Governor had indicated early support for decentralization, he was soon to withdraw from any direct role, although one piece of legislation was proposed by the Regents and the State Commissioner. A pro-union Republican Governor and a Republican-dominated legislative leadership were deciding a thorny issue. Their sentiments on decentralization were ambivalent, and they were not pressured by any constituency able to compete with the influence of the UFT-CSA. The Democratic

---

* The education directors of the poverty corporations in New York City and the boards of each local corporation were also potentially important participants in the decentralization movement, but, except for support at rallies and meetings, they proved to be of minor significance in influencing the outcome of the struggle.

caucus of the State Legislature, largely influenced by the UFT, opposed all of the stronger legislation.

The scenario for decentralization was operational on two political levels, state and local, and the state actors were instrumental in the final outcome.

The Events: Phase 1

Pinpointing the beginning of a political or social movement is always a difficult task, because the roots often reach far back in time and may extend to parallel issues and groups. In the case of the decentralization issue, this is particularly true. Much of the impetus for reform came from the frustrations of the school integration forces, who turned to community control as a policy alternative when integration efforts failed. In this sense, one can say that the IS 201 site-selection controversy ended one era in school reform and began another. Significantly, most of the coalition (with few notable exceptions) of poverty workers, parents, and ministers that demanded control over the school looked upon community control as a consolation prize: Still wedded to the school integration battles of the 1950's, the group initially demanded that IS 201 be integrated; only if integration could not be assured, would they take total community control.

The community control adherents had reason to anticipate that integration was a hopeless cause. Increasingly, schools were becoming more segregated in the large cities of the North. New York City school segregation had doubled in the five years preceding the IS 201 controversy.[10] Other cities were experiencing similar changes. Almost all efforts at integration had failed after a long and arduous struggle, and there is no longer any question that the education bureaucracy played a large role in obstructing implementation of Board policy.[11] The pro-integration forces were unable to secure any meaningful action on any of the proposed plans.

There should have been little doubt of the future thrust of ghetto parents for community control of the schools. One broadsheet circulated in Harlem warned that "the present structure of the New York City school system, not responsible or accountable to the minority community, is guilty of educational genocide." In the neighboring borough of Queens, the predominantly black Federation of Parent's Clubs demanded that teachers be rated according to the standardized test scores their students achieve. Between 1963 and 1967, over a dozen parent boycotts occurred at various ghetto schools. At one point, a self-styled People's Board of Education—which included a Catholic priest, a protestant minister, and a black former school-integration leader—proclaiming itself the true Board of Education, staged a sit-in in the Board members' seats, holding out for two days, until they were arrested. All these demonstrations had a common theme: Parents wanted a say in the running of the schools. "What the parents are asking for is a revolution," Superintendent of Schools Bernard Donovan remarked, "and that doesn't happen overnight."

By mid-winter of 1967, the politics of school decentralization was in full swing. Mayor Lindsay, convinced that the public schools had to show "demonstrably better results" for the city's billion-dollar investment, had openly entered the picture. For the first time since Fiorello LaGuardia, a mayor of the city was openly involving himself as a participant in school politics. In 1967, during the parent boycott of PS 125, the Mayor had let it be known that, in principle, he believed parents should have a voice in selection of the principals and should be given the right to interview candidates for such supervisory posts as principals and district superintendents. Still, the Mayor possessed little leverage for change; his major educational function was to appoint members of the city Board of Education, and, since 1961, the choice was made from a list supplied by a screening panel composed of civic group representatives.

Departing from tradition, Lindsay committed himself to school reform. In the spring of 1967, he succeeded in getting a green light from the New York State Legislature to reshape the city's public school system into five school districts. Bypassing both the city Board of Education and the State Education Department, the Mayor had obtained a mandate to redesign the public school system. In one sense, the law Lindsay obtained was a clever maneuver aimed at getting the city a larger proportion of funding, for, if for educational purposes, the city was considered a conglomerate of five school districts rather than a single school district, it stood to gain an additional $108 million in aid.[12] But, in another sense, the 1967 law went beyond the simple designation of five school districts for the purpose of securing additional money. It was a mandate to the Mayor, stating that:

Increased community awareness and participation in the educational process is essential to the furtherance of educational innovation and excellence in the public school system within the city of New York. . . . The legislature . . . declares that the creation of educational policy for the public schools within such districts will afford members of the community an opportunity to take a more active and meaningful role in the development of educational policy closely related to the diverse needs and aspirations of the community.[13]

The Mayor was instructed to present a plan to the legislature by December 1, 1967. He appointed a blue-ribbon six-member committee headed by Ford Foundation President McGeorge Bundy to draw up a reorganization plan. The membership of the panel included none of the obvious holders of power in the school system (for example, the UFT, CSA, or UPA), which later proved to be of significance in the failure of the panel's recommendations.

Initially, the new law evoked an angry chorus of protest from the city's educational establishment because it empowered the Mayor, rather than the Board of Education, to prepare the study. The PEA decried the "destruction of the city school system," feeling that, "badly as the city's schools need funds, [the law] was too high a price to pay to get them"; State Commissioner of Education Allen's immediate reaction was that the Mayor had exerted a "measure of political control"; the Association of Assistant Principals thought schoolchildren would now be "political pawns"; the Congress of Parents and Teachers feared that "every politician in the city [will now decide] on how our children will be educated"; and *The New York Times* found an "outrageous element in the act of legislative blackmail" that will signal a "forceful reassertion of political fiat as a controlling factor in the schools."[14]

Despite the outcry, no hard lines had yet formed. At that point, educational and civic groups reacted out of surprise, fearing the new law gave political control of the schools to city hall. Lindsay, however, moved quickly to placate these fears; holding forth at a special meeting, which took place in the offices of the Public Education Association and included every educational interest, he assured his audience that he had not the slightest intention of running New York's school system.[15] During this same period, the Board of Education sanctioned the experimental districts, and, coming when it did, their action gave the impression that the city Board favored reorganization along decentralized lines.

Yet, even before the Bundy panel released its decentralization recommendations, alliances were forming. Black school-activists, academicians, some of the more radical, white educational groups, and the Mayor shouldered the greater burden of pressing for school decentralization. On the other side, the professional educational organizations (the CSA and UFT) and the Board of Education submerged their traditional internecine bickering and united in opposition to the growing demand for community control of the schools. If the decentralization alliance united the city's upper class, who had long despaired of the school system and long been leaders in school reform movements, with the city's underclass, who had, as clients, little faith in the schools, the antidecentralization forces largely reflected a coalition between the newly emergent middle-class white civil servants and the labor unions. Ironically, the prospect of school decentralization brought the UFT into collaboration with its past rhetorical foe, the CSA. Although, in union terms, the CSA was an arm of management, on the decentralization issue the protection of professional status made for a common cause.

The Bundy plan, presented to the Mayor in the fall of 1967, crystallized these developing alignments. Essentially, it recommended that the New York City school system be subdivided into from thirty to sixty autonomous school districts, each with elected school boards having assigned powers over budget, personnel, and curriculum. Following the lead of previous studies, the plan recommended abolition of the anachronistic system by which civil service personnel were certified and the replacement of it with a more equitable examination procedure, similar to current state certification, that would admit more minority-group members into teaching and supervisory positions. As to the structure of the local boards, the plan recommended that the majority of members on each be elected by parents of children in the schools.

New York City schoolmen were alarmed. The President of the Board of Education—the sole dissenting member on the Bundy panel—sharply criticized the report: "Serious problems must arise in recasting, in one single stroke, the largest educational system in the world."[16] The professional groups charged that thirty to sixty independent districts would "balkanize" the city system and that local control would impede school integration.

Once the Mayor's version of the plan went, as directed, to the State Legislature, neither the UFT nor the CSA spared any expense in defeating the passage of a decentralization bill based on it. During the 1968 legislative session, the UFT reportedly spent somewhere between $125,000 and $500,000 in a public relations campaign that included hundreds of school meetings, news-paper ads, and radio spots.[17]

On the other hand, the prodecentralization forces split on the degree of decentralization each supported and, lacking tight or-ganizational direction and unlimited funds, were hampered in their attempts to press for a meaningful bill. The two most influ-ential civic educational organizations—the UPA and the PEA—presented their own drafts of a decentralization bill; it departed significantly from the Bundy model by minimizing the delegation of power to the local districts. The net effect of the various ideo-logical differences among black and white reform groups was to enfeeble their collective strength. An umbrella coalition—the Citi-zens' Committee for Decentralization of the Public Schools—was finally formed in early spring, 1968. Nominally under the chair-manship of Radio Corporation of America President Robert Sarnoff, it was set up to lobby for the Mayor's version of the Bundy plan.

In the effort to develop more broad-based support prior to and during the legislative session, the lack of city-wide leadership was significant. The Mayor did not play as forceful a role in pushing for passage of his bill as he had indicated he would. The Citizens' Committee headed by Sarnoff provided little financial or institu-tional muscle; Sarnoff served as chairman of the committee but removed himself from any direct role, the committee lacked funds, and the campaign never got off the ground. (The PEA supplied the only meaningful commitment to the Citizens' Com-mittee, and its staff director—who later resigned to work for the Board of Education—undermined the movement in his public statements and speeches.)

As discussion meetings were set up throughout the city, the UFT and the CSA organized their large membership to cover every one, both on the platform and in the audience. Their ap-proach was blunt: They raised fears about the abolition of the merit system and about black racism, and they quite suddenly became concerned with the terrible problem ghetto districts would have in securing personnel—having previously squashed every plan set up to effect this. Supporters of decentralization were poorly organized and lacked sufficient speakers to cover meetings. Their own differences in point of view and commit-ment also reduced their effectiveness. They made no dent in public opinion and, by and large, allowed public discussion to deteriorate to the level of charges and countercharges. Although there was some recognition of the need to convince white parents that their interests were also to be served by school reform, the meetings and propaganda were not effective in gaining such support. In large part, this failure was a result of the opposition's setting of the stage along explosive racial lines.

In the spring of 1968, a more moderate bill was worked out by State Commissioner of Education Allen and the Board of Regents. It looked for a while as if a compromise bill, with elements of the Regents' plan and the Mayor's plan, could be enacted. The Governor, leaders of the legislature, the State Commissioner of Education, and the Regents supported this more moderate plan for decentralization, though there was legislative backing for the Mayor's version. The more liberal city Democrats in the legislature, and especially the reformers from New York's upper West Side and the few black legislators formed a small coalition operating for passage of stronger legislation. Most state legislators, ill informed on decentralization and viewing it as a city issue, were especially susceptible to pressure from political leaders, colleagues, and the various groups lobbying in the capital. During a two-day period prior to the arrival of the UFT delegation in Albany, it seemed that a compromise would be reached; the issue had narrowed to consideration of central structure—whether to expand the existing Board or to create a new three-man education commission to be appointed by the mayor. Legislative demands that commission appointments would have to be approved by the City Council were rejected by Lindsay, and the controversy delayed agreement long enough to allow the opposition to muster increased forces for the defeat of the legislation.

Although the Governor had indicated his support for the bill both in private and in public, he made no effort to move it through the legislature during the 1968 session. Possibly his generally unfriendly relationship with the Mayor was the reason; possibly his commitment was limited; certainly his inaction was an important element in the failure to secure passage. The Mayor's strategy seemed to be designed to limit his leadership in the undertaking: Staff commitments to the effort were left to the Education Liaison Officer who, though appointed by the Mayor, had almost no contact with him and little knowledge of state or local politics. In fact, the supporting coalition lacked any decisive leadership, and confusion and differences of point of view were constantly evident. At one point, the city coalition (comprised of the more militant city groups, including representatives of the three demonstration districts, with the Reverend Milton Galamison as chairman) sent a telegram to leaders in Albany indicating that they did not support the Regents' plan; yet Galamison was in the capital at that very moment lobbying for that plan as a member of the Citizens Committee. The Bundy panel was virtually nonfunctioning: Panel members had moved on to other activities and were largely inactive in the political arena. Had the panel continued to function, it could have been a source of significant political influence.

In its legislative campaign, the UFT successfully used the threat of political reprisals. As a result, the legislators, all up for re-election in the fall, postponed action for a year, empowering the city school board to draw up another decentralization plan. In order to placate the prodecentralization forces, the legislature increased the membership of the nine-member city Board of Education to thirteen, thus opening the way for the Mayor to gain a more decentralization-minded Board.

The Events: Phase 2

Although the legislative battle was postponed to the 1969 session, a second phase in the campaign was waged in the fall of 1968, when the city school system was struck for thirty-six days. The decision by the UFT to escalate their battle against decentralization, with Ocean Hill–Brownsville as the target, was probably made in the previous spring, when the district ordered the involuntary transfer of nineteen educators.[18] At a meeting of the Education Committee of the Urban Coalition held that spring, UFT President Albert Shanker allegedly proclaimed that he would destroy the Ocean Hill–Brownsville Governing Board and its administrator, Rhody McCoy. During the spring, the union had struck only the Ocean Hill–Brownsville district, with 350 teachers boycotting the district's schools. By September, the union decided that a city-wide strike was the only way to satisfy its demands. It was not until the middle of October, 1968, however, at a tense point in the city-wide strike action, that the UFT announced openly that the cost of settlement of the strike would be abolition of the Brownsville district.[19] Certainly, the union leadership must be given credit for realizing that their newly gained power over policy, won in the 1967 contract, was threatened by the local districts. Tactically, however, all of the UFT's early publicity claimed that the issue in the strike was "due process" for the nineteen teachers who had been transferred—or, as the union put it, fired without adequate charges. (Through the union contract, the UFT had obtained guaranteed job security under a system whereby teachers were to be transferred only with their approval, or in negotiation with the union. An involuntary transfer would be subject to the grievance machinery as stipulated in the contract.) Despite this claim, each union maneuver seemed directed at securing a confrontation with the opposition. In the meantime, between the spring and fall union actions, the Ocean Hill–Brownsville district had, with headquarters approval, replaced many of the staff people who had boycotted the schools.

The union successfully used the levers of fear and intimidation to arouse its own membership and the middle-class white population of the city. A heavy-handed CSA-UFT campaign, charging racial extremism and anti-Semitism in Brownsville, proved extremely successful. Leaflets and flyers, distributed throughout the city by the UFT and the CSA, quoted from materials purported to have been circulating throughout the Ocean Hill–Brownsville district. Some of the content later proved to be false; little of it ever was proven to have come from the district. Nonetheless, mass circulation of the propaganda fed the fuel of existing fears and latent racism, as the atmosphere in the city became more charged with each day of the strike. The Jewish community, in particular, became militant in its demands for redress.[20] Jewish leadership in the city either joined the UFT and CSA in their inflammation of the conflict or sat tight, providing no opposition or rational evaluation of the circumstances. The Board of Rabbis, a rather politically conservative body, became the spokesman for what was accepted as Jewish opinion. At meetings, attended by a wide range of the city's political leaders, the concern of Jewish organizations was voiced.

When the Board of Education directed that schools be opened, even if this meant breaking in (custodians were supporting the strike), the racial split was further intensified. Black parents throughout the city, along with small groups of white parents and teachers, opened schools; generally, however, white parents joined the picket lines. In some areas, "freedom schools" were held for white children, while black children were in the public schools. Reports indicated that UFT militants shouted racial epithets and, in some cases, were violent in their abuse of parents and teachers who crossed the picket lines. Black militants were accused of similar actions.

Although the Mayor attempted to balance the interests of both sides during the strike, he was personally committed to the preservation of the Ocean Hill–Brownsville district and to school decentralization. This pitted him against the UFT-CSA and led to a political stalemate because of the commitment of the professional groups to abolition of the district. The solid alignment of labor in support of the UFT was an additional and important element in the controversy. In fact, the Central Labor Council threatened at one point to call a general strike, according to reports from the Mayor's office. Forced to make various concessions to the union, Lindsay appeared to have no political leverage in dealing with it. His influence was effective only on the Ocean Hill-Brownsville board, and he used it to force them to accept the teachers back as a part of the strike settlement. There is no doubt that many of the participants, including the Mayor, underestimated the strength of the union—greatly enhanced by Shanker's leadership ability; equally underestimated was the full extent of latent racist feeling that was aroused in the white community. Nor was there any question of the mass support for the union: A city-wide prodecentralization rally produced a crowd of 5,000 to 6,000 people while, two days later, a UFT rally marched 40,000 people around City Hall.[21]

The illegal opening of schools, parent sleep-ins, and teacher opposition to the UFT position did produce a new base of support for decentralization, but the numbers were comparatively small and largely confined to elements in the black community that had not been actively involved in school affairs before the strike. Aside from this, efforts to develop institutional muscle for decentralization through the Committee to Save Decentralization and Community Control (the Reverend Donald Harrington was chairman) were slow in getting off the ground, although several new sources, particularly church groups, were successfully tapped.

Most interpretations of the school strike tend to isolate the events of that period from the total struggle for school reform and demands for a redistribution of power in the system. The action of the Ocean Hill–Brownsville Governing Board in transferring nineteen teachers out of the district was an attempt to establish local discretion and to define district power over school resources (in this instance, jobs)—both poorly defined at the time the board was set up. The action or inaction of the local board and its administration was based on their desire to establish independence from the central Board and to challenge the power of the professionals in the UFT and the CSA.

For the most part, the local board was not included in the city negotiations to end the strike. Early in the strike, the board had agreed to take the nineteen teachers back to the district but not to assign them to schools. Later, it supported the creation of a state trusteeship of the district under the Commissioner of Education, because it viewed the state as more friendly to its cause than the city. But any open compromise on the board's powers was viewed as a capitulation.

The strike settlement indicated that the usual power sources had maintained their position. The professional coalition of teachers and supervisory staff succeeded in negotiating a trusteeship status for the district, if not in killing it outright. The Ocean Hill–Brownsville Governing Board and the unit adminstrator were suspended, and, pending negotiation, involuntary transfers were in future to be covered by arbitration machinery.[22]

The Events: Phase 3

The third phase of the politics of school decentralization was played out in the 1969 legislative session. Although it followed the pattern of 1968, there was a clearer indication throughout of the polarization of forces that had taken place during the protracted strike. The manifestation of school policy-making power was more obvious. The lines of battle had been drawn in public. No longer could anyone question the role of the UFT, the CSA, and the Central Labor Council. Support for strong legislation (with delegation of personnel and curriculum powers to local districts) was, once again, weakened by disagreements among the prodecentralization groups. The demonstration districts had become the nucleus of the grass-roots movement for community control, and their experience had led them to a more extreme position. Decentralization no longer seemed adequate to their needs and interests. The Ocean Hill–Brownsville confrontation had indicated that only more complete community control over local resources (jobs and contracts) would provide sufficient power to influence school policy in a meaningful way. City-wide cohesiveness was undermined, however, by concerns community leaders had for their own districts. This reduced their interest in, and commitment to, city-wide decentralization. Supportive community groups throughout the city were unable to organize with the demonstration districts to provide a united front in the black and Puerto Rican communities. Milton Galamison, who had formerly served as the spokesman for those groups, had been appointed to the Board of Education in September, 1968, and was its vice-chairman. It is noteworthy that the demonstration districts and the grass-roots organizations lobbied infrequently —and ineffectively—in the capital. In fact, Senator Waldaba Stewart (representing an area that included Ocean Hill) was a major instrument in the passage of a weak bill.[23] The failure of the districts to play the legislative game was probably a central factor in allowing the 1969 legislative session to go as far as it did in destroying the districts.

The community groups' lack of knowledge of legislative politics explains in part why effective pressure was not brought to bear even when it could have produced some minimal results. It would be naïve, however, to assume that, even given this knowledge and a will to play the game, the groups could have exerted strong influence. These groups did not have the financial resources or political influence to impress legislators. Certainly, events during the 1969 session indicated that the elected state and city officials were extremely responsive to such vested school interests as the unions and the school professionals. Union financial support for election campaigns was not an unimportant factor in their decisions. Only the more radical Reform Democrats from the Manhattan's upper West Side and the Harlem legislators remained a solid force for effective legislation. Early in the legislative session, the Republican leadership was prepared to lend its support to a strong bill but was soon swayed by the regular city Democrats who had begun to talk about the need to compromise with the UFT. Stanley Steingut, the Brooklyn Democratic Party leader, led the downstate opposition to the stronger bill. Many of the opponents of decentralization now had larger stakes in the political struggle—the defeat of Mayor Lindsay in the upcoming election. A resounding defeat of both his board and his decentralization plan would embarrass him and could block his re-election.

The proponents of decentralization repeated their 1968 roles. The Mayor again chose to moderate his position; obviously, he was now also concerned about how developments would influence his re-election. Perhaps he had begun to appreciate why urban mayors had removed themselves from the educational arena. The Governor seemed unwilling to enter the controversy; he wanted a bill, but its content seemed unimportant. He was finally accused by community groups of buying off the Harlem delegation with the legislation creating a Harlem Hospital community board: CORE leaders were informed about the hospital concession in a private meeting with the Governor before he signed the weak bill, and, apparently as a result, CORE agreed not to criticize the Governor's action on decentralization.

The policy output of the three-year period of the politics of decentralization came in the 1969 legislation. The legislation passed in the last day of an extended 1969 session accomplished for the UFT-CSA what they were unable to achieve by a thirty-six-day city-wide strike. The bill not only abolished the three demonstration school districts; it provided a new series of protective devices to guarantee centralization and professionalism. It also removed the first prodecentralization city Board of Education, adding to the total success of the recentralization forces. That Board was replaced with an interim Board, whose members were appointed by the Borough Presidents; they were to remain in office for fourteen months.[24] But, in 1970, the legislature amended the law to allow the Board to remain in office another year. The interim Board was to set school-district boundaries and thus could determine who would control local district boards. School population data indicate that black and Puerto Rican populations represent a majority in eighteen of the thirty-one districts. Shrewd gerrymandering can reduce that control to five or six districts.

Further evidence of the *status quo* aspects of the law can be found in the restrictive provisions regarding personnel appointments. Local boards will have virtually no control over personnel. For example, although many cities have used the "merged list" as a means of increasing the appointment of black administrators, the new law prohibits such lists for principals.* It is likely that the legislation now virtually closes off appointments to blacks for at least five years, because current lists, which must be used first, include few blacks. The bill further provides that any future list of eligibles must be exhausted before new lists are prepared. The impact of this provision is disastrous for the city, especially if there were any plans for breaking new ground in this area.

---

*Under this procedure, new exams are given to qualify larger numbers of minority-group supervisors; their names are then added to existing accredited lists, and they can be assigned jobs immediately. If existing lists must, by law, be used first, there is no way to expand the number of potential candidates and increase minority-group appointments.

The assignment of all personnel who are no longer needed at headquarters to local districts by action of the interim Board will further reduce local options for a considerable time to come. Local districts will not have the chance to elect their local boards until after these assignments are completed. Under the legislation, transfers of personnel are generally more difficult to accomplish than previously, because restrictive provisions are now written into law and appeals machinery is more intricate and detailed. The community superintendent can no longer transfer personnel within his own district, unless certain school utilization criteria are in question. Under the law's procedures, transfers are made at the request of the district superintendent. This provision in itself violates the essence of decentralization and community control: It will be impossible for communities to transfer personnel internally or externally.

The only concession on personnel relates to the possibility of certain districts (those in which reading scores fall in the lowest 40 per cent) appointing teachers who have passed the National Teachers Examination and scored within the average grade of the five largest cities. With this exception alone, the city teachers' examination remains intact, and central assignment of teachers is otherwise retained. Discretion in the assignment of teachers, as noted, is severely limited. The Board of Examiners retains its major role of qualifying teachers; the only change in that procedure is that the chancellor (the new title for the superintendent of schools) now becomes a member of that body.

Budget powers for the community boards as outlined in the legislation, are advisory only. The local boards are, however, to be consulted on budget requests, and their unamended requests are to be submitted with the central budget to the mayor for review. A $250,000 local fund for repairs and maintenance remains controlled by closed competitive city bidding procedures for all contracts over $2,500. The advisory role of local community boards on site selection and expense and capital budgets has been expanded; however, full discretion remains in the hands of the central city Board and the Planning Commission.

The election procedures established for the city-wide Board and the local boards contrast sharply and indicate the political manipulation encouraged by the legislation. With borough-wide elections (all registered voters) for each central Board member, the role of minority groups is completely undermined. The majority of the city's school population is now black and Puerto

Rican, yet these groups cannot effectively exercise political power in borough elections—and this limiting of their power is, undoubtedly, an intention of the bill. Financing of the elections is unrestricted, which should provide the UFT with carte blanche to underwrite campaigns and influence the very people with whom they must negotiate their contract. In fact, in the contract negotiated by the interim Board, the UFT was—several Board members admitted—able to secure all of its demands.

In contrast to the city-wide procedure, the local election procedure provided for in the bill is highly complex and virtually guarantees local minority-group conflict. It requires that only registered voters can vote; parents who are not registered voters must preregister. Voters must be residents of the city for ninety days and be twenty-one years of age. The complexities of the proportional representation system established by the law are extremely difficult to translate to the poor[25] and may well account, in part, for the poor turnout at the first election in the spring of 1970. The most politically astute will have no difficulty in controlling the results of the local board elections. The bill also calls for petitions signed only by registered voters, which seems to exclude parents who are not yet registered as voters. No local resident can serve as a board member if he or she is employed by the district. Thus, all community people working as paraprofessionals in the schools are eliminated as potential candidates. A restrictive clause automatically removes board members who miss three successive local board meetings. It should be noted that no such provision is prescribed for the central Board or any other board in the city.

The support and protection of centralization by the legislation is further reflected in the lack of flexibility of action given to local boards. The law guarantees that no power will be delegated to those boards. In reaction to Ford Foundation financial support to the experimental districts, all outside funding must now be centrally approved, and funds are to be channeled through the central agency and the comptroller's office, thus limiting local control over the power resources of jobs and funds. Textbooks must be chosen from a centrally approved list. All local decisions on instructional materials—and, therefore, on curriculum—must have central approval. Examinations are centrally prepared and evaluated. The central office can change or install new programs in the local district at any time. They can arbitrarily adjust local boundaries and remove local personnel. The legislation is careful to state in several places that the local district is not to be considered a local educational agency; it is, rather, a subdivision of the central agency. While local boards presumably are allowed to operate cafeterias and social and recreational centers in the schools, funds are centrally controlled, and the local board's discretion is, therefore, limited, if not meaningless.

Throughout the legislation, all local district personnel are designated as city Board personnel, an attempt to guarantee their loyalty and obligation to the central agency. Only the community superintendent is appointed by the local board. All personnel are assigned by the chancellor and appointed by the local board. The legislation, however, encourages the chancellor to be responsible to local requests for staff.

The establishment of uniform districts of 20,000 minimum school population creates a further limit on experimentation and local prerogative. Decentralization as outlined in the Bundy plan called for districts of different size in order to achieve diversity and competition; thirty uniform districts denies this goal. The provision limiting size was aimed at abolishing the three demonstration school districts. Ocean Hill–Brownsville, the largest district of the three, has a student population of less than 10,000. All of the programs and personnel appointed by the three demonstration districts have been abolished under the legislation without consideration of their value or accomplishment. Perhaps this indicates most clearly the threat the districts presented to those who hold power in the school system; nothing short of abolition would satisfy their interests.

Who Governs?

It should be evident from this description of school politics that the actors, their roles, and the final policy output all reflect an enormous concentration of power in the hands of the school professionals. It also suggests their wider influence on other power sources in the city and state, and the lengths to which these groups will go to retain their power interests in the system. The complete insensitivity to the demands of the black and Puerto Rican communities and the unwillingness to compromise suggest a continuing and perhaps intensified struggle between these forces. Racial polarization has become more overt and more pronounced.

One should not ignore that city-wide decentralization was initially supported by the Mayor (albeit a reform Mayor with no party support), the Governor, civil rights and grass-roots minority organizations, the PEA, and the Ford Foundation. The Superintendent of Schools was also mildly supportive of the movement. Many a student of politics would predict that there was enough clout in that combination to effect the goal. Instead, not only was decentralization soundly defeated, but the defeat was extended to the political and personal status of the issue's proponents. The Mayor's defeat in the Republican primary election and Ford's retrenchment on its direct ghetto aid policy were by-products of the battle. The extended coalition of the labor unions, the Jewish organizations, and the school professionals demonstrated their enormous power in the city and state political arena.[26] The Mayor, attempting to gain a compromise from among the various forces, found himself faced with a no-compromise issue. One could presumably argue that the decentralization bill did represent a compromise of the various interests—it does create elected local governing boards. On the contrary, however, the centralization forces were served in every aspect of the policy —the larger districts, the creation of the more powerful chancellorship, the restrictions on transfer of personnel, and the complete failure to allocate control of any resources to the local districts. It is clear that the Mayor was not the instrument of compromise, although he attempted to play that role.

In *Participants and Participation* (1967), I predicted that the UFT and the CSA would oppose any decentralization movement, because it would endanger their place in the system. I greatly underestimated, however, the power of the union, its willingness to use any and all tactics to achieve its ends, and the extent that latent racism and fear could be played upon. These were the elements that finally dealt a resounding defeat to school reform and reinforced the *status quo* politics of the system.

In school politics, the insulation of the professionals effectively closes off new power sources. The limited roles and lack of access to power of the new population, which comprises over 50 per cent of the system's clients, has resulted in far more serious consequences. The resistance to change in urban institutions has produced an enormous gap between demands and needs, and policy output.

Notes

1. See, for example, Roger Kahn, "White Man, Walk Easy," in Thomas R. Dye and Brett W. Hawkins, eds., *Politics in the Metropolis: A Reader in Conflict and Cooperation* (Columbus, Ohio: Merrill, 1967), pp. 78–91.

2. The Research Council of the Great Cities Program for School Improvement, *Status Report,* 1967 (Chicago, 1967), p. 7.

3. Irving Kristol and Paul Weaver, "Who Knows New York?—Notes on a Mixed-Up City," *Public Interest* (Summer, 1969), pp. 41–59.

4. Mayor's Advisory Panel on Decentralization of the New York City Schools, *Reconnecting for Learning: A Community School System for New York City* (New York, 1969) pp. 106–7. See attached tables. The failure of the New York City schools has been amply documented. See, for example, David Rogers, *110 Livingston Street* (New York: Random House, 1969); Mayor's Advisory Panel on Decentralization of the New York City Schools, *op. cit.* Marilyn Gittell, *Participants and Participation: A Study of School Policy in New York City* (New York: Praeger, 1967); Queens College, Institute for Community Studies, *New York City School Fact Book,* 1969.

5. Colin Greer, "Public Schools: The Myth of the Melting Pot." *Saturday Review,* November 15, 1967, pp. 84–86.

6. Gittell, *op. cit.,* pp. 23–41. In analyzing school policy in New York City, five areas of decision-making in education were used; these were selected to take in the widest possible range of participation by those involved in education and to prove relevance of the policy selected to the over-all education function. Chosen for intensive study were: (1) selection of the superintendent, (2) increases in teachers' salaries, (3) budgeting, (4) school integration, and (5) curriculum development. Other areas of policy were reviewed in a more cursory way, to broaden the scope of the analysis.

7. Arthur J. Vidich and Charles W. McReynolds, "Study of New York City High School Principals Presented to U.S. Office of Education," *New York Post,* October 27, 1969.

8. It was reported that, in 1969, the UFT spent over $600,000 in Albany to defeat decentralization. *The New York Times,* February 1, 1970.

9. See David Rogers, *op. cit.* (note 4), pp. 15–35.

10. Board of Education of the City of New York Bureau of Educational Program Research and Statistics, *Special Census of School Population,* October 31, 1966, Summary of Tables, Publication No. 286, February, 1967.

11. David Rogers, *op. cit.* (note 9), *passim.*

12. *The New York Times,* March 23, 1967.

13. New York State Legislature, 1967 Session. Chapter 484 of the Sessions Laws of 1967.

14. All quotes from *The New York Times,* April–May, 1967.

15. Address by Mayor John V. Lindsay, entitled "The Mayor and the Classroom," April 27, 1967.

16. Mayor's Advisory Panel, *op. cit.* (note 4). See statement by Alfred Giardino, President of the Board of Education, p. 4.

17. *The New York Times,* May 24 and May 27, 1968.

18. Albert Shanker, UFT President, reportedly said at that time that the transfer of the nineteen teachers was worth about $1,000,000 in publicity. Interview conducted by author with UFT Executive Board Staff Member, October, 1968.

19. *The New York Times,* October 21, 1968.

20. In a voter profile of the November, 1969, city election, a high percentage of Jewish voters indicated that they were voting against community control of the schools in voting against Lindsay.

21. *The New York Times,* October 18, 1968.

22. *The New York Times,* November 18, 1968.

23. *The New York Times,* April 18, 1968.

24. The five borough appointments provided the city with a rather conservative political body. Borough presidents in New York City are of a more conservative cast than city-wide officials. They must be more responsive to local party machinery. Traditionally, borough-wide elections tend to underrepresent minority groups and reform voting because of the distribution of population in the individual boroughs.

25. In several meetings held throughout the city to explain proportional representation, voting responses have indicated the difficulty in accomplishing this task.

26. Nathan Glazer and Daniel P. Moynihan, "How the Catholics Lost Out to the Jews in New York Politics," *New York,* 3 (August 10, 1970), p. 49.

6. Health:
The Community Mental Health Center Controversy

MAXINE KENNY AND

BARBARA EHRENREICH

The Setting and the Actors

Exiting at the 168th Street subway station on Manhattan's upper West Side, one gains a limited but revealing impression of the setting and actors involved in the community mental health center issue; for it was here, in the Washington Heights–West Harlem area, that confrontation politics caught up with the mental health service system in New York City. From 1966 to 1969, minority-group activists, social workers, community psychologists, and avant-garde psychiatrists from storefront agencies were pitted against the power of both the city health bureaucracy and the renowned Columbia Presbyterian Hospital and Medical Center; at issue were the planning policies for a proposed community mental health center. The facility, to be publicly funded and

The authors are greatly indebted to Louise C. Bisogno, graduate student at Hunter College, who put in extensive time and energy in securing material for this study and in revising and rewriting the original draft.

administered by Columbia, was to afford ghetto residents suffering from mental disorders or emotional stress access to professional care in their residential neighborhoods.

In the Washington Heights–West Harlem area, extending from 125th Street to 181st and from Saint Nicholas Avenue to Bradhurst and the Hudson River, 166,443 New Yorkers reside; 45.7 per cent white, 41.0 per cent black, and 13.3 per cent Puerto Rican; 20 per cent of the families have incomes under $3,000, 59.6 per cent have incomes under $6,000; 13.4 per cent of the families live in substandard housing.[1] Census data reveal that these ethnic and economic divisions manifest themselves in the community along geographic lines, and observation confirms this. There is no doubt that the mental health facility issue was exacerbated by these neighborhood demarcations. In the southern section of the region, the population is predominantly black or Spanish-speaking. The West Harlem ghetto, a neighborhood of six-story walkups, burned-out tenement shells, and heavily gated small stores, contrasts dramatically with the fine ancient brownstones and well-kept apartments of the black *bourgeoisie* that line the blocks north of 150th Street. East of 168th Street, *grocerias* and *iglesias* abound, testifying to the dominance of the Puerto Rican, Cuban, and Dominican cultures that thrive there. In the northwestern corner of the region, where Washington Heights meets Inwood, a predominantly white, middle-class population resides, although the neighborhood is changing as these people join the exodus to suburbia.[2]

Throughout the entire area, there exists an acute need for mental health services. District records for 1966 indicated that there were 1,236 terminations from psychiatric clinics and 489 admissions to state mental hospitals.[3] For the sick poor of the neighborhood, the state mental hospital represents the terminus, the end of hope.[4] Entry into the cycle of hopelessness often begins when the disturbed individual "freaks out" and is picked up by the police, who then admit him to a city hospital mental ward, where he awaits psychiatric examination. This examination will determine his future; if he is not released and returned to the streets, and if no criminal charges are involved, he will be sent to a state hospital, from which he may never return.

Alternative forms of mental health care for the poor are almost nonexistent, primarily because the selection policies of private therapists tend to discriminate against those who cannot articulate their problems (and are therefore "unsuitable" subjects for

Freudian analysis), and the poor fall into this category. No large-scale outpatient facilities exist in ghetto communities to fill the gap. The few storefront mental health agencies—operating on tight budgets with skeleton staffs—cannot cope with the epidemic proportions of the problem, as it continues to spread in the heavily populated pressure-cooker environment of the city. On the other hand, the wealthy and the articulate may obtain private care in the city's major medical centers or in dozens of voluntary hospitals and private clinics. Thus, a dual system of mental health service exists, restricting the poor to public institutions, while the wealthy may take advantage of private psychiatric facilities, such as those offered by the Columbia Medical Center.

Towering high over the surrounding structures, covering an area of twenty-six acres, and extending from Broadway to Riverside Drive and from 164th to 168th Street, the Columbia Medical Center represents one of the richest medical facilities in the nation. Beginning in 1928 with a single unit, it has grown to include the Columbia University College of Physicians and Surgeons, Presbyterian Hospital, and the state facility, Psychiatric Institute, and today commands international recognition for medical excellence. Through Presbyterian Hospital, with its clinics for the poor, and through Columbia's teaching affiliation with Harlem Hospital in central Harlem, Columbia monopolizes the medical resources of upper Manhattan. Providing health services, however, is not Columbia's only role in the community, for, in addition, the Medical Center is the chief nongovernmental employer of the area, with 8,000 employees—a number expected to grow to 12,000 by 1975. It is also the area's major landlord, with a redevelopment program that has resulted, in the past decade, in the investment of over $31.5 million in real estate in the community.[5]

In each of its many roles, Columbia has attracted criticism from area residents. As an employer, it has been accused of using counterinsurgency methods to thwart unionizing efforts by workers, many of them residents of upper Manhattan.[6] As the major landlord in Washington Heights–West Harlem, Columbia has been criticized for razing tenements (in a section already suffering from a housing shortage) to make way for offices and apartments for Columbia personnel. As a provider of health services, Columbia has been accused of racism in the management of its municipal hospital affiliate, Harlem Hospital. Angry minority-group members objected to Columbia's abrupt dismissal of black physicians from Harlem Hospital in 1965 (when the affiliation began) and were incensed by rumors of experimentation on unsuspecting patients in that same hospital.[7] In 1968, charges of racism peaked with the revelation by Columbia undergraduates of the university's plan to construct, on public grounds, a gym with two entrances—one for students (white) and one for the "community" (black), and the Medical Center's image suffered by association.

In 1966, several factors combined to provide a climate for controversy and confontation over the closed mental health service system that Columbia epitomized. During the mid-1960's, the war-on-poverty money that flowed into the black and Puerto Rican neighborhoods of Washington Heights served to whet the public appetite for social services of all kinds. The facts of community life meant a day-to-day fight against unemployment, general poor health, decaying housing, garbage, rodents and vermin, lead poisoning, and poor school facilities, all contributing to a pattern of stressful living that resulted in a high incidence of social pathology. When community-action programs failed to turn the tide of decay, residents began to look more closely at the ebb and flow of poverty funds, and militancy centered on the demand for direct control of these funds. Community people realized that even those minimal poverty-program monies that existed were being siphoned off by prepackaged social-service programs, which, in the case of Washington Heights, were often administered by Columbia University. Frustrated by the situation, an angry indigenous community leadership emerged and was joined on this issue by staff members—predominantly black and Puerto Rican—of local social-service agencies.

Agency staff members, many of them residents of the community, had both a deep understanding of their clients' problems and the sophistication essential to extract vital services from the establishment. Fiscally starved and operating out of storefronts, these agencies were, nonetheless, the Washington Heights–West Harlem area's major source of assistance, whether it be in the search for a job, information on health care, or communication links with "downtown" welfare and housing agencies. During the mid-1960's war-on-poverty period, such social agencies proliferated in the area, adding a number of government-linked programs to community-run old-timers such as the Puerto Rican Guidance Center (a mental health service), CAN-DO (a storefront addiction service), the Community League of West 159th Street, the 166th Street Community Improvement Association, the Manhattanville Urban Renewal Study Committee, and the Harlem Parent's Committee. Desiring direct antipoverty funding, a number of these social-service agencies banded together in 1966 to form an elected, "representative" community corporation. Even as funds began to dwindle in 1967, these agency leaders remained in contact, ever on the lookout for new sources of funding for social-service programs for their clients.

The Lindsay Administration, elected in 1965, was amenable to the demands of the minority-group service-seekers. Indeed, Mayor John V. Lindsay's innerborough strategy emphasized the delivery of social services to the residents of the city's ghettos.[8] More important than the growth of grass-roots militancy, the emergence of indigenous leadership, or the climate provided by the administration was the input of federal legislation that offered public funding to localities implementing the community mental health center concept. It was the external stimulus provided by the federal legislation, rather than any intrinsically pluralistic feature of city politics that ultimately led to the attack on the closed mental health service system in New York City.

The Closed System

The public agency responsible for implementing mental health programs in New York City is the Community Mental Health Board.[9] CMHB is the least publicized of the city's health agencies. It presents no public profile of buildings or programs, operates with a small staff, and has usually remained aloof from the routine crises common to other city health agencies. Nevertheless, CMHB's power is considerable. According to New York's City Charter, CMHB has the authority to plan, set priorities, and allocate all funds for mental health services in the city. In recent years, CMHB has controlled an operating budget of over $100 million annually and an even larger capital budget. CMHB does not use any of these funds to operate its own programs directly; rather, since its inception, it has contracted out for direct services.[10] The agency is essentially no more than a conduit, passing on government funds to a wide range of uncoordinated, privately operated health facilities. Until recently, CMHB's internal structure was unique among city agencies. In accordance with the 1954 State Mental Hygiene law, which made state matching funds available for local public and private mental health services, the city CMHB—like its counterparts throughout the state—was set up to administer these funds. Policy for the CMHB was to be set by a nonsalaried board rather than by public officials directly.[11]

The board members of the CMHB represent the interests of the city's major providers of mental health services. Except for the two ex-officio members (the Commissioner of Health and the Commissioner of Social Services), the board is roughly divided between members affiliated with the Catholic Charities of New York and those affiliated with the Jewish Board of Guardians; these are the city's major sectarian charities most heavily involved in funding and operating private mental health services. All these services operated by the Catholic Charities and the Jewish Board of Guardians are under contract to the CMHB for public funds; collectively they absorb a large percentage of the CMHB funds allotted to voluntary agencies. CMHB members are also connected with some of the largest voluntary hospitals with mental health services: Presbyterian Hospital (affiliated with Columbia University's College of Physicians and Surgeons), New York Hospital (affiliated with Cornell Medical College), Brookdale Hospital Center (affiliated with Columbia's psychiatric residency program), Saint Vincent's Hospital in Manhattan, and Saint Vincent's Hospital in Staten Island. Well known to employees in city government but more difficult to document is the extent of affiliation of lower-level CMHB staff with private agencies that receive CMHB funds. Several middle-echelon staff interviewed in late 1968 were found to work part-time for such agencies.[12] The alliance between CMHB, a city agency, and the major medical centers and sectarian charities is well-enough established to raise the question as to whether a conflict of interest exists.

CMHB's public policies have been generally consonant with the private interests of its board and of its largely white middle-class, middle-aged staff and the institutions they represent.[13] A disproportionate share of its funds go to private agencies serving primarily middle-class patients. In 1961, city-run clinics were handling 78 per cent of the city's total outpatient admissions and receiving 45 per cent of the CMHB funds for clinic care. Voluntary agencies under contract to CMHB were handling 22 per cent of the admissions and receiving 54 per cent of the funds.[14] The disproportion has, if anything, increased since that time.[15] Furthermore, voluntary agencies receiving CMHB funds have been virtually unregulated, with contracts specifying little more than the name of the agency and its budget. About five new voluntary agencies have each year gained CMHB contracts, amounting to a total of sixty-six such agencies by 1968. Minority activists in mental health claim it is nearly impossible for a black or Puerto Rican agency to gain support of the CMHB.[16]

The Health Interest Alliance

The close association between Columbia and the CMHB provides a vivid example of the marriage of private and public mental health interests in New York City. The CMHB–Columbia Medical Center alliance began in the mid-1950's, when Presbyterian Hospital received one of the very first CMHB contracts providing public funds for psychiatric services at its clinic. The ties were tightened in 1961 when Dr. Marvin Perkins concurrently accepted the positions of associate professor of community psychiatry at Columbia and Commissioner of CMHB. One of his first acts at CMHB was to arrange for the agency to serve as a "field placement" for psychiatrists in the postgraduate masters degree program at Columbia's Division of Community Psychiatry. One graduate of this on-the-job training program is now Associate Commissioner of the State Department of Mental Hygiene; conversely, several of the CMHB people have moved on to take faculty positions at Columbia and other CMHB-supported institutions.

The next formal link with Columbia was forged when, in the spring of 1963, CMHB asked Columbia's School of Public Health and Administrative Medicine to undertake a household survey on the public image of mental health services in the city. This survey, which was completed in 1965, helped cement the relationship between CMHB and Columbia.

Another vital communication link among the several health interests was Mrs. Marjorie H. Frank, who, more than any other individual, "sold" community mental health to the voluntary hospital sector. Mrs. Frank came to CMHB in 1963 on assignment from the State Department of Mental Hygiene; she was to head the city's Regional Mental Health Planning Committee.[17] The committee's recommendations, published in 1965, which essentially laid the groundwork for CMHB's approach to community mental health, stressed the point that the voluntary sector could best do the job. Mrs. Frank was not new to the world of mental health and medicine; she headed a philanthropic family foundation that had donated heavily to psychiatric research. During the center controversy, Mrs. Frank was to serve as the intermediary between CMHB and Columbia. Early in 1967, she moved on to Columbia to become assistant to Dr. Lawrence Kolb (Chairman of Columbia's Department of Psychiatry and one of the chief policy-makers of Columbia's community-center program) and began teaching in the Department of Psychiatry.

The alliance of the CMHB, sectarian agencies, and private medical centers precluded the participation of the health services constituency until the mid-1960's, when a new input in the form of federal legislation was added to the picture.

The Federal Input

The federal Community Mental Health Center Act of 1963 was a response to the realization that traditional long-term treatment of the disturbed through systems of state hospitals was inadequate, costly, inefficient, and inhuman. Innovation was necessitated by the scope and costliness of the problem: Over half of all hospital beds in the nation are occupied by the mentally ill, incapacitated for periods averaging two years; the bill annually runs in excess of $2 billion,[18] with private care priced beyond the pocketbook of most Americans.[19] The community-center concept offered an opportunity for innovation.

Proponents of the center "movement" in professional organizations as well as in government agencies argued that long-term hospitalization was as unnecessary as it was inhuman and expensive. Mental illness, like physical illness, could be checked by intervention at an early stage of the disease. By making preventive and outpatient services available within residential communities, more people could be saved from entering the state hospitals. Furthermore, with the new tranquilizing drugs, which achieved acceptance in the late 1950's, even formerly dangerous patients could be safely maintained in their communities. The expectation was that, as community mental health centers sprang up throughout the country, state mental hospitals could be gradually phased out. While social reform was not a stated object of the act, the law made possible a dynamic new approach to the treatment of the mentally ill.

For the purposes of the Community Mental Health Center Act of 1963, a "community" was simply a geographically defined target population to which a clearly professional program could be aimed. The legislation defined community mental health centers as agencies providing comprehensive inpatient and outpatient services, including educational, consultative, and day-care programs, and serving an area containing between 75,000 and 200,-000 people. For programs meeting these requirements, the federal government would pay up to one-third of construction costs and, according to a 1965 amendment, would provide a de-escalating share of staff salaries. Community participation in the planning and operation of the centers was encouraged by the federal government, not as an invitation to community control but as a means of securing acceptance of local centers by a public presumed to be hostile to, and suspicious about, mental illness. What made the program politically volatile was not so much the community participation aspect as the inherent vagueness and ambiguity of the community mental health center concept. The law left the concept of the centers open to a wide variety of conflicting interpretations by those concerned—be they from public agencies, private mental health facilities, or the communities to be served.[20] The law's ambiguity was rooted in, and reflected, alternative and confusing perceptions of the problem of mental health. As a result, its programmatic sections were as ambiguous as its definition of the problem it sought to correct. Therefore, although the mandate for local participation gave community representatives roles in the decision-making process (thereby providing a crack in a closed system), the ambiguity of concept and program created the conditions for conflict.

To implement the 1963 act, the federal government looked to New York as the region most likely to succeed in the community mental health center business. For one thing, New York is richer in psychiatric talent than any other American city, and, although most of its psychiatrists are deeply involved in private practice, many are more accessibly deployed in the city's seven medical schools. New York also had the advantage of an established leadership (the CMHB), which could provide the administrative machinery essential to getting the program moving. From the outset, CMHB's interpretation of the Community Mental Health Center Act was closely in line with that of the more medically oriented mental health professionals, who envisioned community centers strictly as hospitals—although the cheaper and more flexible interpretation of mental health centers as networks of services was well within the federal law.[21]

In 1965, the CMHB staff designed a master plan for covering the entire city with such community mental health centers. The plan divided the city into fifty-one areas tailored to fit federal population requirements. Each of these "catchment areas," as they were called, was designed to cover the widest possible range of socio-economic conditions—a feature that not only pleased the integrationists in the Lindsay Administration but also assured that no community mental health center would be too heavily burdened with "inarticulate," poor patients.[22] Once the maps were drawn, CMHB saw no further need for planning: All catchment areas were to have community mental health centers; the only task was to find the institutions to provide staff for them.

In its early efforts to sell community mental health centers, CMHB approached the city's seven medical centers. With maps in hand, Marjorie Frank, CMHB's Comprehensive Services Director at the time, promoted the program with medical schools and teaching hospitals; as a first step, Columbia Medical Center was asked to take Washington Heights, Einstein Medical College to take Throgs Neck in the Bronx, and New York University Medical College to take Manhattan's Bellevue district.[23] Not all the medical centers were enthusiastic about community mental health centers, fearing that such a venture would detract from more academic pursuits, and, according to CMHB, it often required considerable cajoling to involve them. Nonetheless, the incentives for cooperation in the program were high. Public money would be available for staff salaries and, of course, a possible $10 million–$20 million building, which would provide space for private offices and teaching programs as well as for community services.

When the program for community mental health centers got under way in 1966, there was no question but that CMHB would award Columbia a center. Indeed, Columbia was not only to have a community mental health center, it was—through city supplements to federal funds—to have one built almost entirely with public funds.[24]

The Stakes

The diverse interests of the Lindsay Administration, the CMHB, Columbia Medical Center, and the black, Spanish-speaking, and white communities in upper Manhattan converged in the late 1960's on the issue of the mental health center. Each actor in the issue had a vital stake in its resolution. For some, acquisition of funds and facilities was central; for others, maintaining influence in the mental health arena was paramount.

To the Mayor, a center represented more federal money garnered for the city and another milestone in his ghetto redevelopment program. To the CMHB, a center in the ghetto would serve to improve the agency's public image (and, in so doing, enhance its position with the Mayor), while, at the same time, strengthening its ties to the private sector in mental health. CMHB trumpeted Columbia's proposed center as a "model for the nation," one of the first concrete implementations of the Community Mental Health Center Act. Justification for the choice of Columbia as the managing institution was couched in terms of the facility's potential importance as a demonstration project:

> . . . to develop a model comprehensive community mental health center with a balanced program of service, training and research . . . [Columbia's Division of Community Psychiatry] provides training for psychiatrists in community mental health and great potentials are thus offered . . . for manpower development, which is a critical area of need. Linkage would be established with Psychiatric Institute, a special State hospital engaged in research and training, and with the Presbyterian Hospital complex. These factors and many others, including the large body of knowledge of the area and its population gained from research studies, collectively contributed to the decision on the site for this center.[25]

The community mental health center as outlined in Columbia's plans was essentially an expansion of Columbia's existing mental health programs at Presbyterian Hospital and in the Psychiatric Institute. The over-all emphasis was on traditional hospital inpatient services, with only token provision for partial hospitalization services and no provision for more innovative, community-oriented programs. For instance, only 10 to 15 per cent of the proposed 200 inpatient beds were to be for use by night-care patients who would return to work in the community by day. There were no plans to train and employ local people as paraprofessionals, although existing mental health centers in other areas of the city had done this successfully. There were no plans to decentralize outpatient services into storefront offices or to integrate the mental health center's program with programs already offered in existing storefront agencies.[26]

In some respects, the mental health center seemed better designed to meet Columbia's needs than the needs of the community. Preliminary plans drawn by Columbia showed that a large proportion of the building's space was allocated to "allow for

major expansion of [Columbia's] psychiatric residency training."[27]
Moreover, the plans—which have never been made public—included space for 407 private offices for Columbia staff and affiliated psychiatrists. Altogether, the mental health center would cost between $10 million and $20 million, almost all to be paid from the public purse.

Despite the overwhelming benefits accruing to the administering hospital for the community mental health center, some Columbia spokesmen considered the situation potentially volatile. Both Dr. Lawrence Kolb and Dr. Viola Bernard, chief policy-makers for Columbia's center program, expressed reservations concerning the venture. Kolb, who was also president of the American Psychiatric Association, stated some of his reservations in a speech before that organization:

> In our striving for excellence in care for all, we must pose the question as to whether recently discharged, isolated, and impaired individuals are more satisfied with care provided for them in a well-ordered traditional hospital or would prefer "community care," where they may find themselves in a one-room apartment in an urban slum provided by an overworked welfare department.[28]

For Kolb, community mental health centers, if they were at all to be realized, would have to be strictly medical undertakings:

> It is interesting that the [community mental health] legislation in defining [the] structure of a community mental health center is in fact defining a hospital. . . . Yet the words "community mental health center" convey none of that to the general public. Both professional and lay groups seem to be unclear about the functions of such centers. Some have the impression that they are centers for social and political action. [29]

If the centers had a more general social mission than did other hospitals, it was—in Kolb's view—to prevent rather than to foment social action:

> Administrators and deliverers of mental health services will have to sharpen their perception and recognition of their responsibilities in maintaining *social homeostasis*. They bear a social responsibility much in the same way as the courts and other law enforcement agencies do in the support of a healthy community environment for all. [Emphasis added.][30]

Kolb also had deep objections to tying a mental health institution to a specifically defined community, arguing that consumers preferred to shop for the best facility even if it meant leaving their communities or having to "hoard and save to pay for the best."[31] But Kolb also hinted at a much more serious source of difficulty if strict geographic boundaries were to be observed: Such boundaries would conflict with an institution's established "clinical and organizational patterns." Elucidating this concern, a Columbia psychiatric resident noted:

> Perhaps the most threatening [to Columbia] aspect of catchment areas is that they define institutional responsibility. Given a catchment area, an elite private institution such as Columbia is assigned to a community which it must relate to, a public which it must account to. . . . But Kolb's uneasiness about geographical responsibility may stem from an even deeper fear—the fear that his institution could not fulfill this responsibility even if it could accept it. Institutions such as Kolb's Psychiatric Institute have very little to offer a community which is demanding mental health services, as opposed to mental illness "removal."[32]

To the activists in mental health in Washington Heights–West Harlem, a center meant something quite different from Columbia's conceptualization. Coping daily on a case-by-case basis with a variety of environmentally induced mental health problems, storefront agency workers could not conceive of an institutional orientation or the service patterns such institutions subscribed to. The experiences of one community worker at the Puerto Rican Guidance Center provides a profile of the local approach to mental health care. When asked what constitutes a mental health problem, he explained:

> When a child's grades at school drop suddenly and his Spanish-speaking parents can't communicate with the school guidance people, I go up to the school and discuss the problem for the parents and help work out a solution for the child. This is a mental health problem.
> When a disabled Vietnam veteran returns to our neighborhood but cannot find work, he comes to us for help. I call around and use my contacts to get a job for him. This is a mental health problem.
> When a six-year-old child is found crying in a hallway and he is brought to me, I probe what's wrong. Maybe he can't bear to

go home to a three-room apartment filled with a dozen assorted relatives. The crowding and fighting are tearing him apart. This is a mental health problem, and I try to solve it by finding larger quarters for the family and even by marriage counseling.

When a couple can't get any action from a landlord, they come to me and I write a "failure to paint" complaint. Living in dirty cramped quarters with roaches and rats makes people mentally ill. You see, this, too, becomes a mental health problem.[33]

This concept of mental health is all-encompassing and makes the agency an advocate of the citizen in his search for basic services. The storefront agency functions much as did the early twentieth-century settlement house. It attempts to close the communication gap between public service agencies and their clients that often results in a serious service gap for the inarticulate and ignored masses. From one storefront agency to another, the program emphasis varies. The approach of the grass-roots organization depends on the predominant local needs, on the financial resources available, on the expertise of the staff, and on the extent to which staff personnel see themselves as an instrument of social change. Systemic change, to the radical social reconstructionist, is fundamental to a comprehensive mental health program. The radical position rejects total reliance on traditional methods of dealing with mental illness because these treat only the symptoms —for example, alcoholism, drug addiction, and a high crime rate— of deeper social and economic dysfunctioning. Hence, those holding such a view, envision a center that will launch a broad attack on the erosive environmental conditions and on the institutions responsible for them.

The radical position is perhaps best expressed in the following passage:

The major concern is the mental health of the community itself with preventive programs, early detection, treatment, and an effort to change conditions in the community and to make available the mental health "supplies" which enhances [sic] the mental health of all the inhabitants from the psychotic to the healthy individual. Mental illness is to be seen and treated as an intrapsychic, social, and political problem, rather than exclusively a psychological or biological one. . . . [A new social institution—a community problem-solving organization] will not be an institution that maintains the status quo of the community, or reinforces other community institutions which have contributed to the mental illness of the community.[34]

Thus, the spectrum of conceptual approaches to mental health centers extended from the traditional view, represented by Columbia's hospital orientation, to the radical view, which demanded social reconstruction. In the conflict reported here, the traditionalists supported a Columbia-based center and a program emphasizing Freudian theory or drug therapy. On the other hand, the radicals, considering the mental health problem as only part of the larger problem of powerlessness, saw the resources available under CMHB as enabling the community leadership to "control" community resources. Falling between the traditional and radical perspectives were a variety of compromise positions advocating storefront-hospital approaches. Each participating group entered the conflict armed with its own unique perception of what constituted a community mental health center.

Strategies and Actions

It was estimated that almost five years would elapse from the time the CMHB made its initial decision to locate a community mental health center in upper Manhattan to the time a center could be in operation.[35] Key decisions regarding concept and program would be made in the first year. As plans and program became firmer, fewer opportunities for meaningful community participation in planning would occur. In retrospect, one can see that Columbia, aware of the importance of this time factor, immediately established its strategy in the controversy. First, the institution apparently intended from the outset to control the plan regardless of the federal mandate for community participation. Second, Columbia took it upon itself to define the community and to determine which community representatives would eventually participate in the later stages of planning the center. During the course of the conflict that developed, as the professionals from Columbia clashed with local activists, it became increasingly apparent that the latter group was constantly put on the defensive, reacting to Columbia's efforts to control or summarily circumvent community participation.

In September, 1966, Columbia and CMHB jointly submitted their proposal to the National Institute of Mental Health. By November, it had official approval. At the end of that year, interim funds were made available through June, 1967, for a skeleton staff to begin detailed planning; these funds, donated by a private foundation, were channeled to Columbia through CMHB. In June, 1967, CMHB provided another planning grant to Columbia, and the machinery at the Medical Center went into high gear.[36]

The heavy emphasis on inpatient beds in the preliminary plan caused the State Department of Mental Hygiene to observe that the number was sufficient to serve two catchment areas. Instead of recommending that Columbia pare down its plans for 150-plus inpatient beds and reorient itself to outpatient services, the Department suggested that the Inwood section northwest of the catchment area be included in the district. The enlarged catchment area would contain a total population of 281,330 residents, thereby justifying the size of the proposed hospital-based center.[37]

Expansion of the catchment area was welcomed by Inwood activists and local planning board members who, knowing that the size and economic status of their neighborhood excluded them from access to social service money intended for ghetto improvements, had lobbied earlier through their state and city representatives for such inclusion.[38] The alternative for Inwood—private care dispensed by Jewish Memorial Hospital—was unsatisfactory because this facility was ill equipped to deal with complex psychiatric disorders. In the past, Inwood residents seeking mental health services had gravitated toward Columbia; hence, the Columbia orientation was well established when the formal decision was made.

Columbia also welcomed the extension of the catchment areas' northern boundary. The additional constituency not only justified the large in-patient hospital, but also altered appreciably the class, complexion, and conceptual attitudes of the participating community. Compared to Washington Heights (no separate figures are available for West Harlem), Inwood has only half as many families earning less than $3,000 annually and only one-sixth as many tenements considered substandard.[39] The residents, a generally conservative ethnic mix (including German Jews, Irish, anti-Castro Cubans, some Greeks and Dominicans) were expected to support a traditional view of mental health care.

While Columbia planners were designing the center and redefining the catchment area, and Inwood residents were lobbying for inclusion in the district, blacks and Puerto Ricans active in the field of mental health were generally unaware of the proposed community center. They first learned of the program in March, 1967, in an article in *The New York Times*. Angered at the bypass of their newly formed community corporation and concerned that their integrity as community representatives as

well as their access to public funds were at stake, they determined to pressure for minority-group representation on CMHB
and on the planning staff at Columbia. Because it was essential
that community representatives become a part of both the downtown (CMHB) and the uptown (Columbia) decision-making
apparatus, these activists confronted CMHB, demanding an end
to its discriminatory hiring practices, which had resulted in a
staff of 170 employees, only three of them black or Puerto Rican
above the clerical level; they also wanted the all-white CMHB
board opened to minority members. Subsequently, at the request
of Washington Heights agency leaders, the city's Office of Human Relations, headed by William Booth, reviewed CMHB's activities,[40] but, while acknowledging the possibility of discrimination, this agency cautioned that discrimination was a difficult
charge to pin down.

Meanwhile, the Medical Center leadership had mobilized to
"organize" the catchment area. They appealed to the CMHB for
$92,000 for the express purpose of organizing the community.[41]
The assumptions of the proposal Columbia put to CMHB were
that (1) the target population could be identified on a racial
basis and (2) the community was not in fact organized. The
document stated:

> There is little contact or interaction between groups for a variety
> of reasons including cultural differences, antagonisms, rivalries, or
> apathy. . . . There is no broad based organization which speaks
> for substantial numbers of the population. . . . A low rate of par-
> ticipation characterized [all] existing organizations. Therefore,
> the leaders of such organizations are not necessarily representative
> spokesmen for the community. These factors of fragmentation, low
> participation, and limited representativeness of the leaders indicate
> a lack of ready-made channels of communication through which
> to establish contact with local residents for involvement in joint
> planning of needed services.[42]

The leaders of the local social-service agencies wrote a re-
buttal to the Columbia plan, in which they voiced a concern
that:

> . . . the improperly informed invade our community. . . . They have
> submitted incorrect data to secure funds to set up programs on the
> basis of ignorance, when they should have consulted with leaders in
> the community. . . . We are extremely displeased at not having been

consulted in the early planning stages in something that affects both the Negro and Puerto Rican residents of Washington Heights. . . . We recognize the belated interest of Columbia Medical College in mental health needs of the community. . . . The Washington Heights community has received very limited services at the Columbia Presbyterian Hospital.[43]

Their memo specifically indicted Columbia for its racism and questioned the legitimacy of its newly adopted stance as a "community" institution. Pointing to the inclusion in the Columbia proposal of the names of dozens of churches, synagogues, schools, parent associations, health and social agencies, community-planning boards, political clubs, and the like, they argued that the document itself contained the proof that the community was already highly organized and could draw on a wide range of men and women who had proven leadership experience in these organizations.

Within the community, local leaders bitterly resented Columbia's presumption that they were not representative of the area. Living in the neighborhoods that made up the catchment area, these leaders had worked hard throughout the years for community improvement. Many had given up their evenings and their weekends to community-service programs, including those concerned with mental health. When war-on-poverty money supplied the financial support for community-action programs, many of these workers—some volunteers and some paid—had been brought into contact with each other—contact that was reinforced by their overlapping memberships in local organizations. And, while there was some truth to Columbia's charge that cultural differences, antagonisms, rivalries, and antipathies existed among the catchment area's many groups, these differences were neither so unmanageable nor so extreme as to justify Columbia's takeover of the planning of the mental health center—a takeover even CMHB Commissioner Marvin Perkins was soon moved to criticize as "unprofessional."[44]

Area activists, upset by Columbia's arrogance as manifested in the proposal, began to organize to challenge the institution. Dr. Rubin Mora, a psychologist and the director of the Puerto Rican Guidance Center (a small storefront agency on Amsterdam Avenue), was among the first to take direct action. In June, 1967, he went to the CMHB and demanded an interview with Perkins. In response, the Commissioner brought his personal staff and a group of Columbia planners uptown for a July meeting with the

community. Local agency representatives turned out in force
for the meeting, held in the cramped Guidance Center office. Undoubtedly, the large turnout was in part due to the distribution
of more than a thousand copies of the Columbia proposal. A
second meeting, to be held in Perkins's office, was agreed upon.
As that meeting began, Dr. Anna Hedgeman, a black activist,
demanded that available funds be given to the community, not
to Columbia. Although he sidestepped this request, Commissioner
Perkins did agree that local leaders ought to be included in the
planning process, and he proposed the formation of an Ad Hoc
Advisory Committee, which was to be a loose association of
Columbia's mental health center staff people, of representatives
from Inwood, and of activists and reformers from the Washington
Heights–West Harlem area. Perkins also implied that qualified
blacks and Puerto Ricans would be eligible for positions on
Columbia's planning staff. By the meeting's end, two CMHB
staffers had been assigned to work with the Ad Hoc Advisory
Committee, and Perkins (reacting to the "lily-white" charge)
had also asked the group to submit the names of qualified blacks
and Puerto Ricans for possible appointment to any CMHB board
vacancies that might arise.[45]

Skeptical of CMHB's ability to serve simultaneously as con-
fidant to Columbia and advocate for the community, fifty activists
staged, a few days after the meeting, the first sit-in ever held in
the agency. Central to their demonstration was the demand that
minority-group members be on the Columbia planning staff.
Perkins agreed to direct the Medical Center to hire blacks and
Puerto Ricans for certain staff positions, and the demonstration
ended. A short time later, however, the city's Corporation
Counsel cautioned Perkins that such a directive would constitute
a violation of the state's antidiscrimination law. Perkins was also
told by Dr. Sheldon Gaylin, Columbia's planning chief, that finding blacks and Puerto Ricans qualified for the job was difficult.

Gaylin's argument was countered by community spokesmen,
who pointed out that the main qualification for the job was actual
experience working in the streets, hallways, and alleys and out
of local storefront agencies to alleviate suffering in the service-
starved section of upper Manhattan. The embryonic Ad Hoc
Committee backed the activists' demands for minority representation on the planning staff.

In October, Dr. Mora, newly elected chairman of the Ad Hoc
Committee, received word from Commissioner Perkins that, in
effect, he would take no action:

I agree that the selection of personnel most certainly must take into account all relevant factors, including such matters as life experience and the natural endowments that equip one capably to perform the duties of a given position. By overemphasizing at the outset one or another of those individual features which contribute to overall capacity, there is the hazard of a too early narrowing of the field for selection. Furthermore, there is the serious legal question.[46]

In this manner, Perkins closed the issue in October, despite his earlier acceptance of the demand. What pressures had been placed on the Commissioner in the intervening months can only be conjectured.

In the wake of Perkins's reversal, criticism of Mora's confrontation tactics surfaced in the Ad Hoc Committee. The loose association was strained by suspicions. Some moderates believed the radicals were interested in control rather than in services, while the radicals considered the moderates rubber stamps for Columbia. When disgruntled radicals from the southern, poorer section of the catchment area questioned whether Columbia was the proper medical facility to be affiliated with the community center, representatives from Inwood interjected that "this contract is with Columbia and this committee does not have the right to question that."[47] The intergroup tensions were further exacerbated by racial and class conflicts within the group. There were charges of racism and countercharges of anti-Semitism. The class antagonisms surfaced when moderate blacks cautioned the white membership to keep cool while they tried to reach a concordat with the blacks and Puerto Ricans from poor sections of the catchment area.[48]

The CMHB's Chief of Research reported these internal conflicts to Perkins:

The "south" people [below 155th Street] appeared disappointed and later angry particularly at Mrs. [Leona] Feyer, the white community mental health center [community] organizer hired by Columbia, Dr. Gaylin and Columbia for "acting as usual." It appears that Mrs. Feyer contacted and invited her potential supporters of whites, and weakened the Negro and Puerto Rican groups who oppose her. There is a rift and a reaction of conflict can be expected.[49]

On the Columbia community mental health center staff from its inception, Mrs. Feyer was deeply resented by the local leaders, especially the black and Puerto Rican radicals, who saw, in her presence as an organizer for Columbia, an implied insult to the local leaders. Her presence indicated that, despite their years of effort in organizing grass-roots support for mental health care, they were deemed to have failed. Mrs. Feyer's presence also implied a policy of divide and conquer for the benefit of Columbia; as the CMHB correspondence indicated, she had in fact instigated unrest.*

Demoralized by the internal dynamics of the Ad Hoc Committee and the continued circumvention by Columbia, the Puerto Rican Guidance Center took it upon itself to submit its own planning proposal to the CMHB. The proposal requested the abandonment of a Columbia-based center, offering instead a program of decentralized storefront agencies, with an emphasis on prevention rather than on treatment, and with the major portion of personnel to be paraprofessionals, indigenous to the neighborhoods they were servicing.[50] The scheme was rejected by CMHB on the grounds that the small agencies lacked state licenses to operate clinics and did not have adequate professional staffs. CMHB recommended instead that the Guidance Center become affiliated with Columbia's planned mental health center, which was to be ready by 1971. In a letter to the city administration, a CMHB member added:

> If there is indeed a valid [professional] team available [at the Puerto Rican Guidance Center], I am quite certain the Washington Heights Mental Health Center would snap up any offer of affiliation they might make. The proposal though is long on ideals and short on details. That is, it says a great deal about the why and where and practically nothing about the what and how. Because of this lack of detail, it is difficult to determine the depth of thinking of the people involved in developing this program other than their wish to do something very needed and very worthwhile.[51]

The CMHB response to the Puerto Rican Guidance Center's proposal indicates the chasm that exists between the liberal, middle-class, white view of mental health (in both theory and

---

* Columbia, meanwhile, continued to plan without community consultation; by December, 1967, its planning staff had worked up an elaborate proposal for a school mental health program as part of the community health center. But, when Gaylin approached the district superintendent of schools for support of the program, he was turned down on the grounds that the staff was all white.

practice) and the view held by the ghetto activists. To the former, services can only be rendered through a system of facilities staffed by personnel formally educated for the complex task of caring for the mentally ill. The chasm could not be bridged by communication between CMHB and the militants. Despite months of discussion, wide disparities between their concepts of mental health remained.

Rebuffed in their appeal for independent funding, the activists altered their strategy and allied themselves with dissidents from the other ghetto communities. The climate for overt action was favorable. The struggle for involvement in the health service system had by this time taken on city-wide dimensions, with at least a dozen groups battling over other health issues. In early November, 1967, the Washington Heights group called for a city-wide meeting of minority-group health activists—including those from Harlem, the Lower East Side, the South Bronx, and Bedford-Stuyvesant. At the meeting, the Citywide Health and Mental Health Council was formed. The new organization called upon the city to "shift the balance of power from private interest in health and mental health to the interests of the people and involve the diversified segments of this city in *policy-making, planning, distribution of funds and contracts, and in watching for the maintenance of the public interest.*"[52]

This development was not viewed with unanimous displeasure by the "downtown" health bureaucracy. To Dr. Howard Brown, top officer of the city's new superagency, the Health Services Administration, the emergence of a seemingly organized constituency for health services was a potential benefit. Ever since his appointment in early 1967, he had been struggling unsuccessfully to bring together the entrenched health, mental health, and hospital bureaucracies under the common administration of the Health Services Administration. Having few friends in the private medical establishment,[53] Brown's only hope for leverage with the health agencies was from a consumer constituency. As a guest at the founding meeting of the Citywide Health and Mental Health Council, Brown listened attentively to the community charges against CMHB, then told them, "Go to the Mental Health Board and sit there and tell *them* . . . they have the power!"

Following Brown's suggestion, fifty members of the Council staged a sit-in at the CMHB's mid-November meeting. Dr. Harvey Thompkins, chairman of the board, was not unresponsive to the demands for racial integration of the CMHB hierarchy.

Indeed, two vacancies were coming up, and Thompkins promised that the posts would be filled by blacks or Puerto Ricans. After the demonstrators exited, however, Thompkins reversed his position and recommended the reappointment of the two white board members whose terms were about to expire. His recommendation was accepted. Although the sit-in failed in its objective, CMHB was obviously shaken enough to issue a public statement claiming that virtually all of its budget was "directed toward the financially disadvantaged."[54]

The Citywide Council suffered a second setback several weeks later when Commissioner Perkins resigned his post. Though no ally of the blacks and Puerto Ricans, he had been somewhat responsive to their demands. His failure to translate this responsiveness into actual reform in the system was not his own doing, for he was subject to strong pressures from the board, from Columbia, and from the other major voluntary agencies. Dr. Herbert Fill was named Acting Commissioner in Perkins's place, a position he was to hold throughout the remainder of the controversy. At the outset of his administration, he represented an unknown factor, but his initial policies seemed to place him opposite the reformers in the conflict. His first effort at CMHB was to reorganize the staff. He redesigned his "cabinet" so as to exclude the one black member in it—a Washington Heights resident who had served as liaison with the community groups. He also recommended the acceptance of the resignation of the single Puerto Rican staffer. Reorganization, the hope of the militants who felt integration would add sympathetic gatekeepers to the system, had instead eliminated minority-group members from the downtown decision-making apparatus.

The radicals had not yet recovered from the impact of the CMHB reorganization when Columbia made its next move. Issuing a letter in December, 1967, to catchment area residents, Columbia projected an image of the institution trying to bring about community participation. Dr. Gaylin explained:

> By this time you have probably heard about the mental health center to be built in this area. In some cases this letter may represent our first contact with you. Those of us responsible for planning the Washington Heights Community Mental Health Center have been trying to meet with all community groups and their representatives; no doubt we shall accomplish this eventually. But for the time being, an advisory council that is as representative of the community as possible offers the best means by which

we can become aware of the community's needs, discuss with it our mutual concerns, problems and progress as well as plan the programs of the mental health center. For sometime now a small group of interested citizens in the area [has] organized as an ad hoc advisory committee and [has] been meeting to discuss various problems related to the development of the mental health center.[55]

The Ad Hoc Committee responded to Columbia's community mailing with a request for information on the status of the plans for the community mental health center. Columbia's planning staff replied that it had no plans to disclose. The answer was partially true—in the sense that there were no *final* plans. In fact, the architectural plans had proceeded only to the stage of schematic drawings, which Columbia hesitated to throw open for community discussion. At this time, the unrevealed plans included two entrances, one for Inwood and another for Washington Heights, as well as a plethora of private offices, and "a superblock which shall encompass the mental health center and other institutions such as the International Institute for the Study of Human Reproduction, the Institute for Nutritional Sciences, etc."[56]

The Ad Hoc Committee could not help but interpret Columbia's latest moves as threatening. Determined to counter the Medical Center, they took to the sidewalks and collected 4,000 signatures on an angry letter addressed to Columbia's Dr. Kolb, which attacked the institution for excluding local leaders from the planning process. The letter noted that secrecy had created distrust, which was exacerbated by arrogance and a misunderstanding of those community groups interested in developing mental health services, and added:

> We have asked for disclosure, discussion and review of the center's plan and for agreement to revisions so that they may be responsive to our needs. We have found serious impediments to these reasonable requests. . . . Dr. Fill who is Acting Commissioner of CMHB . . . also disclaimed responsibility. *Who* is then responsible? *Who* has the conviction, the courage and the capacity to work out solutions with us as coequals? . . . For these reasons we have appealed to you. It is no surprise to us that the Columbia staff reports no emergency to you. Obviously, they are not sensitive to the crisis nor to the proportions that it may reach. We do have a sense of emergency and will act accordingly.[57]

In response to an Ad Hoc Committee inquiry, Kolb acknowledged receiving the letter, but he denied that 4,000 signatures had been attached. As for the letter itself, he said it "should be addressed to the New York CMHB [since] Columbia had only a developmental grant from the city and was not under contract to manage any community mental health centers."[58] The community workers who had spent days in the streets working for these signatures and explaining their position vis-à-vis Columbia to a generally complacent public could not accept Kolb's explanation. Somewhere between the Ad Hoc Committee and Columbia, the attached sheet had disappeared. Relations between the protagonists were deteriorating rapidly.

Correspondence from Columbia to the CMHB and the Ad Hoc Committee began to take on an ominous tone, conveying the impression that Columbia was losing interest in the center project. The Dean of Columbia College of Physicians and Surgeons warned:

> There has been great concern in the faculty of the Medical School as to whether we would be able to recruit the personnel or whether we could satisfy all the requirements needed for the management of such a center. There has also been considerable doubt as to whether the Trustees of Columbia University [there are many overlapping trusteeships with the medical school] would feel that they were able to take on this additional obligation.[59]

Columbia, like the Ad Hoc Committee, had its factions, too. It was not a monolith. Since the inception of the "center" conflict, some Medical Center staff members had serious reservations; some believed the program would open them up to community scrutiny. Still others, however, saw it as an opportunity to acquire a $10 million–$20 million hospital and research facility. Some radical students in psychiatry found themselves in the same helpless position as the community insofar as influencing Columbia's decisions was concerned; they were able, however, to question Columbia's motives and to assist community leaders by giving them technical assistance in preparing proposals. Those Columbia people pressing to extract Columbia from the controversy would gain support when the Citywide Council was reconstituted in the summer of 1968. In the meantime, it was becoming apparent to the most enthusiastic center supporters that the issue was highly political. The politics of participation and the strategy of confrontation had challenged Columbia's control over the planning of the center, and there was no assurance that participation and confrontation would abate after the center was built.

Concerned that the program was in jeopardy in the upper Manhattan catchment area, CMHB belatedly offered guidelines for local participation in planning the local centers.[60] The guidelines called for the creation of two groups—one to participate in the operational phase and the other in the developmental phase. One group would represent the various health, education, and welfare agencies providing direct or indirect mental health services to the area; the other would be made up of representatives from social, political, paternal, business, parents, religious, labor, and other social organizations in the community. The scheme, no doubt reasonable to the middle-class community the author drew on in designing it, was, to some members of the community, a means of splitting the ghetto into a multitude of competing groups, magnifying the diverse interests, rather than reconciling them, and isolating the leaders of the struggle by adding a large number of participants with other primary interests to the controversy. The program divided the community into agency and consumer groups, and, according to an Ad Hoc Committee statement: "CMHB's guidelines are a trick to divide the community . . . an attempt to rob the community from their own professionals and rob those professionals from their community base. The legitimate community contains professionals as well as anybody else who lives and works with and in the community, not as white planters in a colonial situation, but as equals."[61] The guidelines indicated CMHB's unwillingness to mediate between local militants and Columbia. In fact, the plan called upon each hospital to do the organizing of its own community advisory councils.

Dr. Kolb's first effort to implement the guidelines occurred in mid-July, 1968, at an "other than agency" community meeting. An agency representative meeting was to follow in the fall. To be certain that the division between agency and consumer would be maintained, Columbia sent a special letter "de-inviting" agency people to the July meeting.[62] Instead of discouraging attendance by this group, the letter brought angry agency representatives out en masse. At the same time, word about Columbia's architectural design for the center had reached the community. The plan, which called for two entrances—one for the predominantly white Inwood community and another for West Harlem—Washington Heights, which is predominantly black and Spanish-speaking—produced outrage. (Columbia was eventually to justify the two-entrance idea on the grounds that the facility was actually serving two separate catchment areas, an argument that left community activists cold.) Word of the plan undoubtedly increased attendance at the meeting. During the course of it, Dr. Mora, of Puerto Rican Guidance, declared:

> The Washington Heights Center is a worse offense to this community than the gym in Morningside Heights; because here is involved the mental health care of our people and they are going to have separate facilities within the same building for us in Washington Heights who are a majority of Blacks and Puerto Ricans and for Inwood which is mostly white. This is today gone from the *Deep South* but started as an *"innovation"* by the Mental Health Board: *separate but equal facilities.*[63]

Misperceiving the depth of this anger, Dr. Kolb spoke instead to the discrimination issue, offering visual presentation of staff surnames to prove that Columbia did indeed hire and employ blacks and Puerto Ricans. Instead of calming the audience, this approach increased their dismay, and a large segment walked out on the presentation.

Late in the summer of 1968, the community learned that architectural plans for the center were being completed. Realizing that the time for participating was running out, the dissidents on the Ad Hoc Committee proceeded to line up allies for the September meeting, which had been called by Columbia for the purpose of setting up election procedures by which a permanent mental health advisory council for the area would be chosen.[64] The radicals prepared for the meeting by mobilizing support from the Citywide Health and Mental Health Council membership from the Lower East Side, Bedford-Stuyvesant, and the South Bronx. They also approached Harlem CORE, which, at the time, was concerned with the issue of community control of Harlem Hospital, and, in an unprecedented move, they asked the Columbia University chapter of the radical Students for a Democratic Society (SDS), to join in the struggle.

While the militants were gathering allies, a new issue increased local discontent. The city's Department of Public Works had moved to purchase the Audubon Ballroom on 166th Street, planning to raze the structure in order to clear the site for a proposed Columbia superblock of health facilities. The block was to include the Washington Heights community mental health center. In the view of the community residents, the Audubon was not simply a social center; it was a shrine to black nationalism, for Malcolm X, the Muslim leader, had been slain there. The cry "Save the Audubon Ballroom" was soon added to their demands.

When the September meeting was convened (at 10 A.M., an inconvenient hour for working residents), CMHB representatives and Columbia spokesmen were confronted with an angry vociferous group of mental health militants. The militants soon took over the dais from the chairman and proceeded to turn the meeting into a "teach in." [65] They elected a moderate, William Hatcher (head of CAN-DO, a private addiction service), chairman of the meeting. Hatcher's participation was indicative of the growing distance even the moderates in the center controversy felt in dealing with the health establishment. The meeting that he chaired reflected the broad range of views on the mental health controversy—from radicals demanding full social change to conservatives merely asking to be let into the Columbia program.

But, in the weeks that followed, the anger demonstrated by area activists at the "teach-in" was not sustained, and, once the furor died down, their dynamism dissipated. Later in September, the traditionalists, moderates, and radicals in the Ad Hoc Committee met to decide what course lay open to them. Discussing the alternatives, Dr. Mora argued for militancy, while, at the same time, extending the olive branch to those Inwood residents on the committee. Inwood members, reflecting the spirit of common purpose, indicated their willingness to consider a storefront approach in a center program, but continued to see the program as necessarily tied to Columbia's expertise and facilities. Mora's supporters, cautioning the committee against continued association with Columbia, called the advisory council concept (based on CMHB's guidelines) another of Columbia's devices for subterfuge. Despite these warnings, the majority of members voted to reorganize as the Washington Heights–West Harlem–Inwood Advisory Council. [66]

One of the earliest motions of the council was a call for an end to the funding of Columbia as the administering hospital for the catchment area. Ironically, as one member of the newly formed group alleged that the Medical Center had already collected over $3 million in planning monies, the council members passed around the hat to collect funds to underwrite their attempt to incorporate (a necessary step to gaining access to public funding); they collected $86.00 to launch their campaign against the closed health service system in New York City. [67]

The council's first move was to contact the Office of Civil Rights of the U.S. Department of Health, Education and Welfare with a demand that federal, state, and city mental health funds be withdrawn from Columbia University College of Physicians and Surgeons. The Council planned task forces to determine the most pressing needs of the different areas of the catchment and enlisted the Neighborhood Youth Corps and local social groups in a plan to develop statistics block by block. Previously, the group had relied on Columbia's statistics, but many members believed these reflected Columbia's biases. Throughout those early days, the need to incorporate to gain funding was a pressing problem, and, despite the breakaway from dependence on Columbia, the council made little headway in the next several months. Plans to incorporate hinged on a battle over the semantics of the application at the State Attorney General's Office and the Department of Social Services. The application finally became bogged down on one key issue: The council had included the possibility of running a clinic (although they had no intention of doing so initially) in its application; they were told that, before the incorporation papers could be approved, they must produce a license to run a clinic—*but*, to gain a license, the clinic had to be inspected (and, therefore, had to be in existence physically). The incorporation papers were still pending a year later, in the fall of 1969; only when a group of radical civil liberties lawyers took the case, did processing of the application begin again. Meanwhile, CMHB indicated it would give no grant to the council until it (the council) could be held legally responsible.[68]

Bureaucratic snarls and the machinations of CMHB and Columbia in playing one interest group against another within the council spurred internal disintegration. Within the group, there remained some who felt a program in upper Manhattan had to be connected with Columbia: Columbia had the facilities for inpatient care and the necessary professional resources. Others felt that the experience of the previous several years had proven irrevocably that the community could not participate with Columbia: Columbia would continue to seek control and, failing that, would circumvent the local organizations. The radicals in the council urged the group to be uncompromising in making a definition of mental health that would be relevant to the black and Puerto Rican communities and demanded that the council be allowed to determine the allocation of all public monies received by the Columbia Medical Center for mental health.

CMHB did promise to give the council the meager funds left in Columbia's account (about $9,600), but it delayed turning these over, claiming it could do nothing about the money until the council was incorporated. The financial situation was so desperate that the council had difficulty in even scraping together enough money to send out announcements of meetings to its membership. Columbia had benevolently picked up the tab while it still had the grant but lost interest as soon as the funds dried up. In desperation, the council turned to CMHB for help, but even stamps were not forthcoming without a battle.[69] Acting Commissioner Fill later wrote to the council, explaining CMHB's position:

Since the Columbia contract is no longer in effect, we did not actually have at this time [July 1, 1969] any ready mechanism for funding of even minimal expenses such as stamps, a mechanism which requires some sort of contractual arrangement. I did, therefore, not see any possible way of providing funds for this purpose.[70]

Subsequently—and after the council had disbanded for the summer months—CMHB did offer to share its mailing machine. As the historic first anniversary of the council approached, its Chairman, Bill Hatcher, acknowledged: "Time is on the side of the establishment—they can afford to wait it out." The fate of the council had been predicted in the spring of 1969 when Columbia's Dr. Kolb appeared as a guest speaker before the council: "CMHB is waiting for you people to get yourselves organized. Nothing is going to happen until then."[71]

But the Washington Heights controversy may have made more of an impact on CMHB and Columbia than they were willing to admit. The recognition that there was, somewhere out there, a "community"—structured, vocal, and capable of raising the same kind of community-control demands that were paralyzing the New York City school system at that time—caused a profound rethinking of community mental health by both CMHB and Columbia. For both, the Washington Heights confrontation had been their first sustained encounter with any kind of organized consumer constituency. And, in at least one instance, community action (the teach-in) had come, for CMHB at a particularly trying time: The Mayor had been stalling for nearly two years over appointing Acting Commissioner Fill as Commissioner, and, through the Bureau of the Budget, the Mayor was beginning to

question the more than $200 million city commitment to con-
struction of the fourteen community mental health centers.
Pressed from city hall to come up with a fiscally responsible community mental health program, CMHB brought one message
home from Washington Heights: Community mental health centers did not have to be *buildings.* Ghetto communities could not
wait ten or more years for centers to be built; they wanted and
needed immediate services, in whatever space was available. At
a top staff meeting held three days after the Washington Heights
takeover meeting, Dr. Fill had exhorted his staff to begin to think
flexibly of "integrated networks of service" rather than of centers.
CMHB's 1969 program proposal to the Budget Bureau, expressing this new, cheaper concept of community mental health
centers, met warm praise from the Mayor.

CMHB's new intentions, however, had no effect on its ongoing
plans for the construction of the fourteen centers, including the
one for Washington Heights. It is, of course, a matter of conjecture as to whether CMHB would have had any notion of how
to bring the city's voluntary psychiatric institutions into community mental health programs *without* the lure of expensive, publicly financed new buildings. Columbia, certainly, was not
amenable to a program consisting of a loose "network of services." Its response to the community revolt and to CMHB's less
cooperative stance was to disentangle itself gradually from *any*
commitment to community mental health services in the Washington Heights area. In mid-1968 contacts with Washington
Heights community representatives, Dr. Kolb had denied that
Columbia had any long-term commitment to the community
mental health center. As the months passed and the struggle
sharpened, he began to question the whole concept of community
mental health. In an October, 1968, speech at a professional
meeting, Kolb questioned whether psychiatrists should support
continued federal funding of the community mental health centers program. He also questioned whether it was realistic ever to
hope for the kind of redistribution of services implied by the
Community Mental Health Center Act: "There are clinical and
organizational patterns, not always recognized, that militate
against what we might consider the rational distribution of medical care of any kind, and perhaps especially of mental health
care."[72] And, in his presidential address to the American Psychiatric Association in May, 1969, Kolb did not even mention the
community mental health program, though he did question the

program's fundamental tenet—that patients could be dealt with, in large measure, in their own communities: "Do we place a burden upon the already overtaxed and overstressed community groups in the teeming centers of our metropolitan slums when we force upon them symptomatically improved but far from independently capable persons?"[73] To CMHB, Columbia made it known that it would have to be asked—if not pleaded with—to renew its waning interest in the Washington Heights community mental health center.

Although everyone in the establishment, from the National Institute of Mental Health down, had expressed interest in backing the enthusiastic community participation in mental health that was eventually to be displayed by the Advisory Council, CMHB had taken more than half a year to give the group official recognition. It had taken the same amount of time to cut off the development funds given to Columbia. The CMHB delay was explained as stemming from a need to "justify" the cutoff: According to the Deputy Commissioner of CMHB, the "justification" was arrived at after a review of Columbia's progress report on the Comprehensive Community Mental Health Center Development Project for the period of July 1, 1968, to January 31, 1969. The lack of progress had finally moved the agency to action against the Medical Center.

Trapped in a bureaucratic treadmill, the Advisory Council lost the interest of residents at the grass-roots level. With no increased mental health services to show after almost three years of struggle, they could not sustain their following in the catchment area. In the months and years ahead, it will be this situation, as much as any frontal attack from such establishment institutions as Columbia, that will prove the Achilles' heel of the community mental health center movement.

Who Wins, Who Loses?

The dust has settled on New York City's plans for a Washington Heights–West Harlem–Inwood community mental health center. Columbia University's mental health professionals are once again safe at work among their couches and in their laboratories. CMHB has withdrawn to its offices at the opposite tip of Manhattan Island, grateful that the "Washington Heights incident" evoked as little publicity as it did. And the black and Puerto Rican militants have exhibited their determination to maintain "community control," although the services they sought

to control are now impossibly far out of sight. For the child seeking refuge in drugs, for the family searching for decent housing,
for the disabled Vietnam veteran returning to the pressure-cooker
environment of upper Manhattan, the symbolic victory of "control" has yet to be translated into tangible services.

It was a search for the resources to provide services in the
community that initially motivated the participation of local
leaders in the community mental health center issue. The blacks
and Puerto Ricans did not set out to struggle for "community control." Their involvement was, from the start, far more defensive
than aggressive, but they soon discovered that they were being
planned for, not with, treated as the passive objects of someone
else's plans, not as a community of people. Worse still, the agencies involved in the planning, Columbia and CMHB, had done
nothing in the past to inspire community trust. To the social-
service agency leadership in Washington Heights–West Harlem,
the community mental health center appeared as but another
opportunity for Columbia to use local people for its own academic
purposes and to use local property (in this case, a near shrine to
black nationalism) for its own real estate growth. Community
representatives were propelled into the struggle as much out of
self-defense as out of any positive alternative visions of community mental health centers.

In the struggle to define and control the community mental
health center program, all the initial advantages lay with the
established contender, Columbia. While the community was only
loosely and intermittently organized around the mental health
issue, Columbia interests were strongly integrated and highly
organized along tight, hierarchical lines. Confronted with this
medical power, the community also found it had no public center
to which to appeal: CMHB, the city's mental health agency, was
consistently more integrated into the network of private institutional control than it was into the city's own elected government.
And, in addition to its impressive political power, Columbia
always had the mystique of its professionalism to fall back upon,
so that it could continue to claim that only it had the know-how
to do the job—even if it didn't care to do it. Columbia's ultimate
advantage was its resources—it could outlast the challenge and
the challengers. Salaried and respected, Columbia's mental health
protagonists could hold out long after the most serious community
activists had been demoralized and dispersed.

Once the struggle was under way, all the day-to-day advantages of the established institutions came into play. First, it was up to Columbia and CMHB to set the very stakes of the struggle. The concept of a community mental health center was initially hammered out by the public and private agencies that have traditionally controlled mental health services. Columbia and CMHB not only defined the stakes, they also defined their own adversary, the "community." It was their prerogative to delineate, describe, and, later, to gerrymander the catchment area. Nor did their power end when the stakes were set and the turf marked out. In the struggle that followed, they set the ground rules. Columbia and CMHB defined the forms for "community involvement" to squeeze into—the advisory committees, the agendas of planning meetings, the formalities of representation, and the limits of "participation." Finally, at any point in the struggle, Columbia and CMHB also had the power, to change the rules, redesign the forms of participation, and reshuffle the players.

Yet, for all these strategic advantages, Columbia did not "win." It had not been challenged simply for control of a fixed, well-defined prize—a challenge it might easily have met. Its very concept of community mental health had been challenged, challenged by an alternative vision to which Columbia, for all its labs and drugs and couches, could not relate. For Columbia, the question of the substance of mental health services was as non-negotiable as the question of real control of mental health services. Columbia was not interested in a community mental health center, if having one would mean continual pressure to undertake "preventive" mental health services in a decaying and oppressed community. To do so, Columbia would have had to abandon its own institutional priorities and its exploitative role in that community.

Notes

1. Jack Elinson, Paul Habener, and Cynille Gell, eds., *Community Fact Book for Washington Heights 1956–1966* (New York: School of Public Health and Administrative Medicine, Columbia University, 1968), p. 118.
2. According to "Community Studies for Washington Heights–Inwood" (New York City Board of Education, March 1967), from 1960 to 1965,

white population in the area fell from 92 to 87 per cent, nonwhite population rose from 5 to 9 per cent, and Puerto Rican population rose from 3 to 4 per cent.

3. Community Mental Health Board, *Reports*, 1966 series, nos. 2–6.

4. New York Civil Liberties Union, "Legislative Memorandum," mimeo, December 30, 1969.

5. Committee on Community Health in Washington Heights, *Fact Sheet About Neighborhood Health Programs*, 1968.

6. "New York: The Empire City," Health-PAC *Bulletin*, September, 1969, p. 11. Health-PAC, founded in 1968, is an independent research and education agency dealing with urban health-policy issues. It sponsors seminars and workshops for health-science students and community groups and publishes a monthly *Bulletin*.

7. At this time, Psychiatric Institute was actively and openly involved in drug testing. Interview with Dr. Richard Kunnes, resident, Psychiatric Institute, April, 1969.

8. See, for example, Roger Starr, "Power and Powerlessness in Regional City," *The Public Interest* (Summer, 1969), pp. 3–24. Starr's article provides insight into the innerborough strategy of Mayor Lindsay.

9. In many regions of the country, responsibility has been divided among a multitude of agencies representing different levels of government as well as different approaches to mental health care. Robert H. Connery, *The Politics of Mental Health* (New York: Columbia University Press, 1968), argues that governmental fragmentation was the chief obstacle to the CMHB program nationally.

10. P. V. Lemkatt, Commissioner of Mental Health in New York City, in a letter to City Administrator Luther Gulick, dated June 16, 1955.

11. In the middle of 1969, after most of the events described in this case study, CMHB was reorganized and renamed the "Department of Mental Health," analogous to the Department of Health and the Department of Hospitals. Under this arrangement, CMHB will be reduced to an advisory status, but it remains to be seen whether this will affect the agency's policies.

12. Interviews with CMHB-selected staff members, 1968.

13. Few blacks have been able to influence policy. In mid-1968, CMHB had only three Negro employees (out of 170) above the clerical level.

14. Marvin Lieberman, *The Scope and Role of Public Expenditures for Mental Illness Services in New York City* (New York: Urban Medical Economics Research Project, City University of New York, 1963).

15. Interview with Dr. Marvin Lieberman, political scientist and instructor at the Academy of Medicine, April, 1969.

16. It has been nearly impossible for a black- or Puerto Rican-run agency to gain CMHB support. Two minority-run agencies, offering preventive services to blacks and Puerto Ricans in Harlem and the Washington Heights area are still smarting from their initial rebuffs by CMHB. Because the agencies are in the process of reapplying for support, their identities cannot be revealed.

17. Community Mental Health Board, *Annual Report,* 1965, p. 55.
18. U.S. Department of Health, Education and Welfare, *The Comprehensive Community Mental Health Center: Concept and Challenge,* PHS NIMH, April, 1964.
19. The cut-off income for "psychiatric indigency" or the inability to meet psychiatric expenses, has been estimated to be about $12,000 per year for a family of four. In New York City, the median income is approximately $7,000 per year for a family of four. See Kogan, Leonard, and M. J. Wantman, "Estimates of Population Characteristics, New York City, 1964–1965–1966," *Population Health Survey Research Bulletin,* City University of New York, 1968.
20. Various interpretations occurred in New York City. Maimonides Hospital (Brooklyn) and its community mental health center offer an example of extreme decentralization. This "center" program consisted of a small storefront facility. The approach to mental health care was interpreted as a broad attack on environmental conditions. The "center" worked with area activists in such programs as rent strikes.
21. The hospital emphasis is peculiar to New York City. In the country as a whole, only 49 per cent of the existing community mental health centers are hospital based. 51 per cent are under clinics or local government units. For further information on this note, see Stanley Yolles, "Community Mental Health Services: The View from 1967," *American Journal of Psychiatry,* 124 (October, 1967) supplement, pp. 1–7. See also CMHB minutes, April 15, 1967.
22. For a discussion of the difficulty of applying psychotherapy to poverty patients, see Viola W. Bernard, "Some Principles of Dynamic Psychiatry in Relation to Poverty," *American Journal of Psychiatry,* 122 (1965), p. 254.
23. *Psyching-Out the City Scene,* Health-PAC *Bulletin,* May, 1969, p. 5.
24. CMHB, *Annual Report,* 1966, pp. 18–27. A complex system of financing would cover the costs of center construction. The federal government would pay one-third of the construction cost plus a de-escalating share of staff salaries. State and city grants would cover the remaining cost.
25. CMHB, *Annual Report,* 1965, p. 68.
26. Department of Psychiatry, Columbia University College of Physicians and Surgeons, unpublished draft of "Proposal for the Development of a Comprehensive Community Mental Health Complex Under the Professional Direction of a University Medical Center," 1966.
27. *Ibid.,* pp. 11 and 12.
28. Lawrence Kolb, "The Community Mental Health Centers: Some Issues in Their Transition from Concept to Reality," *American Journal of Psychiatry,* 125 (1968), p. 4.
29. *Ibid.,* p. 54.
30. *Ibid.,* p. 43.
31. *Ibid.,* p. 54.
32. Richard Kunnes, "Will the Real Community Psychiatry Please Stand Up," unpublished paper, 1969.

33. Interview with community worker Mrs. Juana Lopez, Puerto Rican Guidance Center, May 5, 1970.
34. Washington Heights–West Harlem–Inwood Community Mental Health Council, Proposal Committee, "Proposal for Washington Heights–West Harlem–Inwood Community Mental Health Center," undated mimeo.
35. Unpublished CMHB paper, "Estimated Time Table to Construct a CMHC From Inception of Its Planning," September 25, 1968.
36. CMHB, *Annual Report,* 1966, p. 26. According to the Attorney for CMHB, the Rosenthal Foundation was the private fund mentioned in the CMHB report.
37. On the community reaction to this (as well as the CMHB rationale), see CMHB minutes of the July 30, 1967 meeting (dated July 31, 1967). Among those present at the meeting in Dr. Perkins's office were Dr. Gaylin of Columbia and Dr. Hedgman of the Washington Heights–West Harlem community. Dr. Perkins responded to a request from Dr. Hedgman that the catchment area be narrowed by explaining that federal and state approval of the package was contingent on a broader catchment area. Nonetheless, as early as December 9, 1966, Dr. Gaylin wrote Michael Cohn, of Inwood, in reference to community involvement with the development of the program, and, on February 4, 1967, Cohn wrote Gaylin summarizing his efforts to round up an Inwood steering committee to work with Columbia.
38. Information on Inwood involvement in this issue with Michael Cohn comes from conversations, in May, 1970, with a member of the local planning board and an activist on this issue.
39. New York City Board of Education, "Community Studies for Washington Heights and Inwood," March, 1967.
40. Letter written by Dr. Ruben Mora, Executive Director, Puerto Rican Guidance Center, to William R. Valentine, Regional Director, Office for Civil Rights, U.S. Department of Health, Education and Welfare, New York City, circa February, 1968.
41. Ironically, it was later revealed the Columbia community development proposal was actually written with the assistance of a CMHB staff consultant.
42. "Proposed Community Organization Program for the Washington Heights–West Harlem Comprehensive Community Mental Health Center—CONFIDENTIAL," unsigned and undated mimeo.
43. "Rejection of the Proposed Community Organization Program for the Washington Heights–West Harlem Comprehensive Community Mental Health Center," mimeo, July 6, 1967.
44. CMHB, interoffice memorandum: "CONFIDENTIAL—For the Record," July 11, 1967, unsigned. Subject: "Meeting of July 6, 1967, at the Community House, Washington Heights, 510 West 159th Street. Discussion of the proposed plan for the Washington Heights–West Harlem Community Mental Health Center."
45. CMHB, interoffice memorandum: "Notes on Meeting in Commissioner's

Office of Washington Heights Community Mental Health Center on July 30, 1967, 1–3:00 P.M.

46. Letter from Dr. Marvin E. Perkins, CMHB Commissioner, to Dr. Ruben Mora, Chairman, Ad Hoc Advisory Committee, October 9, 1967.

47. Ad Hoc Advisory Committee, Washington Heights Community Mental Health Center, minutes of September 22, 1967, and October 9, 1967, meetings. Signed: Leona Feyer, Community Organization Specialist (a social worker on Columbia's community mental health center staff).

48. Interviews with former members of the Ad Hoc Committee.

49. Letter to Commissioner Perkins from CMHB Chief of Research, October 10, 1967.

50. According to Mrs. Lopez, of the Puerto Rican Guidance Center, the proposal was not a new one but rather a program advocated by the Guidance Center even before the decline of the Ad Hoc Committee.

51. Letter written by a member of CMHB (unsigned) to Dr. Timothy W. Costello, Deputy Mayor—City Administrator, October 2, 1967. A copy was transmitted to Dr. Mora, October 13, 1967.

52. Citywide Health and Mental Health Council, "Open message to elected and public officials and citizens of New York: The need for a sound health and mental policy for the people of New York City," undated mimeo.

53. Interview, Dr. Howard Brown, Health-PAC, February, 1969.

54. Untitled mimeo issued by CMHB, shortly after November, 1967, community sit-in.

55. Letter written by Dr. Sheldon Gaylin, Planning Director, Washington Heights Comprehensive Community Mental Health Center Project, Division of Community Psychiatry, Columbia University, to "Community Members," December 15, 1967.

56. Undated mimeo, "Progress Report, Washington Heights Comprehensive Community Mental Health Center Development Project—July 1, 1967, to February 29, 1968," submitted to CMHB.

57. Open letter and petition, signed by 4,000 Washington Heights residents and submitted to Dr. Lawrence Kolb, April 3, 1968.

58. Letter written by Kolb to Mora, Chairman, Ad Hoc Committee of the Washington Heights Community Mental Health Center, June 14, 1968.

59. Letter written by H. Houston Merritt, MD, Dean, Columbia University College of Physicians and Surgeons to "Dr. A. Rubin [sic] Mora, Chairman, and Mrs. Vinia R. Quinones, secretary, Ad Hoc Committee of the Washington Heights Community Mental Health Center," June 11, 1968.

60. Letter written by Kolb and Fill to area activists, August 20, 1968; Xeroxed copy of guidelines attached.

61. Notes prepared for use at the July 11, 1968, meeting at Psychiatric Institute by members of the Ad Hoc Advisory Committee.

62. Letter written by Kolb to "Rueben [sic] Mora, Ph.D., Director, Puerto Rican Guidance Center," July 1, 1968.

63. Notes prepared for use at the July 11, 1968, meeting at Psychiatric

Institute by members of the Ad Hoc Advisory Committee. At the time, the decision to proceed with construction had not been made. In mid-August, in response to a telephone call from Mora on behalf of the Ad Hoc Committee, William R. Valentine, Regional Director, Office of Civil Rights, Department of HEW checked into the status of the building plans of the Washington Heights community mental health center. He wrote the following information to Mora: "I have checked and obtained information regarding the meeting of July 25, 1968. Present at the meeting were representatives from the National Institute of Mental Health, State Department of Mental Hygiene, New York City Mental Health Board, City Planning Commission and the architectural firm. The discussion concerned architectural considerations for the proposed building for Washington Heights–West Harlem project. No decisions were made at that meeting. Another meeting is being planned for the Fall, for further discussion regarding basic problems, and the Board of Estimate's concern about expenses."

64. Letter written by Fill and Kolb, August 20, 1968.
65. Washington Heights–Inwood Community Mental Health Project, minutes, September 20, 1968, meeting. Submitted by J. Robinson, Acting Secretary, Harlem CORE.
66. *Ibid.*, October 21, 1968. Submitted by Winifred Winikus, Secretary.
67. Washington Heights–West Harlem–Inwood Community Mental Health Council minutes, November 15, 1968. Submitted by Winifred Winikus, Secretary.
68. Letters written by Vivian F. Bucknam, Associate Social Services Consultant, Adult Institutions, New York City Area Office, State of New York Department of Social Services, to Joseph A. Bailey, attorney for the Washington Heights–West Harlem–Inwood Community Mental Health Council, March 26, 1969 and April 24, 1969. Attachments: Certificate of Incorporation of the Washington Heights–West Harlem–Inwood Community Mental Health Council. Drafts #1, #2, #3, and #4, written during the period of March, 1969, to August, 1969.
69. Minutes of June 18, 1969, meeting. Washington Heights–West Harlem–Inwood Community Mental Health Council.
70. Letter written by Fill to William Hatcher, President of CAN-DO, July 1, 1969.
71. Kolb, in a taped speech, Washington Heights Community Mental Health Council, March 18, 1969.
72. Kolb, *op. cit.* (note 28).
73. Kolb, "Presidential Address," *American Journal of Psychiatry*, 126 (1969), p. 44.